C000246015

SHOWMEN, SELL IT HOT!

SHOWMEN, SELL IT HOT!

Movies as Merchandise in
Golden Era Hollywood

John McElwee

GoodKnight Books
Pittsburgh, Pennsylvania

GoodKnight Books

© 2013 by John McElwee

All rights reserved. No part of this book may be reproduced or transmitted in any form or by any means, electronic or mechanical, including photocopying, or by an information storage and retrieval system without permission in writing from the publisher.

Published by GoodKnight Books, an imprint of Paladin Communications
Pittsburgh, Pennsylvania

Printed in the United States of America

First Edition

Library of Congress Control Number: 2013934827

ISBN 978-0-9711685-9-6

frontispiece: Judging by the ceiling display and the November 1929 release date of Gloria Swanson's *The Trespasser,* this is likely January 1930. The Loew's crowd looks to be feeling effects of the Crash three months previous, ragamuffin kids having got the worst of it. Could this be some kind of orphans' benefit? Never mind Gloria Swanson—these urchins could use a good scrubbing.

To Ann, who says I ignore household matters but am vitally interested in what Boris Karloff might have said on some street corner back in August 1933, to which I reply, *Well, what did he say?*

CONTENTS

SHOWMEN, SELL IT HOT!

In 1983 local artist Brad Floyd Davis painted this view of the Liberty Theatre circa 1955.

Prologue

UNSUNG HEROES

A big mystery about movies for me was how people responded when they were new. Was 1931's *Dracula* in theatres the same big noise for my father's generation that it would be for mine watching on late-night TV? What of exhibitors getting what we now call classics brand new and having to devise ways to sell them? Theirs was the task of convincing a local public to forfeit dimes and quarters in exchange for what may or may not be an evening's entertainment. Uphill was the climb for picture-show men and women who'd change marquees three times a week and face the renewed challenge of filling seats for each program.

It's too bad the experiences of showmen, distribution folk, and field reps went unrecorded during their lifetimes, for they had the real movie story to tell. Ones I knew and spoke with lent perspective utterly different from critic and historian accounts on what made movies tick. Colonel Roy Forehand was the manager of our Liberty Theatre, that being the 700-seat "picture show" in my hometown of North Wilkesboro, North Carolina, where I embarked upon a lifetime of show interest. Over the 30 years he ran the place, Col. Forehand never once watched a feature. To him, the Liberty was a selling counter where the product was pictures, and aesthetics never entered into it.

North Wilkesboro was home to no more than three indoor theatres at one time, called "hard-tops" in the trade, and there was a like number, at most, of drive-ins, or "ozoners," around us. All these but the Liberty would perish over time. I was an adult before realizing it, but the Liberty was one of the best small venues in Southeast operation, this a result of ownership and oversight by day-to-day manager Col. Forehand, and by owner Ivan Anderson, a veteran of every aspect of show business, including vaudeville, where he'd gotten his start performing. I never knew Mr. Anderson and regret missing him, but surely got benefit of momentum from glory days of the '40s and '50s when his were the best-conceived shows in our region.

Showmen, Sell It Hot! is partly a lament for such lost ways of showmanship, at least as it was practiced on community levels, before media's wider reach made grassroots merchandising passé.

Movies today are more intensely promoted than ever. You could produce a whole season of '30s features with the money spent to advertise a single one today, but exploitation in our modern marketplace is wholly impersonal. Everyone receives the same pitch to see new movies once a campaign is locked in. It wouldn't occur to a modern exhibitor to go off message and use individual initiative to promote his show, not with a barrage of effort already expended on behalf of 4,000 other theatres opening the same film and on the same day.

We seldom hear the word "showmanship" anymore for its being largely expunged from the vocabulary of exhibition. Film promotion has taken on a nationwide sameness not unlike generic fronts of fast-food establishments. This wasn't always so, of course. Theatre managers were once artists of a sort. They customized advertising to suit their hometowns. To them fell responsibility for preparing all-important ads for the local newspaper. Poster displays were hung at entrance and lobby areas with the precision a curator might bring to outfitting a paintings gallery.

The best "fronts" were celebrated in trade magazines recognizing a most creative effort toward success at box offices. It was all geared toward selling tickets, and what worked in one town might fall flat in a neighboring community, the result being that no two campaigns were alike. Similar, yes; identical, never. If *The Wizard of Oz* (1939) played 5,000 theatres, which it did and many more, rest assured it was sold 5,000 different ways. MGM could suggest merchandising ideas in a lavish pressbook sent to showmen, but in the end, managers relied on their own judgment to put a show over with local patronage.

Ad campaigns were nearly always devised by company personnel other than the filmmaker. Exceptions to this were rare. Pioneer director D.W. Griffith was known to follow through by way of supervising road shows for his silent epics, and Alfred Hitchcock was closely involved in merchandising the thrillers he made. Otherwise, the distance between production and marketing was that which separated an east from a west coast. In brief, California made them, and New York sold them, Gotham being nerve center for all the major film companies.

Selling arms weren't always congenial with creative heads: many in New York felt Hollywood was out of touch with what a paying public wanted to see, and more than one "dog" was put to sleep by sales departments that couldn't be bothered with selling of product they thought unpromising.

Showmen, Sell It Hot! is the result of a lifetime's fascination with movie merchandising, even as it barely scratches the surface of exhibition and what it took to fill seats when film going was our dominant mode of recreation. Most secrets of showmanship stayed with the generation that played Golden Era favorites for the first time. I regret not meeting and getting stories when more exhibitors were still around to tell them.

These were unsung heroes from a flush era of moviegoing that *Showmen, Sell It Hot!* looks to honor. They were the ones, after all, whose next meal turned on whether they could sell what we today call classics. Some of the latter, like *King Kong* (1933), *Jesse James* (1939), and *Psycho*

In 1935 the Liberty Theatre in North Wilkesboro, North Carolina, is ablaze in light to welcome *Harmony Lane*, a down-south musical ideally suited to us.

(1960), bought groceries. Others along the lines of *Citizen Kane* (1941), *Ace in the Hole* (1951), and *The Red Badge of Courage* (also 1951), set a Spartan table for management. Still, it was a showman's job to promote, no matter the product's potential—or lack of same.

As actors and directors were found and interviewed, the showmen who placed their output before a mass audience were ignored, then forgotten. The names of Terry Turner and A-Mike Vogel aren't known even in rarefied film circles, but the efforts of these two, among many others, were what kept turnstiles spinning and made possible continued success for motion pictures in the United States, and it's time we recognized them.

I never wanted to operate a theatre because it was *too much work*. Plenty satisfaction for me came by way of festooned entrance areas and further delight waiting in lobbies. The Liberty, built in the '30s, was gutted by fire at least once but rose again to host decades of moviegoing. It is, in fact, still operational, one of the few Main Street theatres left in North Carolina (or anywhere, I'd suspect).

I'm not unreasonably nostalgic about the place. Sometimes the floors were sticky. Friends swore they saw mice, and using the boy's lavatory entailed more risk than relief. Old Frank at the concession window would

A typical Liberty Theatre afternoon in 1948, with locals milling about the front and dapper Colonel Forehand holding court in sport coat and tie with ever-present cigarette. These frame grabs from a documentary about North Wilkesboro merchants captures the small-town movie-going experience and the theatre's function as informal gathering place.

slam down a nickel bag of M&M's with force enough to break the outer shells, and I stayed a little timid of formidable authority figure Colonel Forehand even as he generously shared pressbooks with me and patiently endured pleas to book *The Haunted Palace* and *Horror of Dracula* yet again.

The Liberty was like thousands of small-town theatres across the United States during the middle half of the century, and that, I think, makes it relevant to this book. Certainly the account ledgers Col. Forehand kept reflected the hits/misses that other showmen experienced, and the budget crunch he often felt was a bane as well for counterparts throughout the country.

I devised my own imaginary theatre, the Parkland, at age 10, and I misspent many a school hour conceiving programs for it. I had kept scrapbooks of theatre ads since kindergarten. My 8mm film collecting from 1964 segued to 16mm accumulation in 1972. Like a lot of movie buffs, I put on film shows in college and did displays inspired by ones I'd seen Colonel Forehand arrange for the Liberty.

Poster and memorabilia collecting became a focus and an excuse to cut classes and travel through North and South Carolina in search of closed theatres and attics filled with treasure. That's where I began picking up merchandising lore from showmen long or lately retired from the biz.

Much of what is in this book originated at my webpage, Greenbriar Picture Shows, more or less a latter-day variant on the Parkland theatre of my childood imagination and site of further meditation on how movies were merchandised during a golden past. Just Google the name for access to a backlog of posts dating from December 2005 when Greenbriar opened its doors.

A lot of people lent valued assist toward completion of *Showmen, Sell It Hot!* Much of that help—and rare images made available—goes back years to when I collected stuff that's reproduced here. Speaking to that, the real architects of this book are Robert and Mary Matzen. Robert's experience told him just how and where ads and photos should be placed for maximum effect, assuring a result attractive to look at, whatever the worth of my words. Sharon Berk designed the book inside and out, and graphics consultant Valerie Sloan brought many long-damaged images back to life.

Karl Thiede is the most knowledgeable film historian I know. He has spent a working

From top: Air conditioning in Carolina summers is another draw for the Liberty; birthdays are rewarded with two free admissions, and the nearby ozoner, the Starlite, offers Ladies' Night on Thursdays.

life in the very field this book is about, and was unsparingly generous with facts, corrections, and details to enhance each chapter. His expertise in business and financial aspects of film history is very much that of an insider. Karl knows the picture trade in real-life terms.

Others whose expertise I greatly respect were gracious enough to review *Showmen*'s text. They are Richard M. Roberts, James D'Arc, and Lou Lumenick. One day I hope to know as much about movies as these three.

To paraphrase Orson Welles in the *Citizen Kane* trailer, I could say a lot of nice things about the following, but they deserve more, and many who shared and gave particular guidance are repeated among *Showmen's* ending chapter notes. The list of benefactors, which I hope is complete, but probably isn't, includes some who have passed on, but all were helpful to a fault and there'd be no *Showmen, Sell It Hot!* without their input. Roy Forehand, Dale Baldwin, Garland Morrison, Eddie Knight, Homer Hanes, Mike Cline, Don Jarvis, Tom Osteen, Moon Mullins, Bill Wooten, Wesley Clark, William Sears, Dan Austell, and Geoffrey Rayle showed me what it is to be an exhibitor. Also, Bill Cline and Phil Morris represent a showman's world. Mary Ann Brame and Bill Moffitt introduced me to marvels of nontheatrical bookings, as did Professor Ellis G. Boatman at Lenoir-Rhyne College, whose first campus run of *Gone With the Wind* at LR in 1974 made me pea green with envy (I'd hoped to get it first for my classic movie series). John Comas was the Program Director at WSJS in Winston-Salem who was very indulgent when I dropped in at age 14 to tell him how to run his TV station. Mr. Comas taught me the realities of programming black-and-white oldies during the color-crazed '60s.

It would take another volume to tell what many more contributed: Norman Stewart, Marty Kearns, Doug Johnson, Scott MacQueen, John Setzer, Ernie Shepherd, Richard Bojarski, Conrad Lane, Lou Valentino, John Millen, Jean Cannon, John Story, LeRoy Bawel, Phil Johnson, Eric Hoffman, Richard Watson, Jerry Williamson, John Newman, Russ McCown, Gerald Haber, Dr. John Schultheiss, Fred Santon, William K. Everson, Suzanne Kaaren Blackmer, Laura Boyes, George Feltenstein, John Beiffus, Dave Smith, Mark Vieira, Edwin T. Arnold, and Eugene L. Miller.

And finally, Mary Matzen edited my text and put right my sometimes peculiar turns of phrasing, succeeding where English and grammar teachers failed for years. I only wish she were on hand to correct everything I post at Greenbriar Picture Shows. Now *that* place could sure use a professional's touch.

The auteur theory thrived in my hometown circa 1951, as director Howard Hawks' name adorns the marquee of the Allen Theatre, which was, unfortunately, lost to fire 10 years later.

Kids pack the house for a Saturday matinee at the
Parkway Theatre in West Jefferson, North Carolina.

CHAPTER 1

ABOUT THOSE SO-CALLED "GOOD OLD DAYS"...

This is a book about movies as merchandise. Some view film as art, more (especially those who finance them) as commerce. Many would say that to look at classics in such terms is to demean them. To that might be added that were it not for the money, there'd have been no Hollywood.

The selling aspect of movies is what always fascinated me most. A theatre's front entrance and lobby were often the show I'd remember longest. How many screen attractions lived up to posters and lobby cards that promoted them? To fall down on the job of merchandising meant dollars lost and maybe theatres gone dark.

Competing for Americans' leisure time was the never-ending occupation of theatres. There was plentiful recreation to challenge them, much of it cheaper, if not altogether free. Local sporting events, a school pageant, any local activity that drew communities together to be entertained could wreck a night's business.

An early challenge was radio, a nationwide and popular presence by the 1920s, followed by more distractions to siphon off patronage. Miniature golf was a brief fad, but it chewed into receipts, as did night baseball enabled by lighted fields after World War II. Migration to suburbia cleaved downtown business, and attendance to large auditoriums, by half or more. Most calamitous was television.

There really were no "good old days" for exhibitors to look back on, for they faced a nonstop struggle against every threat imaginable to their break-even (let alone profit) goals. Get yourself squared with the bank and along come talking pictures, wide screens, or stereo sound to borrow further toward, each transition calling for screen and/or equipment updates. Status quo was a thing largely unknown to showmen. Any manager's goal was filling seats to feed his family. As to particulars of what was shown, that mattered less than patronage turnout and no complaints over what they'd seen.

Colorful publicity material and pressbooks supplied by distribution helped exhibitors. Pressbooks had varied ads that could be placed in local newspapers, plus suggested ballyhoo tie-ins that might stimulate customer interest in the product—movies being mere merchandise, after all.

Exhibitors generally weren't movie buffs, but businessmen who displayed film as their neighbor merchant might a lawnmower or cold remedy, except showmen had to be more cautious, owing to the close tabs local gentry and would-be censors kept on their wares. This was largely reason for movie houses positioning themselves as community centers, open and available to citizenry whenever a gathering place was needed. Small-town cinemas hosted school graduations, beauty contests, functions of every sort; some were the site of church services during otherwise dark Sunday mornings. Such accommodation was essential to establishing goodwill.

Metropolitan theatres were not so affected, though pressures upon them came as varied. The larger the auditorium, the greater were expenses to maintain it. Filling 300 seats in a small burgh was its own nightly challenge. Imagine the pressure to sell 3,000 tickets in a picture palace where weekly expense ran to five figures. An independent operator's failure to put over his program cost groceries and rent; a circuit manager's continuing downturn could mean his job. Changing a marquee and displays began anew the race they all ran.

Shows were measured on drawing power and little else. Management might concede the quality of a picture, but who cared if it delivered no profit? All-time best lists are loaded with now-classics that first-runners disdained. We revere *Citizen Kane* and *Vertigo*, but the showmen didn't. These were, to borrow parlance from long-ago exhibitor commentary, "clucks" or "weak sisters."

Sometimes an aggressive enough showman made money with a said cluck that tanked elsewhere. Visionary Eddie Marks of Charlotte, North Carolina, ran a string of houses and could make lemonade from the sourest fruit. He teamed with American-International merchandisers in 1966 to put over the woebegone *Ghost in the Invisible Bikini* after parades had passed for AIP's once-successful beach blanket series. *Ghost* stunk, but Eddie sold it like *Gone With the Wind*, or better put, Elvis combined with the Beatles. What he got for grassroot effort was socko biz for *Ghost*. Rival showmen scratched heads in amazement that he could pull it off.

Local effort could often goose a product limping elsewhere. Certain territories rang the bell with attractions that specifically pleased their regulars. How else could North Carolina theatres and drive-ins go on repeating *Jesse James* (1939), *Tobacco Road* (1941), and *Thunder Road* (1958) right into the '70s?

Early ballyhoo includes poster displays on a bucolic street pushing the 1914 serial, *The Million Dollar Mystery*, at a small-town theatre well named the Dream.

Rural exhibs developed genius instinct for luring locals. In these situations, a program lasted two days tops. Three or more indicated a Second Coming, and indeed, it would take a *Ten Commandments* to command such extended playing time. Chicagoans might have 12 weeks to catch *Miracle at Morgan's Creek* in 1944, but counterparts in a Midwest farm community had to make tracks for the one day a new Gene Autry or Hopalong Cassidy ran.

Thousand-seat cathedrals might shun "B" cowboy Sunset Carson, but for rural patronage, he was Ty Power and Gable rolled into a packed house. Saturday was hands-down the best attended of a rural venue's week. Exhibitors rented westerns and serials at reasonable flat rates as opposed to big studio specials that often commanded a percentage of receipts. More than one small theatre's attic I searched held nothing but cowboy and

By 1936 picture shows used colorful displays and as many images as possible to lure patrons.

cliffhanger advertising that management had kept in belief, mistaken as it turned out, that such product would stay evergreen for generations to come.

Baleful weather could wipe out even a most promising bill. *Little Caesar* on the local screen was as nothing against drought or snow. Attendance rose or fell with local economies. When times were hard, movies suffered, as evidenced by falling receipts once the Great Depression took hold.

Basic comforts weren't taken for granted either. Most theatres, particularly in small towns, lacked air-conditioning during Hollywood's otherwise "Golden Age." A lot of them simply closed when hot weather took hold. Others soldiered on to empty seats and hope that things might improve with season change. Air-conditioning proved a better investment than wide screens and 3-D; ads from dates of installation featured the theatre's name encased in icicles. A lot of people went to the movies just to cool off, never mind what was playing. Urban palaces were first to lower temperatures, their example—and increased ticket sales—inspiring smaller locales to similarly upgrade.

The so-called "Big Five" producers/distributors owned or otherwise dominated the largest urban houses. Big Five meant MGM, 20th Century Fox, RKO, Warner Bros., and Paramount. These set a tone for picture handling down the line. With enough trade ads and drum-beating, they could disguise a flop and make subsequent daters think a big hit was coming. Smaller-town showmen needed but little experience to recognize snake oil as pitched by major company sales folk. Distrib/Exhib negotiations could be testy, but more often came to mutual back-scratching and satisfaction, if guarded, for both.

Crack field men used a glad hand to peddle what they and customers often knew was junk. Any distributor's sales force had to realize that, in the picture business, excellence was an anomaly. Mostly they got wares to market and never mind how stale they were. In 1951 the Warners rep who could inveigle small-town management to take oldie *Captain Blood* (1935) in addition to much-wanted *A Streetcar Named Desire* would return to his home office a hero and up for a bonus.

It fell then to the local showman to give customers a good time for their dimes. All bucks (hopefully) stopped at his box office. A theatre owner could only pray that his attraction would satisfy. Otherwise, it would be tepid greetings and limp handshakes from townsfolk the next day. Small exhibitors in particular were responsible to their neighbors for a good show. More than one manager would hide out in his office as patrons filed out of a weak program. The law of averages as to quality was seldom tilted toward excellence since most movies, then as now, were just average, if that.

Saturday matinees were but one then-popular format that would thrive, then disappear. There were also late shows, some that ran from dusk till dawn. Lady-shopper matinees were well received, then stopped being so. Giveaways of everything from dishes to dogs were tried. So-called "bank" and dish nights amounted to bribing a public into theatres, but in desperate enough times, how else to get them there?

Local disc jockeys and TV personalities would moonlight as masters of ceremony at teen-slanted conclaves where rock 'n' roll bands performed and onstage dancing was permitted. This was fertile ground for merchant tie-ins. A record store down the block might supply platters for prizing

A 1948 North Carolina showman directs the cameraman photographing him in front of his house. Today's fare is a Republic western, with a Warner Bros. comedy playing late. Such men have little interest in watching the features they run; their focus is on selling product, and instead of Buicks or sewing machines, they happen to be pushing celluloid.

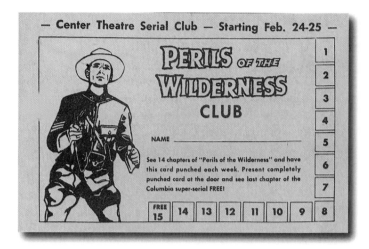

Clockwise from left: Lash La Rue has churned out nine PRC westerns in 1947 and pitches many of them in a personal appearance at the Ritz; a punch card encourages attendance at the first 14 chapters of a Republic serial (the 15th is free!); speaking of free, a free pass, gift, or automobile is the draw for a Randy Scott oater; and always popular is an opportunity to dance onstage, as with the Granada's Twist contest.

in exchange for lobby display of wares, and weeks leading up to the show saw both the theatre and the music retailer promoting each other at their respective sites.

Theatres were very much about orderly presentation. Management wore coat and tie as did ushering staff. Larger theatres issued uniforms. Military precision and daily drilling at urban venues insured discipline and kept dark auditoriums safe. Flashlights were cast upon rowdies, with warnings to behave issued but once. It was imperative for better theatres to maintain an image of cleanliness and order. That included rest areas, which were kept spotless.

Tendering themselves as community baby-sitters made theatres responsible to parents for their child's weekend welfare, this accomplished by way of programming keyed to distract youth from early morning start until parent pick-up or the walk home in late afternoon. Theatres served as convenient warehouses for children who might otherwise be underfoot at home. Cartoon marathons anesthetized moppet mobs gorging on sugared treats. It was in fact concession areas where showmen realized the most profit, with popcorn proving to be salvation for many a struggling site. Cheap and bought by bushels, popping corn became the showman's truest friend. Patronage could fill up for a dime, then order sodas to relieve thirst induced by the salty treat. Many spent more for concessions than for tickets to get in. Eating could indeed be a motivation for going to the movies.

Enterprising houses established Mickey Mouse or Popeye clubs to which youth applied for membership and privileges thereby conferred. What was on screens was less vital than the weekly ritual of being there. Many a youngster's social outlet was the Saturday movie show where they'd get to know fellow attendees as all shared familiar and ongoing series westerns, serials, jungle dwellers of Tarzan or Bomba extraction, mysteries resolved by Charlie Chan or Sherlock Holmes—whatever could be flat-rate (and cheaply) rented by management.

The concessions area hasn't changed much since this 1954 photo and continues to represent profit central for exhibitors.

Outright horror or monster subjects could be problematic, however. Parents kept awake by Junior's resulting nightmares might spread word that too-scary content was being inflicted upon their young. Some exhibitors adopted a no-chills policy or restricted gothics to late-night schedules only, the assumption being that youth below teen-age would not then be in attendance.

A biggest event for the knicker set was personal appearances by cowboy stars who rode on screens and now were performing live for fans in their own hometowns. Many brought well-known mounts to execute tricks on stage—for instance, Ken Maynard and his horse, Tarzan. Harnessing two- and four-footed guests fell to exhibitor hosts; a businesslike Bill Elliot or Johnny Mack Brown made management's duty easy to fulfill. Others could be as troublesome as heavies they fought on screen. A close-by exhibitor told me of sidekick Al "Fuzzy" St. John's thirst for moonshine whisky, satisfied by an obliging state trooper who brought him hooch. Ken Maynard was often as not a drunken sourpuss, hard not only on theatre staff, but on beloved Tarzan as well.

What if a ghost shows up in your town and nobody cares? With a window card taped to his back, this 1940s theatre worker can't seem to scare up business.

Remarkable was the fact that patrons could see all such for as little as a dime and seldom more than a quarter's admission, as theatres had to keep prices low to sustain regular business. People were at movies to pass time and be amused, so it mattered not at what point of a show they arrived. Not uncommon was getting there halfway through and then sitting from a movie's start to the point where you "came in." Did moviemakers realize how easily customers caught on to a story even when starting from latter stages of it? Patronage didn't like being told when to show up at theatres, and **Please See It from the Beginning** was a request, never a demand—except when Hitchcock enforced arrivals at *Psycho*'s start time for 1960 first-runs.

A lot of moviegoers came to sleep or hide out. Dark auditoriums were congenial to ducking wives, husbands, employers, truant officers, or cops; after all, where could Oswald run for cover in November 1963 if not the local theatre? One could generally stay all day if it suited purposes, and some would leave after a long siege and not remember what played on screens in front of them. Showmen had reason to rue theatre seats made too comfortable. Rocking chairs installed in deluxe '60s houses invited slumber, and by-then cooled air made trips to a land of nod that much quicker.

Projection was an unseen aspect of theatre going. You'd not notice the man in the booth unless something went wrong. Operators were generally guys who'd been at it for decades, having assumed a sickly pallor for sunlight denied over a lifetime. Prints these men handled, and it was almost always men, would arrive in varied states of distress. Some would not even thread while others were scratched, spliced, or otherwise beat beyond the capacity to run from start to finish. Theatres toward the end of the distribution line often got junkers like this, and sometimes a show had to be cancelled simply because the print was unusable.

A showman had his product delivered by truck from wherever a nearest distributor exchange was located or, if he was close enough, would simply drive down and pick up the cans, thereby saving expense of transport. At least one city in most states had its so-called "Film Row," a street along which distribution hung shingles and supplied programs. Film exchanges were the selling office and a shipping point for a given territory. During the '30s and '40s, there were 30 exchanges in the United States and 6 in Canada.

North Carolina's Film Row was on Church Street in Charlotte. There were trade screenings of newest movies for theatremen, then haggle over playdates and terms. It was understood policy that all prints had to be returned after an engagement, but some exhibitors wangled a feature, or three, to keep as backup in case of nondeliveries or aforementioned beat-up prints.

More than one North Carolina showman had his own warehouse of movies to fill late or all-night schedules. These shows were unauthorized, but who knew? A particular theatre in a North Carolina college town ran pornographic features during the '70s as regular policy, but used squirreled away prints of classics like *Treasure of the Sierra Madre* and *Yankee Doodle Dandy* to clear the house come closing time, audiences for *Deep Throat* having little interest or patience with Jim Cagney or Humphrey Bogart.

This minor clash between old and new would have been one of many, as traditional ways of showmanship gave way to modern, more impersonal exhibition of filmed entertainment. What we come to celebrate, then, are the long-gone years when movies we now call classic were sold at both nationwide and grassroot levels to a public for whom they were brand new and untried. Some worked commercially, others did not, and very often, merit would have nothing to do with it.

Above right: School's out in 1958 with a family picture, *Snowfire*, plus freebies. Below right: Even in 1964, Batman serials from the 1940s lure in the kiddies, as does the chance to dance on stage (always big). Opposite page: By 1966 the pictures being run are sometimes overshadowed by stage shows and major giveaways or, in some cases, a mere free booklet with instructions on "How to Embalm a Corpse."

ON STAGE!

IN PERSON!

"THE MUNSTERS"

(Character Portrayals Of Your Favorite TV Personalities)

PLUS
2 HORROR HITS!
IN WEIRD COLOR!
"HERCULES IN THE HAUNTED WORLD"
"TALES OF TERROR"

FREE CAR!

GIVEN TO BRAVEST PERSON!

CAR

GIVEN COURTESY OF

BOYLE CHEVROLET, INC.

We Invite You To Stop In And See Our Complete Line of 1966 Chevrolets:

☆ CAPRICE ☆ IMPALA ☆ BELAIR
☆ BISCAYNE   ☆ CHEVY II
☆ CORVAIR ·CHEVELLE·

ONE DAY ONLY!
SAT., DEC. 11
CINEMA
■ THEATRE ■
BENNETTSVILLE, S. C.

FULL OF FRIGHT AND DELIGHT!

Erich von Stroheim and Mae Busch exchange come-hither looks in his 32-reel *Foolish Wives*. By the time Universal is done with the cutting, von Stroheim will look upon the film as "the skeleton of my dead child."

CHAPTER 2

ALL ABOARD THE MUTILATION EXPRESS

Erich von Stroheim would have called it Universal's butcher shop on wheels. The *Foolish Wives* train from L.A. to New York City served as publicity's relay toward a long-awaited January 11, 1922 opening of the studio's first million-dollar picture. EvS said it cost more like $600,000 to $700,000, though inter-office memos indicate $1,124,498 was needed to complete *Foolish Wives*. Whatever the expense, Universal got as much from the free press and patron anticipation they'd been whipping up over a two-year period. Von Stroheim had begun a directing career with continental exotics. The first two, *Blind Husbands* and *The Devil's Passkey*, looked like beginnings of a profitable and ongoing thing. *Foolish Wives* would mark his first dive overboard. Universal wanted lavish, but not eight hours of it. Von suggested that audiences report over two successive nights at four hours per shift, an idea sure to fail.

There had never been a movie half so long shown in the United States, said the front office. People were still getting used to feature-length pictures in the early '20s. In early September 1921, invited studio previewers sat a one-time marathon beginning at 9:00 P.M. and letting out at 3:30 A.M., little realizing they'd be sole eyewitnesses to the *Foolish Wives* that Stroheim intended. Realist Carl Laemmle noted the excess cargo, if not sore backsides, and delegated shearing duties to Arthur Ripley, a remarkable biz figure whose lifetime in film would see him writing for Harry Langdon, directing W.C. Fields and later Robert Mitchum in *Thunder Road*, then founding the UCLA Film Center after years of serving on its cinema school faculty.

Ripley's whittling brought *Foolish Wives* down from 32 reels to 18, still a four- to five-hour sit and beyond what Universal was willing to open on a date, January 11, set in stone. The rush was on.

Ripley and his cutting team would get a $40,000 bonus provided they finished cleaving in time. Publicists seized on that urgency and organized a cross-country race against the clock. *Foolish Wives* would be shortened in transit on a day-and-night schedule, sleep aboard the juggernaut be damned. Stroheim lamented the rape of his art by brainless hacks and Puritans, but as to degrees of that, he'd seen nothing yet. Armed marines accompanied the so-called first print, itself insured by varied carriers for $1,078,000 against fire, wreckage, theft, and other loss and mutilation—Universal might yet collect on that last item had it not been their own editors' handiwork. Coverage premiums for the trip were said to total $12,000. L.A. officials and hordes of press said bon voyage as train left platform with a specially re-equipped baggage car for cutting and screening convenience.

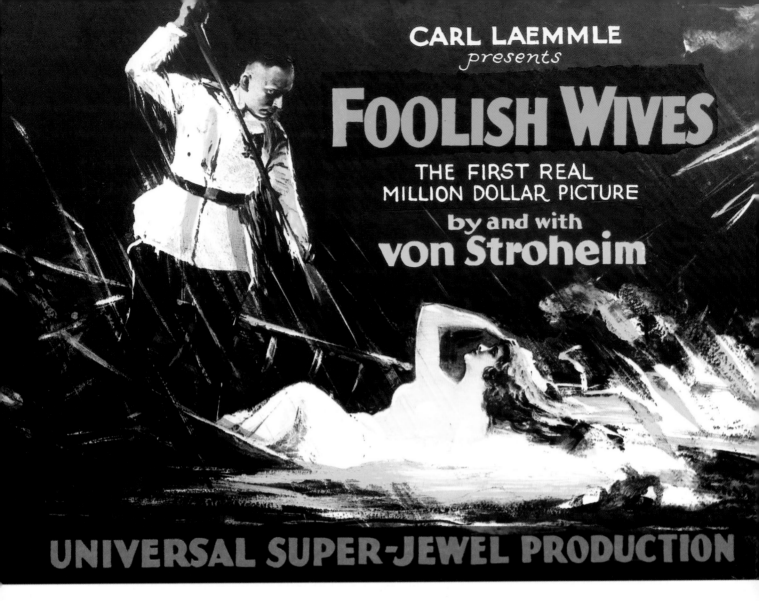

Ads boasted of "the first real million dollar picture," but Universal boss Carl Laemmle lacked faith in *Foolish Wives* and ordered more than half of von Stroheim's narrative to be cut.

The locomotive was said to have traveled at "top speeds." Stops along the way were met by Universal exchange representatives and curious locals. Ripley issued progress reports as his editing crew applied scissors in what must have been a sweltering boxcar. Three-thousand feet had to go, he said, and a new set of titles would be prepared during transit.

Von Stroheim had meanwhile decamped to New York under separate passage, as no invitation was extended for him to join the group dismantling *Foolish Wives*. Relations between EvS and Universal had soured over cost overruns and the director's unwillingness to endorse a less-than-two-part *Foolish Wives*. Whole sections and subplots would have to be junked.

By the time the train reached New York, more than half of *Foolish Wives* was gone. Universal's reception committee arranged for a ritual trucking of film cans to the company's home office at 1600 Broadway. Noted composer Sigmund Romberg was hired to arrange a score for the premiere, an august commission befitting Universal's biggest-ever opening.

Foolish Wives, at 14 reels, played to its first paying audience at the Central Theatre. The program lasted about three-and-one-half hours. Many felt it was too long, and some laughed in the wrong places. Stroheim said that wouldn't have happened had they left alone the version he'd submitted. Universal gremlins worked mischief in the Central's projection booth by continuing to cut *Foolish Wives* throughout the theatre's engagement. What started with 14 reels was eventually whittled to 12. Patrons would actually see less at an evening show than counterparts did at the same day's matinee.

The *Foolish Wives* roadshow was a shrinking affair, but how was anyone to notice with footage disappearing by increments? Vandalism imposed by regional censors and exhibitors anxious to maximize daily screenings denuded *Foolish Wives* still more. Now there were 10 reels. Stroheim called it "the skeleton of my dead child." Euro decadence he revealed was so much castor oil to showmen accustomed to the rural-friendly serials and westerns that Universal customarily supplied. Inflated rental terms made exhibs froth at the mouth. Laemmle had little choice but to sell, if he could, *Foolish Wives* at advanced rates. The picture still lost money. The critical standing it later gained would not be supported by prints even more truncated than what 1922 general release patrons saw. This would appear to be one silent classic that we'll never fully reclaim.

What if, by some miracle, we did find *Foolish Wives* in its entirety, or *Greed*, or *The Wedding March*? Would the legend of Erich von Stroheim survive our modern scrutiny of running times extended to, as with *Greed*, 42 reels? His reputation was actually enhanced from having been broken on the wheel of crass industry, being the directing surrogate of critics who flattered themselves for never bowing to philistine tastes.

Stroheim had the looks and manner of a tyrant and big spender, but that only conferred greater majesty when he fell. Much of his reputation was folderol cooked up by studio publicists. The intractable director that studio bosses loved to hate was an arresting figure always good for colorful anecdotage. Like Orson Welles, Stroheim seems never to have had a picture turn out his way. Pygmy hordes forever seized Von's negatives and locked him out of editing rooms. Arthur Ripley and east-bound minions have the look of functionaries no more qualified to assess Von's work than janitors clipping studio hedges, thus absolving Stroheim of responsibility when the films they cut didn't work.

Top: Universal literally called in the U.S. Marines to guard the EvS payload on its way to New York. Center: Arthur Ripley sits amongst his cutters on the Mutilation Express. Bottom: Ever-shorter versions of *Foolish Wives* are screened en route.

Von Stroheim's sets for *Foolish Wives* include the full-scale replica of Monte Carlo seen here, constructed on the Universal backlot.

What's left of *Foolish Wives* makes sense enough. You'd not think a feature at less than half its intended length would emerge so coherent. Indeed, some advocated trimming it still further. I watched the Kino DVD release, a reconstruction supervised by writer and historian Arthur Lennig in the early '70s and a large improvement on the seven-reel travesty in circulation since Universal again shortened *Foolish Wives* for an aborted music-and-effects reissue in 1930; all previous U.S. versions are lost.

Stroheim's martyrdom was such as to secure a place for *Foolish Wives* on all-time best lists despite its sole survival as the truncated edition he saw and renounced at a Museum of Modern Art showing during the '40s. Critics had to proceed on faith and plenty of imagination when lauding any Stroheim beside many silent favorites that have survived intact. The *Foolish Wives* of Lennig's heroic effort runs to 111 minutes (with a sound track), as he combined the leavings of U.S. footage with materials from an Italian archive. The end result was said to approximate what audiences saw in the film's 1922 general—and shortened from its roadshow—release. Like a lot of silents dragged from the abyss, it requires faith on our part to divine the impact that the glistening 35mm nitrate would have had many decades ago. You couldn't reasonably expect to win new converts to the Stroheim cause with such a battered specimen as what remains of *Foolish Wives*, but for those willing to make considerable allowance, there is still much reward to be had.

Erich von Stroheim died in 1957, and there were once coffee-table books devoted to him. I don't think there will be again. Something about EvS must have appealed to that pioneering generation of film historians, since four of them took up the subject in a number of works, all out-

14

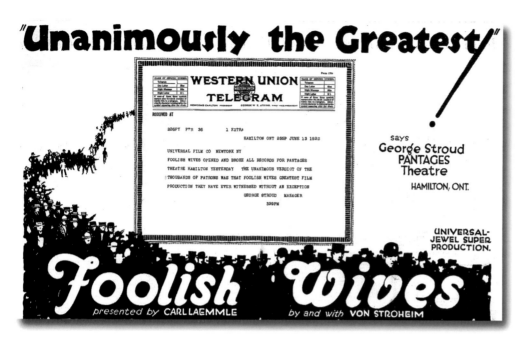

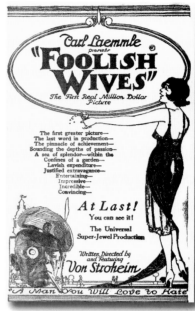

Above left: Universal builds its own prestige for *Foolish Wives* to justify inflated rental terms. The picture, or what is left of it, will still lose money. **Above right:** Ads build new terminology into the American lexicon as EvS is labeled "a man you will love to hate."

standing. Herman G. Weinberg contributed three. Richard Koszarski wrote *The Man You Loved to Hate*, published in 1983. Thomas Quinn Curtiss was a friend of Stroheim's, and his 1971 book was the result of collaboration with the director. Arthur Lennig's comes latest of the bios, having arrived in 2000. Successors to these are few.

Who's caring much about Von these days? Is it the fact so much more cinema is available to look at now, or just that Stroheim is out of fashion? Weinberg had been a champion for EvS since *Foolish Wives* first ran. He'd known the director and took receipt of fanciful Stroheim accounts as to what became of his approved version. According to Von, there was a super-complete *Foolish Wives* shown in South America with a 24-reel running time. He also spoke of an uncut *Greed* having been in the private collection of Benito Mussolini!

Weinberg would chronicle Stroheim struggles to the end, paying tribute with picture books on *Greed* and *The Wedding March*. Both were deluxe editions. *Greed* carried a $50 cover price in 1971, surely a record for any film book published to that time. A 1974 photo presentation dedicated to *The Wedding March*, nearly as hefty a tome, cost $20. These classics illustrated were as close as fans could get to a full-length *Greed* and *The Wedding March*. It's unlikely we'll see a similar photo reconstruction of the complete *Foolish Wives*, as original images from that title are challenging to come by.

One could rent *Greed* from Films, Inc., but *The Wedding March* was something that required travel to see. Both features were renewed by their copyright holders, unlike *Foolish Wives,* which went into the public domain early on and was available to collectors in 8 and 16mm for years before Kino and Image released the Lennig restoration on DVD.

At only 28, Clara Bow made her final appearance in the 1933 feature *Hoopla*, produced during the heyday of pre-Code pictures. Here she plays it risque with Minna Gombell.

CHAPTER 3

TITILLATED TO DISTRACTION

When my mother was 11 or so, her favorite actress was Clara Bow. One day she asked my grandmother's permission to see Clara's newest for 1928 at the within-walking-distance Joy Theatre. Just then my aunt and some other kids showed up and reported seeing a poster in front of the Joy depicting Clara Bow in a bubble bath. That slammed the door on anyone's trip to the Joy for that day.

My grandmother could scarcely have shielded her daughters from the avalanche of pre-Code once talkies unleashed those sights and sounds of moral abandon. It might have been as well for staunch Victorian folk to forbid children to attend movies altogether during the early '30s. Indeed, the only film Grandmother had let my mother see as a small child was Mary Pickford's *Pollyanna*.

Had youth ever been exposed to such sustained attack upon morality as pre-Code? What they learned on screens represented polar opposite of lessons taught at home. With sound's arrival, Clara Bow made way for Helen Twelvetrees in my mother's scrapbook. Something about her must have appealed to a by-now 14-year-old girl fascinated by the infusion of adult themes into movies learning to talk. Did lurid graphics and tag lines inspire parental edicts against youngsters wanting to attend pre-Code movies? Times were sufficiently hard as to disallow lavish promotions for theatres serving smaller markets. It was all most of them could do to buy space just for announcing titles and start times.

American movies lost a third of their audience during 1930. The Depression and an eroding novelty of sound put theatre going among lower leisure-time priorities. You could listen to radio a lot cheaper, and outdoor activity during summer months appealed more than sitting in theatres devoid of air-conditioning. The only way out for Hollywood was product with sex and confession themes. How else could someone like Helen Twelvetrees have sustained a career—hers would last no longer than the pre-Code era itself.

Naughtiness too could be staged with greater economy. Negative costs on sex dramas were minimal. RKO spent $338,000 and $339,000 respectively on Constance Bennett vehicles *Born to Love* and *The Common Law*, with eventual profits of $90,000 and $150,000. An epic like *Cimarron* took $1.4 million to finish and lost $565,000 despite its Academy Award for Best Picture. You might gamble a reputation making sex dramas, but they were otherwise a near sure thing.

Producers hastened to lay in a supply for the 1931–32 season (September 1 a first year to August 31 of the following year) once lines began forming. It was plain enough they'd be testing boundaries in

17

CREATION'S GREATEST DRA-
MATIC PROPERTY...BROUGHT
IN ALL ITS SPLENDOR TO
SHOWMEN OF THE WORLD!

Wonder of the Show World—Known
to a Hundred Million—Yet Never Till
Now Laid Before Human Eyes with
the Spread and Spectacle the Talking Screen Alone Allows!

Production Towering to a Scale Un-
dreamed of—Throwing Its Colossal
Shadow Across the Screen's Gloried
Achievements of the Past.

RICHARD WALTON TULLY'S VOLCANIC

BIRD OF PARADISE

DOLORES DEL RIO
AND THOUSANDS IN THE CAST

The influence of pulp illustrators is seen in a trade ad for *Bird of Paradise*, which promised a bare-breasted Delores Del Rio...and delivered!

order to survive. Trade ads borrowed leaves from lurid pulp and magazine covers to stimulate patronage. An ad for *Bird of Paradise* promised island beauty Delores Del Rio au natural and indeed delivered via nude swims she undertook in the feature as released in 1932.

Exhibitors not boarding up, and many did, called for spicier fare. Adapt or perish, whatever the punitive measures of local censors and bluenoses. If Mae West filled houses, damn the complaints. Small exhibitors took some knocks, doubling as they did as community centers and presumed safe haven for local youth. Urban centers could easier enjoy dollars pouring forth from largely anonymous patrons. Mae West and *She Done Him Wrong* shot down "Mr. Low Gross" on behalf of downtown palaces needing to fill thousands of seats daily just to keep such barns open.

Everyone involved played a wink and nod game, with showman shorthand telling customers what to expect. "Give me a job—at any price," says Loretta Young to Warren William in a teaser ad for *Employees' Entrance*, and by February 1933, customers knew Warner Bros. wouldn't let them down. *Hold Your Man* bade audiences to **Learn how to do it in one easy lesson**, with Clark Gable and Jean Harlow more than capable instructors. These were the sorts of come-ons that got crusaders hottest under collars. After all, kids were checking out heralds distributed around town by theatres even as Mom and Dad made efforts to prevent them from seeing such films.

18

States rights hustlers went beyond even the relaxed protocol observed by the majors. States rights was a method of distribution where a producer sold to an independent exchange the rights to rent that picture for his territory. Shows like *Blonde Captive* hurled kerosene upon community standards already aflame, serving up **A White Woman "Gone Native" Among Descendents of the Oldest Human Race**. Venues hawking such product fairly begged for padlocks, but as long as doors stayed open, thrill seekers rewarded them where it counted most.

Things got bad enough as to oblige showmen to acknowledge over-the-line outrage and make even that pay, leading to backhanded selling that was as clever as it was insincere. **With Shame Our Screen Unfolds the Worst Picture Ever Made** was how Robert S. Guiterman of Manitowoc, Wisconsin's Capital Theatre peddled *Freaks*. The scheme filled Guiterman's house. Well, he warned them!

Free and easy screen content attracted lots of kids, especially for the horror shows. Will Burns managed the Princess Theatre in Joliet, Illinois. He mounted a four-day run of *Freaks* with full circus trappings. Barkers out front promised never-before-witnessed monstrosities inside, as a local midget rendered cornet solos for passers-by. Barker and midget then drove a pony cart to visit schools and playgrounds during recess time, urging youngsters to catch *Freaks* on Saturday. Cunning then was this ad for the engagement, which expressly forbade kiddie attendance: **Warning! Children Positively Not Admitted—Adults Not in Normal Health Advised Not to See This Picture**.

Of course, Burns had no intention of enforcing that. "We haven't heard of anyone dying from heart failure," he laughed. But were parents and city fathers amused? Studios and their racy output weren't alone in bringing on the inevitable crackdown. Showmen turned cynical by the wild and wooly stuff they played invited civic scrutiny even as *Freaks*, *Blonde Captive*, and the rest kept wolves of bankruptcy and closure at bay. Wiser heads had to know chickens would soon be home to roost.

The moral ambiguity of motion pictures soon spilled over into newsstands, where two kinds of fan magazines could be found in the '30s. *Photoplay*, *Screen Romances*, and dozens of

Above and below right: Newspaper ads for Loretta Young's *Employees' Entrance* and Helen Twelvetrees' *Millie* left no doubt as to salacious content. And *Hold Your Man* offered the additional enticement of learning how to "do it."

Above: The alter egos of *Photoplay*, *Motion Picture*, and the other sanitized Hollywood fan magazines offered up images to fire the imagination of the male moviegoer. Below left: MGM queen of the lot Norma Shearer strikes a seductive pre-Code pose. Below right: Mayo Methot and Carole Lombard paint a Sapphic picture in the Columbia picture *Virtue*, as advertised in the pages of *Film Fun*. Opposite page: Warner Bros. siren Joan Blondell epitomizes the earthiness of pre-Code Hollywood.

POSED BY MAYO METHOT AND CAROLE LOMBARD IN "VIRTUE," A COLUMBIA PICTURE.

"I never can sleep if I take a bath before I go to bed."
"Well, if I left the shades up I suppose I'd have a guilty conscience, too!"

like formula served readers with movie news, star profiles, and reviews of upcoming films. Their disreputable cousins went by names like *Stage and Screen Stories, Saucy Movie Tales*, and *Film Fun*. With these you got the same bang for your dime and quarter that pre-Code movies gave in the theatres, only more so. Trashy movie mags went for outright cover nudity and hotter-than-hot stories within. **Hollywood As It Really Is** pervaded text, which emphasized perils awaiting young girls should they venture west in search of film fame. Femmes braving Hollywood jungles laid bare shame of the casting couch and off-the-set seductions. Studios furnished legit fan publications with dope on stars and films in release, but there were also supply lines open to the scavengers. This is where

Barbara Stanwyck promises hot, gartered times in her break-out picture, *Baby Face*, and the warnings are stark: PLEASE DO NOT BRING YOUR CHILDREN.

naughtier pre-Code images got their first exposure. Portraits and even swimsuit art of Carole Lombard appeared routinely in *Photoplay*, but a tawdry pose of her and *Virtue* co-star Mayo Methot was more to the rarified tastes of *Film Fun* readers and was seasoned further with a spicy limerick.

Teen girls and single women mostly bought *Photoplay*. Dad and little brother snuck *Film Fun*. They're hard to find today, as most were left behind in corn cribs, outhouses, and whatever hiding place beckoned to periodicals you'd rather not bring indoors. No telling what neat stuff a complete run of these would reveal. Sometimes in old scrapbooks I find snaps of contract players way edgier than what mainstream publications were using. Stars were the stuff of fantasy after all, and who could blame pre-Code viewers wanting to take idolatry to the next level? Venturing to that ninth ring included stops under the counter where notorious Tijuana Bibles, which were made up of pornographic comic strips featuring movie stars, took pre-Code licensure to its sometimes unnatural conclusion. These comic speculations fed darker patron appetites titillated to distraction. Monitors stumbling across such magazines and drawings would naturally figure movies to be an industry badly in need of fumigation.

National Screen Service called it *Love* in the trade ad shown here, but it was purest sex that their trailers sold, and talk about wiring into fantasies! **When Lupe Velez throws those lips against the hot ones of her lover, every guy in the house is imagining he's right there.**

The text within the advertisement reads:

Love

How are you going to sell your audience those tempestuous love moments in your coming attraction with MERE WORDS or STILL PICTURES? It can't be done—not 100%.

When Garbo nestles into her leading man's arms—A-h-h-h! Joel McCrea puts a head-lock on the girl of his dreams. WOW! Marlene Dietrich glides into a half-nelson with the handsome army officer. WHAM! Clark Gable gets a strangle hold on a jungle maiden in a tropical love scene. ZAM!

That's the REAL THING—the PULSING, VITAL-IZED ACTION that will get every femme in your audience—flapper, matron and grandma. Do the MEN GET IT TOO? Boy—and HOW! When Lupe Velez throws those torrid lips against the hot ones of her lover, every guy in the house is imagining he's right there.

ACTUAL SCENES—ACTUAL DIALOGUE—RIGHT FROM THE PICTURE ITSELF—AND YOU'VE GOT A SAMPLE THAT SELLS.

NATIONAL SCREEN SERVICE

NEW YORK · CHICAGO · LOS ANGELES · DALLAS · ATLANTA

National Screen Service baits the hook in 1932 for moviegoers with the hottest scene stills available for pre-Codes about to be released. NSS was at this time renting movie trailers to theatres. Film companies also had trailers available for exhibitors.

Paramount literally brandishes a smoking gun in appealing to showmen.

Many theatres didn't use trailers and preferred glass slides to announce coming attractions. Independents supplied graphics-only previews with still glimpses of stars and tentative appeals to patronage. NSS baited its hook with actual scenes and naturally used ones likeliest to excite anticipation for hot content.

Trailers as we now know them would blossom here. Some turn up as extras on DVDs; previews for *Tarzan, The Ape-Man*, *Footlight Parade*, and others almost became productions in themselves. With its newly streamlined trailer service, NSS had red meat it could toss to sensation-hungry lions: "That's the real thing—the pulsing, vitalized action that will get every femme in your audience—flappers, matron, and grandma."

Most trailers produced during the pre-Code era are lost now. No telling how many of these would have been censorable once Code enforcement took effect in July 1934. Racy previews walked hand-in-hand with posters out front. There were days you'd think those were burlesque houses on small-town Main Streets. Parents did complain and often forbade movies altogether for offspring. Exhibitors took heat for little ones venturing too near a Mae West.

Comments in the trades acknowledged scenes and dialogue a little warm, but seldom did showmen attack product they played. Maybe those running and watching pre-Code on a regular basis got used to being treated as thinking adults. Theatre advertising in 1931 credited readers for knowing the facts of life.

Our ancestors didn't come away from pre-Code product without a few worldly tips. It was the ones who seldom if ever attended movies that stirred up trouble. Urban markets had organized censor bodies ready to pounce when offending product hung in their net. Rural houses played shows through for a night, maybe two, spat them out, and threaded up the next. Even dedicated community crusaders had not the time to flag down trucks delivering half a dozen or more shows a week to the local Bijou, thus pre-Codes played mostly uncut in underpopulated territories. When church ladies and town councils took action, it was mostly confined to Blue Laws closing theatres on Sunday. The push-pull couldn't last, with mid-1934's crackdown as inevitable as many felt it was overdue. Movies would be cleansed, as would advertising of same. A lot of fun would go out of showmanship with pre-Code's passing.

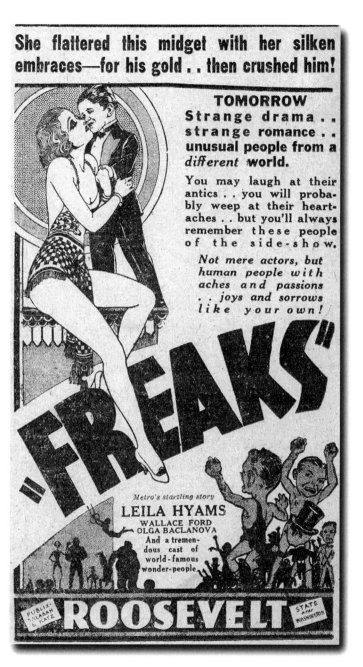

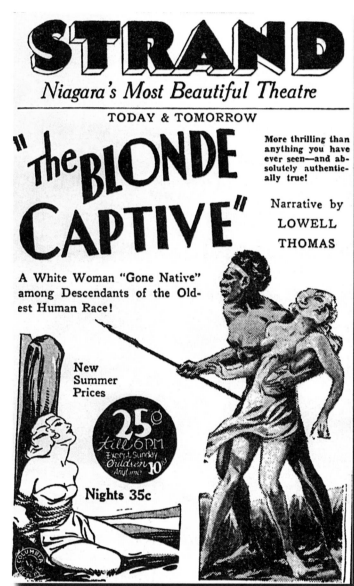

Above left: Admen protest too much in begging audiences not to subject themselves to *Freaks*, knowing all the while that the allure would be irresistible. Above right: Long before Lowell Thomas *remembered*, he narrated a salacious little pre-Code called *The Blonde Captive*, which featured "A White Woman 'Gone Native.'"

Young and fresh-faced, Ginger Rogers and Fred Astaire make their screen debut as a team.

CHAPTER 4

WHEN RKO
FLEW DOWN TO RIO

There was an exhibitor living close to me who'd been in the business some 50 years when I interviewed him for a Winston-Salem *Journal* piece in 1985. Garland Morrison and wife Virgie knew exhibition cold and handled seemingly every pic released for most of the talking era and a few silents besides. Garland had gotten a start pushing peanut wagons down aisles before concessions began selling out front. Then he wanted in on management and was given the chance to prove himself by getting word around the county on *Flying Down to Rio*, this to be accomplished largely on foot and whatever conveyance with pedals he found.

Hard times were everywhere in 1934 but nowhere so much as the backwood this aspiring showman ventured into with heralds and the promise of good times for a dime. What did North Carolina foothill dwellers know from Rio or flying there? Garland remembered climbing fences into pig yards to convey the joys of RKO's extravaganza set in the clouds. I kept waiting for his anecdote's payoff of being scatter-gunned or done ways dramatized in *Deliverance*. Instead, there was success at the Amuzu's ticket window, and young Morrison got the job. For that reason, *Flying Down to Rio* would be one of his favorite movies for all time.

I guess the foregoing is to say how regions, patrons, and reactions could differ for a single show as it fanned out across early 1930s America. Agrarians who'd barely traveled off the farm saw *Flying Down to Rio* as foreign indeed, a musical set amidst Latin high-life resembling import from another planet for any similarity it had with the lives rural folk led. Well, exotic was what RKO was selling. How many patrons anywhere had flown on passenger planes, let alone piloted their own like Gene Raymond here? He made the procedure look so simple that any of us might do as much given a private craft. Even a forced landing is cake for Raymond, smooth beaches at the ready when engines misbehave.

Moneymen and those who governed were allied as to the bright future that air travel promised. From the evidence they saw in *Flying Down to Rio*, movie patrons would figure that planes *never* crashed. In fact, there was passenger service from Miami to South America's coast by 1932, and the goal among providers was to make the public feel safe boarding clipper ships. Harnessing movies to popularize air travel was an investment beyond what *Flying Down to Rio* brought back from theatres. Merian C. Cooper served as production chief at RKO when the project went aloft and was on the Board of Directors for Pan-American Airways, so he profited on every air trip down and back, plus got a percentage of the

$480K profit realized by *Flying Down to Rio*. The man's genius clearly extended past *King Kong*'s creation.

Flying Down to Rio is the one to pull out for guests wanting a dose of Hollywood silly, confirmation of what old movies have become to modern eyes. It might be Fred Astaire's best, just for being his first as featured player; there had been *Dancing Lady* before, but that was for a single number and no participation otherwise.

Broadway success in partnership with his sister, recently retired to marry, would contribute little toward recognition by moviegoers. For most he'd be a fresh and untried face. RKO placed Astaire first and in largest type among cast members announced in the company's 1933–34 product manual sent to exhibitors. Was Fred Astaire initially slated to headline *Flying Down to Rio* rather than eventual Gene Raymond? Helen Broderick was listed also, but she's not seen in the finished show at all. What emerged for late December 1933 release was Fred as sidekick, a prominent one, and kibitzer to the romance that Raymond shares with Dolores Del Rio, those two forevermore characterized as nominal *Rio* leads. Astaire was so good as to foreclose anyone else being noticed, other than Ginger Rogers, his to-be partner introduced as such here.

Everyman Fred happened to be, from this moment, the most accomplished dancer in movies and nailed a screen persona from his first warning of dog-food diet to come for the band. He's loose, funny, and utterly unself-conscious of his amazing skills on the dance floor. We're well used to the magic that Fred and Ginger conjured, but imagine how patrons flipped when it was all done the first time. No wonder a dancing public went "Carioca"-crazy for Christmas '33 and afterward.

Yes, the dance was essential, for its catching on would be key to word of mouth and hopeful repeat trade. After all, *Rio* was where you had to go to see it done. RKO pushed the newness and naughtiness of this closest-up fad since Valentino's tango, the first of many moves two could do that sold nearly every Astaire-Rogers teaming to come, including *The Gay Divorcee*'s Continental and *Top Hat*'s Piccolino.

Trade ads preceding *Rio*'s release called the Carioca tantalizing and mesmerizing, standing Fred and Ginger tallest among the images shown; Raymond and Del Rio might well have been casting insurance in the unlikely event that Astaire wouldn't click. Fred was a different sort for sure, far afield of a conventional leading man, so tentative use of him in *Flying Down to Rio* was at least understandable, even as first glimpse of him and Rogers dancing settled any question as to whom customers would go home talking about. The two as sardonic Greek Chorus seemed also to point toward a new flavor

The dance sensation Carioca provided crossover appeal for the exotic picture and assured that the *first* impressions of Fred and Ginger were *sexy* impressions.

STARLITE DRIVE-IN
N. WILKESBORO, N. C.
Highway 115 — Phone 3913-M

Week of June 7th to 13th

WE ARE CELEBRATING OUR . . .
SILVER ANNIVERSARY!
IN THEATRE WORK TOGETHER!

Garland Morrison   Mrs. Garland Morrison

We Have Selected "MARDI GRAS" For Your Entertainment The First 4 Days of Our Anniversary!

☆ ☆ ☆

Every 25th Car ADMITTED FREE!
DURING OUR ANNIVERSARY WEEK!

they'd soon be serving in musicals. RKO, perhaps divining this, devoted ads to Astaire singly, promising in its *Rio* pressbook, "You are going to see more of this Broadway star. He makes the hit of your life."

Hard-luck RKO had dropped from profits of $3 million in 1930 to negative $10 million for 1932, with receivership a next stop come 1933, despite turnstiles spinning for *Little Women* and *King Kong*. Those were but two of a largely desultory lot numbering 49 released in 1933. Most had been done for smaller change per volume goals set by head of production Merian C. Cooper, and eight were independent productions that RKO distributed.

RKO was backed by corporate giant RCA, but limitless dollars didn't come with it. Profitable for '33 was *Morning Glory*, *Ann Vickers*, and *Professional Sweetheart*, with *Christopher Strong*, *Sweepings*, and *The Ace of Aces* representing loss. Biggest spenders of the year would be *King Kong* at $672K and *Flying Down to Rio* at $462K. A lot rode on getting the musical into a money class with Warners' *42nd Street* and *Golddiggers of 1933*, two that had revitalized this genre over a just-past season.

Above left: Showman Garland Morrison got his start drumming for *Flying Down to Rio*. As seen in the flyer, Garland and his wife Virgie would spend decades in theatrical exhibition in North Carolina. Above: RKO trumpeted its offbeat new triple threat Fred Astaire for the Big Apple premiere. Below: In other Radio City ads, the aerial circus and girl show takes center stage.

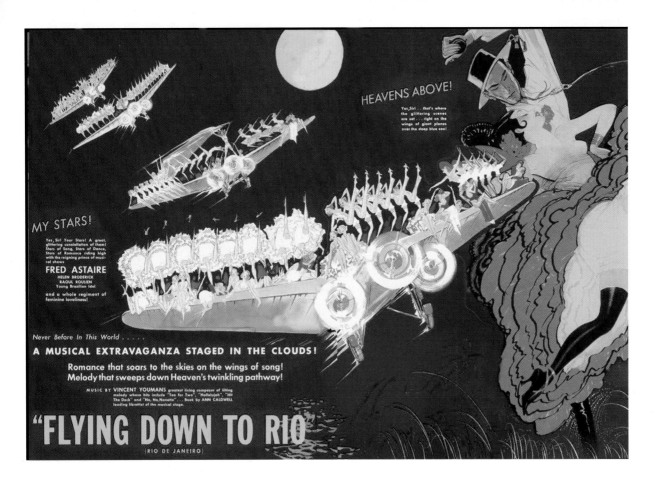

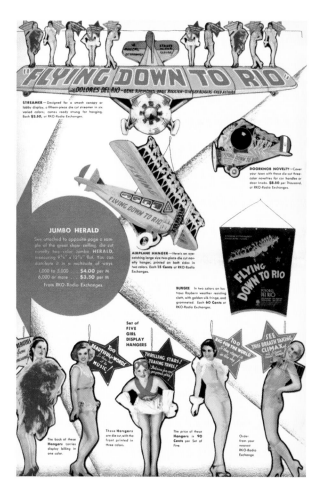

RKO exploitation for *Flying Down to Rio* centers around scantily clad, wing-walking chorines on tri-motor airships (as in the poster assortment above left) and the herald handed out by showmen (above right), but also features the carnival atmosphere of Brazil. In an age long before Rio becomes a vacation destination, advertisers know they have to add the parenthetical (Rio de Janeiro) for clarity.

FOX TROT STEP   HEEL & TOE SLIDE   THE ROLL *(FoxTrot Step)*   CROSS STEP & TOE BEAT   CIRCULAR ROCK *(Foxtrot Step)*   HEEL & TOE CLICK

The pair that will become synonymous with dancing perfection get their start as supporting players in *Rio*. As-taire and Rogers click from the first moment and easily eclipse "stars" Dolores Del Rio and Gene Raymond.

Flying Down to Rio called itself "the first indoor aerial circus and girl show ever produced," this referring to chorines on plane wings that climaxed the film and dominated most of its publicity, all faked in airplane hangers with aircraft suspended off the floor, thus the "indoor" aspect of the circus. Still, it was sporting of RKO to reveal the tricks behind their third-act spectacle, *King Kong* having given them the basis for pride in FX work done on the lot.

The company had sent cameramen to Brazil for background shots to establish locale and supply footage for process screens that the actors could stand before. What came back was effective enough to make some think a whole cast and crew had made the trip.

Finished product to rival *Rio Rita*'s stand-up box office was the hope expressed by RKO. Certainly they'd not had a musical so successful since that 1929 blockbuster, which returned $2.4 million worldwide.

For *Flying Down to Rio*, a premiere at the 5,945-seat Radio City Music Hall was deemed appropriate; *Rio* would serve as the palace's Christmas attraction. Surface-wise, this looked to be a printing machine for cash, what with holidays and infinite space within New York's most celebrated venue, but size was the rub for this biggest and most expense laden of barns.

Variety assessed the situation a few weeks ahead of *Rio*'s opening, calling Radio City's "the largest fixed overhead of any two theatres in the history of the business," its pair of screens including the Music Hall and a smaller RKO Roxy. RKO was obliged to tender a million-dollar yearly rental to the Rockefeller family, and there was debt of $600,000 beyond this payable to the Rocke-fellers and to RCA. The year's operating deficit had already run up to $135,000 on a venue that ate up an estimated $105,000 per week just to stay open, and these were Depression dollars.

Flying Down to Rio was the feature part of a two-and-a-half hour yuletide gala that would become a Music Hall tradition. Best seats brought $1.65 and there wasn't a more lavish revue in town. Notable among the supporting bill was Walt Disney's latest Silly Symphony, *The Night Before Christmas*, a Technicolor reel amounting to an event in itself, as there were no short subjects so eagerly anticipated as Disney's. This one was especially well received as a follow-up to *Santa's Workshop*, the previous year's first leg of St. Nick's journey with his toys.

Radio City engagements were generally limited to a week, few shows able to fill so many seats beyond that. *Flying Down to Rio* would be only a second to be held over, according to *Variety*, with *Little Women* the first. Its initial week's receipts of $100,000 translated to *Rio* seating approximately 165,000 patrons. "This number removed from prospective customers explains why a second week is invariably doubtful," said the trade, "except where the hold-over session includes a holiday."

Closest Broadway competition was the Paramount Theatre's *Alice in Wonderland* bow, at which Mary Pickford appeared to perform a brief sketch and convey holiday wishes to packed houses. The deal gave Pickford a guaranteed $10,000 plus a split of grosses past $60,000. It took big money, even then, to launch films upon waves of perceived success, that impression vital to bookings and terms negotiated down the line.

Two weeks at the Music Hall put *Flying Down to Rio* in a winner's circle and gave it a start toward worldwide $1.5 million in rentals. Some have written that the picture "saved RKO from bankruptcy," though receivership was under way by the time of *Rio*'s release. The Carioca rage kept the film on public radar, RKO touring their 50 "Original Carioca Dancers" from the film through presentation houses during 1934.

Flying Down to Rio would be remembered as the musical that invented Fred and Ginger while its other merits became more obscure. MGM's *The Band Wagon* in 1953 harked back with reference to lead character (played by Astaire) Tony Hunter's "Swinging Down to Panama," Hunter's artifacts being sold now that Tony and his hopelessly old-fashioned movies are in eclipse. If *Flying Down to Rio* was a relic, at least folks still had fun watching, with television having taken '50s receipt of most '30s song-and-dance features. *Rio* would maintain distinction as the one placing scantily clad girls on airborne wings, irresistible kitsch that endeared camp-seekers and kept *Rio* flying on revival screens. The iconic one-sheet, among most sought after by collectors, fetched a whopping $239,000 at auction in 2008. Double that, and you could have made the movie again in 1933 dollars. Original *Rio* elements seem happily to survive, if HD streamings of late are any indication. Nice to know there are at least some vintage RKOs that can put on a modern glow.

Ballyhoo for *Flying Down to Rio* includes instructions for how to stage a Hollywood-style premiere guaranteed to snarl traffic. Another stunt features a "projection car" to take the *Rio* trailer to the masses, neighborhood by neighborhood, as had been done successfully with Dolores Del Rio's *Bird of Paradise*.

WAYS TO EXPLOIT YOUR SHOW WITH NIGHT STUNTS

The Hollywood stunt is by the Smoot Theatre, Parkersberg, W. Va., and the projection car is from the Stanley, Pittsburgh, Pa., both as done on "Bird of Paradise."

"Hollywood Opening" (left)

Stage a traffic-stopping opening night, with show music to whoop things up. Have the flood lights trained on parking places for arriving taxis, with movie cameras for special shots of local celebrities. A night plane flight with fireworks display or amplified "Flying Down to Rio" music will work in nicely with the Hollywood opening.

Projection Car (Right)

A car equipped with projection equipment will get your trailer before thousands of people. Crowds will be milling around this five-minute show all evening.

METRO GOLDWYN MAYER

Marx Brothers

CHAPTER 5

METRO AND THE MARXES

I don't happen to believe that the Marx Brothers sat naked in Irving Thalberg's office and roasted potatoes, but show business legends die hard, so who am I to spoil everyone's fun by saying this particular anecdote creeps me out and always has? Still, it dovetails nicely with '60s-era protest gestures applauded in yellowed editions of *Ramparts* magazine. Maybe Groucho understood this when he repeated the tale for a legion of collegiate disciples who dogged his senior years. Who among the team's army of madcap scribes dreamed up this offscreen japery, and when? I'm figuring it was planted in a column just prior to release of *A Night at the Opera* or soon thereafter. If the team was to be gelded in front of Metro cameras, then at least preserve some vestige of Marx madness behind them.

This viewer enjoyed a boyhood diet limited to their Paramount features. I didn't come by way of *A Night at the Opera* until 1973. Funny how you remember best those classics that *don't* deliver. At 19, I wondered if it was me or the movie. Groucho playing Cupid—that seemed a violation of everything he stood for. Harpo the happy clown smashes his fingers under a piano lid, and gaggles of Metro moppets laugh themselves silly—sacrilege!

Songs, dancing, and romancing. This was the dreaded laxative after a bountiful meal of *Duck Soup*. So what of the alleged flop of the latter? Did *Duck Soup* curdle and resolve Paramount to rid itself of Marxes? I don't have gross figures any more than writers who've accepted received wisdom—itself dating back to columns of the day—but I do have a few numbers for *Horse Feathers*, and that one was sure enough a hit for the company in 1932. At a negative cost of $647,000, the college comedy took a gratifying $115,000 in profit. That was significantly better than runners-up *Shanghai Express* ($827,000), *The Big Broadcast* ($775,000), and *Love Me Tonight* ($685,000). Co-ed hijinks spiced with Thelma Todd in negligees and a climactic football game would seem a safer bet than political satire, but could *Duck Soup* have been a total bust-out? I'm as curious as any Marx fan, and lest Paramount open their ledgers to researching, will probably remain so. One elusive number *has* surfaced, however. Turns out *Duck Soup*'s negative cost was $765,000. Did Paramount spend itself into a corner?

Rife had been conflict between stars and studio since business manager for the team Gummo Marx visited from New York and discovered monkey business on the part of Paramount bookkeepers during shooting of the same-named 1931 feature. Seems they'd forgot profit percentages due the Brothers; after all, **Your Profit Is Assured**, said Paramount in its trade ads.

Above: Would you trust these gentlemen to assure your profit? Gummo didn't, and demanded an accounting. Below: Groucho, Zeppo, and Gummo return on the Twentieth Century from their New York reckoning. They are soon to begin *Duck Soup.*

The matter simmered through much of 1932 as Gummo sought a proper accounting before inevitable civil actions brought things to a boil. The team then decamped to New York despite preparations being made for *Duck Soup.* Paramount's countersuit claimed the Marxes owed them a picture and were refusing to honor their contract. By May 1933 matters were uneasily settled, and the comedians returned to California to shoot *Duck Soup.* Overhead was thus piling up before summer filming began.

The Marxes were at least the most expensive comedians on this studio's payroll, with *Duck Soup*'s $765,000 exceeding money spent elsewhere on bigger pictures. Consider that MGM had $695,000 in *Grand Hotel*; Warners managed *Golddiggers of 1933* on a $433,000 negative cost; and RKO finished *King Kong* for just $672,000. Paramount's own investment in other comedies was considerably less than *Duck Soup.* The all-star *International House* came in at a mere $337,838. Monies needed to wrap Mae West's hit, *I'm No Angel*, amounted to $434,800, and W.C. Fields in *Tillie and Gus* was done for a modest $235,000.

The fact is that Paramount, even if it maintained a solid following for its Marx Brothers series, could never hope to profit in the face of expenses like those incurred on *Duck Soup.* Besides, there were plenty of other laugh makers on hand to fill the void. Word was out that *Duck Soup* was a flop, but this wasn't altogether fair to the Marx Brothers. The long wait of three or so decades to have their final Paramount offering declared one of the greatest sound comedies was hopefully worth it; Groucho acknowledged as much in old age.

The deal for *A Night at the Opera* seems to have had its genesis during bridge-game conversation between Chico Marx and Irving Thalberg. The comedians had been off movie screens for going on two years, and their confidence was shaken. A proposed independent start-up had piled on financing rocks, and it was figured the Marxes had lost their momentum. Speaking to Groucho, Thalberg made clear that

Above left: The Marx Brothers honed their screen performances with countless hours on the stage. Here they are in Cleveland in 1930. Above right: An ad for their 1932 Paramount picture, *Horse Feathers*.

his was a salvage job. These were comedians in need of new direction, and any deal with Metro would be conditioned upon their acceptance of same. *Duck Soup* was lousy, said Thalberg, to which Groucho could but meekly disagree.

"I can produce a Marx Brothers comedy with half the laughs that will do twice the business," promised Thalberg. His idea was really nothing new. He'd simply reapply the stage formula used in *The Cocoanuts* and *Animal Crackers*, only this time romantic subplotters would figure more prominently. There *was* such a thing as *too* many laughs, after all.

Morrie Ryskind would sum it up while the team was still on Broadway: "You didn't have ice cream all the way through, you know." Feckless stage juveniles had been a necessary conveyance for songs an audience might whistle going home and buy sheet music for the next day. Love stories functioned quite apart from the Marx Brothers, and they seldom overlapped. Thalberg was resolved to

integrate the two, even if it meant watering down the comedy. This would, at the least, have greater appeal for women. Unrelieved laughter was best left to two-reel fillers. *A Night at the Opera* would deliver on the promise of its title. There would indeed be opera, and per Thalberg's dictum, we'd take it and like it.

It's a shame no one referred back to the Paramount model, for they had fixed whatever needed fixing with the Marx Brothers. *Monkey Business*, *Horse Feathers*, and *Duck Soup* ironed out wrinkles inherent in too-literal adaptation of Broadway hits now passé to increasingly sophisticated talkie viewers. Each was better than the one before, with *Duck Soup* the most polished diamond among them.

Thalberg and MGM determined to reinvent that wheel. They sent their newly hired comedy team on the road to get live audience confirmation of what exhausted writers hoped might be funny. A half-dozen features could have been made from screenplays discarded by Thalberg. How does one honestly know what works after a hundred or so readings and redraftings? One of the writers auditioned some material for his producer; Thalberg scanned the pages without cracking a smile, then turned to the man and announced, "This is the funniest material I've ever read."

That story's been told to Thalberg's disadvantage, with emphasis on his tin ear for comedy, but many's the feature and short I've watched without outright laughing, yet some rank among favorites for me, evidence that we don't necessarily guffaw at everything we find funny. Sometimes an approving smile is expression enough, though comedies shared with an audience, preferably large, do have a way of breaking down inhibition.

The Marxes were agreeable to taking *A Night at the Opera* routines on the road for testing before

Above: A theatre herald handed out to patrons introduces the "new and improved" MGM Marx Brothers. Their gelding is not mentioned. **Below:** Irving Thalberg allows the Marxes the appearance of running amok.

Above: Metro brings its stable to bear on Marx Brothers messaging to showmen. Below left: The Marxes follow best practices and try out material on the road. Below right: More outreach for exhibitors touts early success *for A Night at the Opera*. Next spread: Bally ideas for "the most important comedy attraction in 10 years!"

HIGHLIGHTS OF M-G-M'S BIG SHOWMANSHIP CAMPAIGN in BALTIMORE and ST. LOUIS

M-G-M put on these campaigns for **you**, to show **you** how to break records with the most important comedy attraction in 10 years! You can add practically every stunt to your own town and pack **your** theatre, too

BALTIMORE BUSTS RECORDS!

EARLY (OR LATE) SANTA CLAUS
Santa Clauses placed on principal corners of downtown section with signs announcing that they had come early this year to see Marx Bros. (If you play it after Xmas let your sign read, "Santa stayed in town. He didn't want to miss the Marx Bros!")

PRESS IDEA
Columnist in News-Post ran specially prepared imaginary letter from Groucho Marx.

STUDIO COOPERATION
Wires from stars on M-G-M lot obtained from studio for press stories, and lobby and department store displays.

RADIO
Radio spot announcements daily, for week in advance of opening, obtained gratis from Radio Stations WCAO and WCBM

OPERA CONTEST
Radio contest identifying operatic recordings with passes offered as prizes, arranged with Radio Station WFRB.

NEWSPAPER TIE-UP
Promotion ad in Baltimore Sun showing photo of Groucho Marx reading paper's WIRE-PHOTO page.

COAST INTERVIEW
Long distance telephone interview with Groucho from M-G-M studios arranged with Sunday Sun, with two full columns of space guaranteed for five day advance break.

PHONE COMPANY
Co-op ad from Bell Telephone Company, based upon long distance phone interview with Sun.

Stooges in Nut Container at Food Show.

HOW MANY NUTS ARE IN THIS CONTAINER BESIDES THE 3 MARX BROTHERS?

10 GUEST TICKETS AWARDED DAILY

MARX BROS. in A Night at the Opera Opening with Halloween Midnite Prevue at Loew's CENTURY plus BIG STAGE SHOW

Groucho Marx appearing in A NITE at the OPERA World Premiere Loew's CENTURY

Imagine

having a cigar and no 5c--but if you think that's bad imagine having 5c and no

ROI-TAN

AUTO TAGS
Maryland automobile tags for 1936 were presented to Marxes Commissioner of Motor Vehicles of State of Maryland, all th sets bearing number, 000-000.

WANT ADS
Want ads offered ten dollars cash to town's meanest, gloomiest dividuals who could sit through picture without laughing.

MAIL TIE-UP
Rubber stamp plugging picture used on all outgoing mail from main office of Baltimore & Ohio Railroad to destinations within one hundred mile radius.

CITY COOPERATION
Placards announcing World Premiere, attached to lamp posts in downtown area, through special permit from City Hall.

STORM WARNING
A HURRICANE (of hilarity)
A TORNADO (of stillation)
Will Hit St. Lou FRIDAY, NOV.
It's the Midwestern Premiere of the Funniest Picture in '10 Years.
"A NIGHT AT THE OPERA"
Starring
THE MARX BROS
and St. Louis' Own
ALLAN JONES
AT
LOEW'
(of course)
P. S.—ALLAN JONES WIL BE HERE IN PERSON FRIDAY!

THE MARX BROS LOEWS N

Ushers all made up like Groucho.

THIS WEEK
ARUNDEL
Special

MARX BROS. NUT SUNDAE

Made with the NEW Almond Krax Ice Cream
Nuttier than THE MARX BROS.
in "A NIGHT AT THE OPERA" at *Loew's* CENTURY

"Marx Bros. Night" at Dance Palace.
Prizes for Best Marx Costumes.

STREET CARS

Dashboard cards attached to all city street cars.

RACE TRACK

Marx Bros. Handicap scheduled at Pimlico Race Track with trophy presented in name of stars to winner of feature race.

CUT-OUTS CUT UP!

Cut-out figures of Marx Bros. (specially rigged) crawled up walls of two department stores located at town's busiest intersections.

TOP HATS

Old model top hats, secured from manufacturer, and lettered with playdate, etc., worn a week in advance by theatre service staff.

PEANUTS TO YOU

Army of pushcart peanut vendors each displayed a background blow-up of the Marx Bros. captioned: "Nuts to You!"

100 Peanut Stands.

GIRLS' HELP

Girls, dressed in nurses' uniforms, distributed capsules on downtown streets with tissue paper fillers captioned: "A laugh a day keeps the doctor away!"

HOSIERY TIE-UP

Tie-up with Real Silk Hosiery based upon national ad written for them several years ago by Groucho Marx, with all local agents distributing heralds.

GROUCHO'S CIGARS

Co-op ad and window streamers promoted from cigar manufacturer on basis of Groucho's cigar smoking.

SONG HIT

Window displays in music and department stores plugged song hit from picture, "Alone!".

TRAILER OUTDOORS

Huge screen painted on wall of downtown office building to show sound trailer each evening.

"I'm upside down from laughter."

...ners on prominent corners.

NUT SUNDAES

Nut sundaes featured for week at two dozen of town's busiest soda counters with fountain strips and special employee badges suggesting Marx Bros. nut sundae. Passes were given to employee in each store selling most sundaes during week.

FREE STUNT

Men wearing opera hats and full dress tails were admitted free on opening day as guests of Baltimore News and Post.

LAUGHMETER

"LAUGHMETER" installed at box office with amplifier carrying a special laugh record of audience reaction.

CUCKOO CLOCKS

Lobby display of cuckoo clocks borrowed from jewelry stores with tie-up copy and Marx Bros. blow-up photos.

Choice painted board locations.

A. & P. STORES

Co-op ads and window streamers in 250 A. & P. stores featured special sale on nuts in honor of Marx Bros. engagement.

NUT BREAD

Bakery co-operative ad and window strips featuring nut bread and cake dedicated to Marx Bros.

Truck load of nuts, with 24-sheet.

(That's not even the ½ of it. Go on!)

Above left: Street bally for *A Night at the Opera* **includes tandem bikes and a headless Groucho. Above right: The United Artists Theatre in Los Angeles hosted** *Opera* **in December 1935. Between shows, theatre manager Thomas D. Soriero demonstrated a four-ton, $75,000 contraption called "television." Claimed Soriero, "Some time in the future one will sit at home and watch the latest movies as well as current events and stage productions." It was a strange intersection of the Marx Brothers and technology that would, in 15 short years, finish off Hollywood's Golden Era of leisure domination.**

audiences. After all, they considered it a vote of confidence on the part of Thalberg and MGM to spend considerable amounts toward fine-tuning material for eventual use in the feature. *A Night at the Opera*'s live act was 50 minutes, give or take, preceding onscreen programs. The team, with writers assessing and revising, generally played four times a day and spent intervals figuring out what to save for the movie. Audience response determined the keepers.

If corporate-applied scientific principles got maximum efficiency out of car assembly plants and grocery chains, why not comedy? Thalberg assured control by assigning "a humorless functionary," so-called by Groucho, Sam Wood, to direct. Wood was instructed to shoot repeatedly from every conceivable angle, with 30 or more takes the enervating norm.

The Marx Brothers must have been sick to death of this material once they finally got it all down on film. *A Night at the Opera* was specifically edited for packed houses. Pauses for laughs break up each routine, much as they would in the later Hope/Crosby road comedies, also designed for large audiences. No wonder some of these play so sluggishly when you're watching alone.

For all the trouble Thalberg had taken, his formula would work only once. *Opera* had a negative cost of $1 million to recover, not an easy thing for a comedy team who'd peddled similar onscreen wares since 1929. Then as now, you either liked the Marx Brothers or you resolutely did not. The ink was probably dry on trade raves weeks before the picture opened. The majors had a knack for creating the perception of a hit; never mind what Mr. and Mrs. Patron really thought. Reviews not corrupted were often ignored. Photos of lines outside Broadway theatres conveyed a more forceful message.

Year-end accounts told the real story, and that wouldn't be shared with the press or public. *Opera* earned domestic rentals of $1.1 million, surely a peak for the Marxes, but less than MGM specials of that year were typically bringing. Foreign was $651,000. Worldwide rentals totaled $1.8 million, yielding final profits of only $90,000.

Thalberg sought the Marxes because he felt the lot needed comedians. Season commitments from independent exhibitors came with expectation of a balanced program. Undoubted disappointment over *A Night at the Opera* would not discourage Thalberg, but would he have stayed with the Marxes had he lived to see the losing numbers *A Day at the Races* generated? That follow-up to *Opera*, still in production at the time of Thalberg's death, took a considerable bath in red ink. A negative cost of $1.7 million was not equaled by domestic rentals of $1.6. The eventual loss was $543,000. Subsequent Marx Brothers features would be downgraded in budget and prestige. *At the Circus* lost $492,000; *Go West* (at a cost of $1.1 million) came up short by $206,000.

The Big Store's trailer depicts crowds howling for the team to come out of announced retirement to do one last comedy, but how many cared by 1941? *A Night in Casablanca* was said to have been made at Chico's behest, as he was in serious dutch over gambling debts. The 1946 independent released through United Artists would surprise naysayers and become the biggest grosser in first-run that the comedians ever had. In fact, it would be *A Night in Casablanca* that paved the way for *Opera* to finally become an unqualified hit.

The Marxes could scarcely have picked a better time for an encore, with 1946 a U.S. summit for theatre attendance. Seems everybody spent a first year back from the war going to movies. *A Night in Casablanca* may not have been prime Marx Brothers, but turnstiles spun to the tune of $1.8 million in domestic rentals, with $894,000 foreign. A worldwide final of $2.7 million suggested possibilities for a real comeback. The Marxes were surely in for a percentage. Were they fully apprised of how well this picture did? Looking back on the Paramount dispute, I wonder. By now, these comedians were showing some age, and may have been thinking that picture making had become more trouble than it was worth. At least for Groucho, solo work seemed preferable.

Would a major studio have embraced the team after *A Night in Casablanca*? MGM tested the waters with a December 1948 reissue of *A Night at the Opera*. Its New York sales team must have noticed the revival of old Paramount Marx Brothers features in newly burgeoning art houses around Manhattan. Flat rental peanuts to be sure, but what if the company really got behind *Opera* with an all-new campaign and top-line bookings? MGM's newly christened reissue program "Masterpiece Reprints" had led off with the stunning success of *A Rage in Heaven*, a 1941 feature that took $1.2 million in profits during 1946. This was followed with more library favorites and further profits:

After separating from MGM, the brothers split up and Chico hit the road with his orchestra; among his gigs was this one at Chicago's Oriental Theatre in 1942. Chico's gambling debts allegedly led the boys to reunite one more time.

Boom Town ($862,000), *The Great Waltz* ($1.0 million), and two Tarzans—*Secret Treasure* ($410,000) and *New York Adventure* ($434,000).

A Night at the Opera was trade-shown, ordinarily the exclusive province of new releases, and sold on a percentage basis. Domestic rentals were an outstanding $633,000, with foreign an additional $435,000, for a worldwide total of $1.0 million. The profit was $746,000. Save the 1949 *Love Happy* and its unremarkable $1.0 million in domestic rentals, there would be no further Marx Brothers starring features, and you could argue that Groucho's appearance in that one was but an extended cameo.

I'm guessing a lot of readers have been watching the Marx Brothers as long as I have. Maybe for *too* long. There's a point at which I stop laughing and start wondering what it is that's making *other* people laugh. I've long forgotten what first appealed to me about the team. I spent most of *A Night at the Opera* trying to remember. You get to a certain age, and too many favorites from youth become objects under a microscope, all of which keeps them interesting and maybe more stimulating, but comedies wilt on cross-examination, and too much analysis of the Marx Brothers drains every laugh out of them. I confess to having paused several times to remind myself, Ah, yes, this is supposed to be one of the funniest parts, and indeed, maybe it would be again were I part of a larger and, more important, younger audience.

In comedy, timing is everything. The Marxes finally enjoy perfect timing at United Artists, where they earn a stellar return with *A Night in Casablanca*.

It isn't fair to blame any movie for one's overexposure to it. *A Night at the Opera* is fascinating for what it reveals of a comedy act trying to hang on for a changing public. And *Opera* certainly has some of their best routines; that bed-moving sequence is a marvel of timing genius. But did viewers in 1935 want to see the Marx Brothers humanized, and worse yet, associated with normal, functioning, dull characters such as Allan Jones and Kitty Carlisle?

The last three Marx Paramount features were filled less with people than foils, stereotypes as opposed to individuals. Louis Calhern and Edgar Kennedy in *Duck Soup*, Nat Pendleton in *Horse Feathers*, and Thelma Todd in *Monkey Business* belonged in a Marxian universe. The Brothers interact with these figures only to torment and bedevil them. Human contact is the last thing they need or we want. Allan Jones and Kitty Carlisle are all the more distressing for friendly gestures they extend toward the comedians, surely the antidote to their being funny. The Marx Brothers must act in opposition to all things if they are to make us laugh. Whatever it is: I'm against it. But Grou-

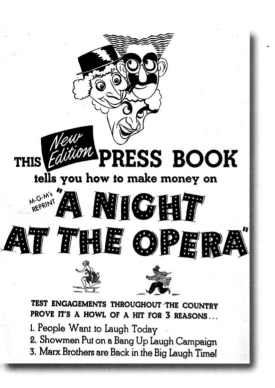

Riding *A Night in Casablanca* coattails, *Opera* returns for another run and finally becomes an unqualified hit.

cho delivering love notes from Allan to Kitty and rewarded with a kiss on the cheek that sends him into bashful retreat? Chico pledges unswerving loyalty to seemingly incompatible friend of long duration Jones. Both these plot devices were, and are, anathema to Marx followers.

"All those years we studied together at the conservatory," recalls Allan's character.

"We're still young, we got our health," replies steadfast Chico, who then volunteers to manage his buddy's career, for nothing. Chico was many things prior to landing at Metro, kindly and reassuring not among them. Worse still is Harpo's transformation. The edge, if not danger, he posed at Paramount is replaced with kiddie-host geniality, a forerunner to harmless fools who'd smuggle bananas past Captain Kangaroo. Brats guffawing around Harpo's piano would not have taken such liberties in earlier films.

Accommodations made for these and other tender sensibilities make it harder for the Marxes to play off each other successfully. Soft hearts once revealed are less credible in the guise of anarchists. The loss is most keenly felt at the end when the team goes about demolishing the opera itself, simply because they are the Marx Brothers and this is what they do, or once did. Going through the motions of destructive acts both pointless and forced—why wreck the opera when they were otherwise so determined to enable Allan Jones to sing in it?—the comics seem lost in a polished MGM universe, wherein Marx madness would be all too studied in application and conventional in results.

This still, taken on May 25, 1937, seems to show Clark Gable contributing to the studio's efforts to keep Jean Harlow looking vital under lots of makeup and wardrobe. In fact, Harlow is already dying and won't last two more weeks.

CHAPTER 6

METRO'S JEAN HARLOW CLOSEOUT SALE

Code enforcement had signaled the end for Jean Harlow's established sexpot image as surely as it had for Mae West. The character may have been played out in any case, but clearly something had to be done to accommodate the Code and maintain Harlow as a viable ongoing attraction.

Hold Your Man was produced and released before the crackdown of mid-1934, but already MGM was softening content, perhaps in response to the outcry over *Red Dust*. This second Gable–Harlow co-starring vehicle was like two wildly disparate movies under a single wobbly umbrella. A first 35 or so minutes of bare-knuckle pre-Code devolved to a final half that doled out excessive punishment to both the characters and their audience, as if to chastise us for having enjoyed what went before. It was a harbinger of worse things to come, not only for Jean Harlow, known affectionately around the studio as "Baby," but for a generation of actresses who had defined themselves in terms of pre-Code freedom of expression. Things would never be the same for any of them after this.

It was a testament to her public's confidence that Harlow maintained popularity despite the neutering, though a $125,000 loss on *Reckless* and $63,000 down with *Riff-Raff* suggested their patience might be thinning. Metro's answer was to polish off some rough edges. First, the hair had to change, which was good because it was nearly gone anyway, having been coarsened and ruined over years of mistreatment. The new brownette look went hand in hand with gentler Jean, no longer the barbed wire that wrapped herself around leading men (see *Red-Headed Woman*), but an unassuming helpmate, best exemplified by a subdued turn in *Wife vs. Secretary*. This was 1936, and adulterous games she'd played on-screen during pre-Code years were now a deadly serious business with grave consequences for those who transgressed. Jean's secretary was a nice girl living at home with Mom and Dad, her gelded suitor a just beginning James Stewart. Whatever sizzle audiences recalled with co-star Clark Gable was lost in the mists of time, as PCA prohibition against reissues of forbidden titles kept embargoes firmly in place.

Harlow's compensation was now increased to $3,000 a week, but her suffocating mother remained a problem, and the star never girded up sufficient will to fight back. Alcohol became a hidden crutch, though it seldom interfered with work. But what about the nagging health problems that plagued her? Impacted wisdom teeth led to a procedure that almost proved fatal, and photographers who'd once tabbed Harlow's a flawless face and figure now applied retouching to both. Romance with urbane William Powell held the promise of eternal commitment, only Bill didn't want to commit, and that re-

Above: Platinum bombshell Jean Harlow poses at home in Beverly Hills. Close inspection of this photo shows retouching to smooth out some of the Baby's baby fat. Below: Two years later, *after* the Code, a family-friendly, "brownette" Harlow is reborn in pictures like *Riff-Raff*.

sulted in public embarrassment for Jean. This was the world's most desirable woman, after all.

The image modification seemed to have worked. Profits for the next several pictures were up. *Suzy* ($498,000), *Libeled Lady* ($1.1 million), and *Personal Property* ($872,000) promised glad tidings to come. Jean was young enough to sustain at least another decade of success, unlike older thoroughbreds in the Metro stables. As Shearer, Crawford, and Garbo were maturing out, Harlow ascended to first chair among female talent. A forthcoming loan to Fox for their spectacular *In Old Chicago* promised to team her with man of the hour Tyrone Power.

That she would die at this moment was unimaginable, but that's what happened on June 7, 1937. Her kidneys had been degenerating since a scarlet fever episode in 1926. The crisis point was upon Harlow, and nothing could undo years of cumulative damage. A lot of friends and co-workers blamed the crazy mother and her Christian Science-inspired determination to avoid doctors, but Mayo Clinic couldn't have saved this girl. The shock was all the more palpable because Harlow was genuinely liked among peers, and no one imagined such a dire outcome for her. Death was lingering and painful. The official cause was uremic poisoning—total organ shutdown and a ghoulish tableau that visitors would never get over. She was just 26.

It was *Variety*-announced the next day that Harlow's in-production *Saratoga* would be "scrapped" to a loss of $500,000, as the film could not wrap satisfactorily minus further scenes with her character. Imagine corporate reaction here. They were close enough to a *Saratoga* finish line to sniff the receipts. Banner obit headlines referred to her last film so near done. A resigned Louis Mayer figured to cast a new leading lady and reshoot *Saratoga* in toto. What else could his company do?

From here, events moved fast. The following week saw "more than 500 fan letters" demanding

Above: Jean Harlow's decline is visible day to day due mostly to fluid retention. Costumes hide some of it, but she looks less and less like herself. Below: A swollen, tired-looking Harlow with Walter Pidgeon, Lionel Barrymore, and director Jack Conway shoot what will turn out to be her last scenes for MGM's *Saratoga*.

the pic be released as is, with Harlow. New York's sales arm for Loew's wondered if another player, Rita Johnson, could pinch-hit for a departed Harlow in those scenes left to film, "with fact of this peculiar situation explained in [a] note under the main title"; this according to *Variety*.

Others suggested that perhaps co-stars Clark Gable and Lionel Barrymore could simply explain the balance of the plot from the point where Harlow dropped out. W.R. Hearst's Los Angeles *Examiner* took the lead among press pleas for Metro to do whatever was necessary to share *Saratoga* with an eager and waiting public.

Earlier Harlow films were meanwhile flying off exchange shelves and into theatres fairly desperate for anything of her they could play. *Personal Property* had been sub-running, nearly wrung out, when the actress passed. Now it was back as if new. "Nabes [slang for neighborhoods] are putting on Harlow weeks with three or four of her films in a row," reported *Variety*. Even oldies *Bombshell*, *Dinner at Eight*, and *Hell's Angels* came roaring back, exhibs in many cases pairing them to promote JH double-feature tributes.

By June 17, 10 days after Harlow's death, Metro had "understudy" Mary Dees before cameras to double the late star in long shots and filmed-from-behind action. One scene had Dees holding binoculars to her face as others spoke necessary dialogue. The impersonator was a practiced one, Mary Dees having been yanked off Canadian vaudeville touring as an ersatz Harlow to do *Saratoga*. MGM gave her a term contract for the forfeit, but issued no Dees publicity so as to keep her doubling low key.

Volumes of ad copy rationalize the release of Harlow's last picture. The gamble of completing *Saratoga* returns substantial profit to MGM.

MAKE YOUR PROMOTION CAMPAIGN
A Final Tribute to Jean Harlow!

AVOID SENSATIONAL OR THE MORE OBVIOUSLY COMMERCIALIZED EXPLOITATION METHODS. JEAN HARLOW'S SUDDEN DEATH LEFT SUCH AN IRREPARABLE ENTERTAINMENT LOSS THAT AT LEAST 50% OF YOUR CAMPAIGN SHOULD BE IN THE NATURE OF A TRIBUTE TO HER PERSONALITY AND POPULARITY. HANDLE IT WITH DIGNITY AND RESTRAINT SO AS TO CAUSE OFFENSE TO NO ONE.

W. R. FERGUSON, *Manager of Exploitation.*

Exhibitors face the difficult task of acknowledging the passing of one of Hollywood's biggest stars, while still managing to promote their product.

And so they came to ponder Jean Harlow graveyard bound in *Saratoga*, the talking screen's first post mortem for all to enjoy. What else but pure morbid fascination drove attendance numbers higher than any yet recorded for a Harlow film? Trades called the *Saratoga* push "a natural," what with public interest at a fever pitch. A dark side of movie going was—and still is—that desire to ponder idols in the grip of mortal concerns visited upon us all. What was the crowd response to Wallace Reid's posthumous offerings? He and Harlow shared the lure of having been gravely sick, yet reporting still for work. In effect, the public watched them die on the screen. That was as intimate a glimpse into celebrity private life as fans could hope for.

MGM press would hammer two points: The public's insistence that *Saratoga* be released, and the technical brilliance applied toward making that possible. You'd think they were remaking *King Kong* for so much emphasis on camera effects. Beyond a Harlow-esque dye job with sunglasses and floppy hats on Mary Dees, there were script changes for act three taking the JH character largely out of action. Fortunately for MGM, they'd done a Gable/Harlow two-shot to cap the final scene, so crowds could enjoy a happy fadeout clinch with their departed favorite.

Metro's *Saratoga* trailer host Lewis Stone gave assurance that all had been conducted with dignity and decorum. Again it was our demand that his employers were accommodating, not MGM's desire to reap profits from a star's premature exit.

Clark Gable and Walter Pidgeon flanked the Harlow ghost and must have spent by far the creepiest days of their respective careers doing so. Neither appears to have spoken of it later, but imagine how they felt plodding through shots jerry-rigged to cover for this essential presence now absent. Making it worse was the fact that Metro's workforce, Harlow allies all, were put off by these not-so-magic tricks.

Saratoga was sneak-previewed in Pomona on June 30 and "went over in grand style," according to *Variety*. Two days later, Al Lichtman and Howard Dietz winged in from New York to organize sales and exploitation. The *Motion Picture Herald* didn't list a release date until July 10, and then the announced August 6 bow was moved up when Metro booked *Saratoga* into their New York flagship, the Capitol, for July 23. Time as essence was upon them, for how long would patrons' grim curiosity abide?

There was another preview in Glendale, California—the very town where Harlow would rest for eternity—during mid-July. "A respectful burst of applause greeted the title, cast listing, and Miss Harlow's first appearance," said a trade reviewer. "It was obvious the audience was watching every move she made." No doubt, since folks knew by then how ill she'd been and wanted to diagnose the patient for themselves. "Yet this interest did not prevent moviegoers from enjoying the picture as a whole and being appreciative of the efforts of the other stars and members of the supporting cast." It was as though press coverage wanted to let viewers off the hook for gaping at Harlow as she approached death.

"The audience psychology seemed to denote that the picture would be a potent box-office feature," was the *Motion Picture Herald*'s summation. Here was tactful assurance to Metro that they were in the chips. "MGM Breathes a Little Easier" was a follow-up headline for July 31 after *Saratoga*'s conquest of the Capitol became apparent.

In fact, they'd seldom seen crowds like these at the Capitol, where the Loew-Metro management stationed several police guards at all points of the lobby "to prevent souvenir hunters from carrying away Harlow photographs or other materials." Summer was ordinarily dog days for show going, that owing to most theatres' lack of air-conditioning. MGM boasted all-year-round hits and made good, as reflected in trade ads, with stellar attractions that would highlight any venue's season.

Captains Courageous, *A Day at the Races*, and *Broadway Melody of 1938* were offered during those warmest 1937 months, and now there'd be a bonus of *Saratoga* and waiver of

GET FLORISTS TO PARTICIPATE

THE phrase, "Lest We Forget", should be the keynote of all theatre and outside observances planned for Miss Harlow's final picture, "Saratoga". It can be handled delicately with framed photos of her in florists' windows which can also show scenes from her past pictures. Omit the usual tie-up copy and let the store state it is their tribute to a very great star who achieved immortality among the motion picture fans of the world.

Above: MGM suggests tie-ins with florists, deepening the funereal pall over the picture. Below: A Fort Worth newspaper has some grisly fun sorting out which scenes feature Harlow and which employ her double, Mary Dees.

Which Is Jean, Which Is Double?

Jean Harlow—or double? Which is which? These screen performance photos, snapped by Press Photographer Wilburn Davis from the fifth row at the Worth Theater, show you how Metro-Goldwyn-Mayer completed "Saratoga" after the death of Miss Harlow, star of the film. Top, left, is the real Miss Harlow in a merry scene with Clark Gable. On the right and below, enter a double. The cameraman, shooting from long distance, covers the switch in the upper right photo. Below, the double cleverly keeps a pair of binoculars to her eyes, concealing most of her face. "Saratoga" will be at the Worth all week.

the run/clearance policy that kept smaller showmen at the back of the line. Leo was committed to make more prints and get them into circulation faster—a saturation play-off long before such strategy was generally embraced by distributors. These were "unusual circumstances," per MGM's trade declaration, unique to a feature that mere weeks before looked as though it would have to be abandoned or completely reshot. An unprecedented 360 prints (nearly double the customary number for a major release) were manufactured for nationwide day-and-date openings.

Word got round fast that *Saratoga* was a must-see. *Harrison's Report* called it "just fair as entertainment and quite choppy in the bargain," but critics maybe failed to realize that patrons' fun of watching was bound up in just that, for *Saratoga* quickly evolved into a nationwide hide-and-seek for the real Harlow versus the woman impersonating her. Newspapers got in on the grisly game.

Which Is Jean, Which Is Double? asked Fort Worth editors as they dispatched a photographer to capture shots supposedly snapped from the Worth Theatre's fifth row, these published for readership sport of spotting Metro's gambit. So went dignified tribute into a cocked hat, despite ads promising same.

At least the money was good. Since when had MGM collected anything approaching $3.2 million worldwide for a Harlow pic, let alone profits exceeding a million? To Clark Gable's benefit, *Saratoga* provided welcome fumigation for theatres having just played *Parnell*, a stench still fresh in viewer nostrils. The windfall blew through by the close of 1937, and *Saratoga* remained vault-bound from there until release to television in 1956, by which time most had forgotten the fluke success, and reason for it, that had accompanied Jean Harlow's last film nearly 20 years earlier.

United Artists seizes upon Harlow's death and reissues *Hell's Angels* using art from the 1930 campaign, including this lobby card dated 1937. Suddenly, Jean Harlow is a raw teenager again and very much alive.

Individually they provide chills; together
they will prove unstoppable.

CHAPTER 7

THE PAIR THAT CURLED YOUR HAIR

There was a time when giants filled the theatres, two being *Frankenstein* and *Dracula*. Both embodied brand names; together they were unstoppable. Think mashed potatoes and gravy, football and beer…American institutions. No, *Frankenstein* and *Dracula* are *world* institutions. Both had literary origins overseas. They've pinballed cash registers here and over there for more generations than any of us have been around. Universal draws blood yet from these early '30s stones that play more profitably than anything else so old. A *Frankenstein* or *Dracula* one-sheet in your attic will buy a new house.

For seven years after their initial release in 1931, showmen regarded them separately. Playdates were infrequent as Universal provided sequels (*Bride of Frankenstein*, *Dracula's Daughter*) beginning right where originals left off, but there were gold deposits untapped even as the mine's route lay not hidden, but in plain sight. The magic was in combining them, but nobody thought of that until seemingly bungled reissues of *Frankenstein* and *Dracula* suddenly caught fire together in August 1938.

For months running up, talking picture revivals were an idea just beginning to come into their own. To have heavily circulated oldies prior to this would have meant either pictures too recent, or, heaven forbid, silents. Thus, 1938 became the first season for heavy studio exploitation of vault product. A lot of that came of patron and showman requests. The trades said that a shortage of new product was what catapulted demand.

Universal counted 21 favorites that fans wanted back. Most of these were supplied by whatever prints an exchange might have on hand. An official re-release necessitated a fresh campaign and submission of the feature for a Production Code seal, then test engagements determined levels of interest in proposed titles. Universal tested *Frankenstein* during March and April '38 with three others, *All Quiet on the Western Front*, *Lady Tubbs*, a 1935 comedy with Alice Brady as a madcap crashing society, and *Love Before Breakfast* with popular Carole Lombard. These were floated in both single and combo berths, but response was mixed. Harold S. Eskin, head of Eskin Amusement Enterprises, was impressed. "You may unreservedly tell your men in the field, if you wish, to sell this show [*Frankenstein* and *Love Before Breakfast*] to the exhibitor as a unit, that it did for me more than 75 percent in excess of business ordinarily done in my theatre."

A New York booking of *Frankenstein* at 42nd Street's Liberty Theatre was something else. "It played off during April without causing much excitement," said the *Motion Picture Herald*. The few-doors-down Rialto repeated *Dracula* the same month, without impressive results. Owner Arthur Mayer spoke of both pictures having played singly every "shooting gallery" (a term for grind theatres) in town.

Universal still regarded *Frankenstein* as promising enough to warrant an official May 15 re-release date along with the three other tested oldies. *Dracula* became number five of these for the company's 1938–39 season in early June. Trade ads promised accessories, including fresh trailers, but nothing was suggested with regard to pairing the monsters. Showmen drawing from the list took so many pigs from a poke. B. Hollenbeck of the Rose Theatre in Sumas, Washington, tried *Dracula* with *Lady Tubbs* and, said Hollenbeck, "These two reissues were a complete flop here. Didn't make running expenses."

Is it safe to say *Dracula* was damned on this occasion by the company he kept? Both horrors got into some pretty horrific combinations. One theatre ran *Frankenstein* and *Dracula* on separate programs in support of "B" westerns; a lot of houses normally dark during summer months because they lacked air-conditioning kept their lights burning with such cheaply bought fare. Universal's monsters were clearly not being sold properly. As is so often the case, it was the singular effort of an ingenious showman that saved their bacon.

Tests in the spring of 1938 indicate evergreen strength for five Universal oldies, but results prove to be mixed...until the horror boys are packaged together.

FIVE TOP FILM FAVORITES RE-EARNING PROFIT GROSSES ALL OVER THE COUNTRY!

Exhibitors report test runs turning in record receipts!.... Each picture a power-charged, money-making vehicle!
YOUR UNIVERSAL RE-DATES FOR PROFIT!

DRACULA
with Bela Lugosi...The Vampire Bat Strikes Again! Feasting on the blood of the living!

ALL QUIET ON THE WESTERN FRONT
Twice as timely NOW! Every word of the title super-charged with interest by front page events!

FRANKENSTEIN
The top grosser of them all!...The Power Thriller they can't resist! Karloff! Colin Clive! Mae Clarke! Boles!

LADY TUBBS
Comedy smash that's pulling them in like magic in a dozen test spots! With Alice Brady, Anita Louise, Alan Mowbray and Douglass Montgomery.

LOVE before BREAKFAST
with CAROLE LOMBARD, the comedy and star a delighted nation went crazy over!

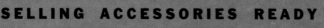

SELLING ACCESSORIES READY   .....PUT THEM TO WORK!

Above left: *Dracula* and *Frankenstein* are paired to shatter records in L.A. and Seattle. Above right: Patrons of the Joie are dared to see them together (note segregated late-night showing for "colored folks"). Below: Audiences at the Regina in L.A. are among the first to respond to the unique pairing.

The Regina was an 800-seat theatre at Wilshire and La Cienega in Los Angeles. It had opened on April 21, 1937, with a combo of *Black Legion* and *That Girl from Paris*. With seats at 25 cents for adults and a dime for children, the Regina got by mostly on sub-runs and reissues. Peter Lorre dropped in once to catch *M*, the German thriller that had made him famous, third on a bill with *The Black Room* and *White Zombie*. Lorre fell asleep in his seat waiting for *M* to start.

A lot of patrons slept through parts or all of such double and/or triple bills at the Regina. Their booking of *Frankenstein* and *Dracula*, along with RKO's *Son of Kong*, was intended to be a four-day run beginning Thursday, August 4, 1938. I'm specific about that date because it made history. Crowds jammed the front, and manager Emil Umann found himself adding late, and later, shows to accommodate them.

Legend persists that Umann rented long-neglected prints of *Dracula* and *Frankenstein* at a film warehouse, but these titles, having been available on reissue for several months, were less neglected than mishandled. The inspiration, and a brilliant one, lay in combining them for the first time with a marquee challenging patrons: **DARE YOU SEE?**

Umann's masterstroke was no one's idea but his own. Universal bookers driving to work watched him smash records daily with pictures they'd sold the Regina at flat rate. Within a week, trades carried accounts of the theatre's smash biz and nightly stop-ins by Bela Lugosi, invited by Umann to appear with his star-making (once again) hit.

"I owe it all to that little man at the Regina Theatre," said Lugosi of his showman benefactor. "I was dead, and he brought me back to life."

A belatedly alerted Universal began laying plans of its own. "Following the local stint," said the company, "Lugosi will go on a prolonged personal appearance tour with the horror films, first taking in the west coast, then extending it throughout the country."

Being a producing firm without its own theatre chain, Universal's reach was exceeding its grasp. Bookings, let alone favorable ones in "A" houses, came hardest to those below the integrated radar of the Big Five, which included Paramount, MGM, 20th Century Fox, RKO, and Warner Bros. They each owned theatres and together dominated every worthwhile territory in the nation. Universal faced its usual selling challenge with *Dracula* and

Frankenstein, despite the combination's remarkable success at the Regina.

A second August run at Seattle's Blue Mouse Theatre disabused notions that monsters in tandem were a fluke. **UNABLE HANDLE CROWDS OPENING DAY**, reported manager John Hamrick in a telegram. **COMBINING THESE PICTURES SHOWMANS DREAM OF GOOD TIMES HERE AGAIN**.

The Seattle Board of Theatre Censors crabbed the party somewhat when it barred children under 15 from attending on grounds that the intense excitement was harmful, a minor bump in Universal's road toward a "profit epidemic," now confirmed. A September 3 trade ad promised runs for Denver, Salt Lake City, and hundreds of other cities. Terms were generous to start as the company continued seeking wider traction. They got it after riots at Salt Lake City's Victory Theatre all but necessitated that state's militia. The house was sold out by 10 o'clock in the morning. Said one trade observer: "Four thousand frenzied Mormons milled around outside, finally broke through the police lines, smashed the plate glass box office, bent in the front doors, and tore off one of the door checks in their eagerness to get in and be frightened. Management was forced to rent an empty theatre across the street to seat the overflow."

Reels of *Dracula* and *Frankenstein* were bicycled back and forth in 20-minute intervals throughout the day. The Victory's triumph was bittersweet for Universal, as this theatre, like the Regina, booked its monster rally at a flat rate and therefore kept a lion's share of bounties. With their fad blossoming for a lucrative autumn, Universal would stiffen its terms and swing for the fences.

Small-timer Umann took the brunt of Universal's bounce when they yanked the Regina's prints after a fourth week, and *Frankenstein* and *Dracula* moved to downtown palace digs with more seats and percentage

Top right: A window card for the 1938 reissue is among the first posters to feature both monsters. Bottom right: Homespun bally for a successful combo run at the Blue Mouse Theatre in Seattle is designed to inspire other showmen to follow suit for "sockeroo" business.

FRONT
The Blue Mouse front was a sockeroo. Colors were red, yellow, purple and green. The main banner was 50 feet long and 4 feet wide. This carried the "DARE" copy and the names of the features. On each end of the banner was a huge compo-board figure - 10 to 14 ft. high - one of the MONSTER and one of DRACULA. Easels were constructed with stills on a panel shaped like a bolt of lightning. Easel background spider webs of purple, black and green with flitter on the webs were also used. Cutout heads of FRANKENSTEIN and DRACULA were used on the easels. All glass doors, panels, etc. were painted with the spider web effect.

payoffs. It seemed a raw deal for the man who'd conceived such a winning plan, as Universal sale staffers were given (and took) credit for the company's monstrous success when newspapers began recognizing the phenomenon.

Throw Away the Books! read trade ads on October 15. **You Play Them Together! You Dare Them to See It! And Then the Crowds Break Down Your Doors!** Salt Lake's fulfillment of the latter helped get the big circuits on board as of that month.

Dracula and *Frankenstein* played Fox west coast theatres plus major houses nationwide, and at last Universal was in for a piece of the action. The New York *Times* wrote up that town's opening at Broadway's Rialto Theatre and expressed the mainstream's customary bemusement over a public's frenzy for horror. Rialto manager Arthur Mayer had been Harvard educated and knew how to milk the press for coverage of goings-on at his all-day-and-night grindhouse.

Those 600 Rialto seats provided refuge for kids playing hooky, husbands who were supposed to be out looking for jobs, and guys on the run from cops. They had an entrance door from the subway and through a basement arcade known as a hangout for troublemakers. Mayer was called the Merchant of Menace and relished the tag; his Rialto had been premiering Universal chillers over the past several years.

If you've heard anything at all about "Big Business" pictures—you've heard about this pair of horror babies. They work automatically. You play them together. You dare people to see them. Anywhere, any type of theatre, any day of the week—THEY HIT!

"DRACULA" with BELA LUGOSI ...AND... "FRANKENSTEIN" with BORIS KARLOFF TOGETHER!

BOOKED BY BALABAN & KATZ, ESSANESS, FOX-WISCONSIN and OTHER LIVE-WIRE SHOWMEN

THE LIVING DEAD with GERALD duMAURIER GEORGE CURZON Belle CHRYSTALL A FIRST DIVISION RELEASE

A BRAND NEW RELEASE

SHE WAS NOT DEAD ... NOR ALIVE ... Just a WHITE Zombie Starring BELA LUGOSI

Because Horror Is the Pay-Off!
Book These Two Outstanding Horror Hits
SUPERIOR PICTURES, INC.
CHICAGO — MILWAUKEE — INDIANAPOLIS — ST. LOUIS

Opposite page: The formula for success: "play them together" and dare your audiences to see it. Clockwise from above: Once paired, *Dracula* and *Frankenstein* spell big business; box-office success ushers in two more pairings "Because Horror Is the Pay-Off!" Not only does *White Zombie* reappear, but also a *Bride* and a *Daughter*; bally for a reissue combo of *The Walking Dead* and *Revolt of the Zombies* includes skeleton on a gurney.

You dared them to see "Dracula" and "Frankenstein"... now defy them to see "Drac and Frank's" sister team... The answer is the same... the grosses are the same... the appeal is there!

"DRACULA'S DAUGHTER" with OTTO KRUGER · GLORIA HOLDEN ...AND... "THE BRIDE OF FRANKENSTEIN" with COLIN CLIVE · VALERIE HOBSON ELSA LANCHESTER · UNA O'CONNOR Directed by James Whale

CAN YOU TAKE IT? ads for *Frankenstein* and *Dracula*, plus imaginative front ballys, delivered $12,000 in the Rialto's first week against an average weekly gross of $5,500. It was inevitable that others would try scaling Universal's castle walls. Lacking names the equal of *Frankenstein* and *Dracula*, they nonetheless copied selling tactics of a we-dare-you sort with results satisfactory but nowhere near what the first team was fetching. RKO came closest with its first major revival of *King Kong* since 1933, but most competing shows ran along the lines of pretenders *Revolt of the Zombies* and *The Walking Dead*.

Exhibitors who knew better clung to the originals, however. "These two pictures together [*Frankenstein* and *Dracula*] have all the rest of the horror pictures cheated a mile," said P.G. Held of Griswold, Iowa's New Strand Theatre.

Halloween meanwhile provided another surge for Universal's monster merchandise. The Orson Welles *War of the Worlds* broadcast on October 30, along with "upset conditions in Europe and the Orient, further whetted a public's appetite for shudder pictures," according to the *Motion Picture Herald*. Universal announced *Son of Frankenstein* for production starting November 9, with January 1939 release to follow. A pastiche culled from a *Flash Gordon* serial, *Mars Attacks the World*,

The success of the 1938 combo reissue of *Dracula* and *Frankenstein* ushered in a new cycle of Universal chillers, including the landmark *Son of Frankenstein*, which featured Karloff's return for one more interpretation of the Monster, and his marquee co-headliner, Lugosi, this time portraying broken-necked Igor.

was released in the wake of Welles' news-making event. This went into theatres right behind *Frankenstein* and *Dracula*, where it often scored 80 percent of the combo's business.

To maintain flows of reissue cash, Universal test-ran a merger of *Dracula's Daughter* with *Bride of Frankenstein* at the Uptown Theatre in Kansas City during November '38. Results proved sufficiently gratifying to earn this new pairing a nationwide re-release later that month. Everything horrific was hot again, but just how long were legs for 1938's monster boomlet?

The dearth of new horror films during 1937 and 1938 explained much of Universal's success. Patrons frankly missed being chilled and wanted that old goose-bump feeling back. December '38 saw *Dracula* and *Frankenstein* still harvesting off money trees. Universal boasted of "a thousand bookings for the combo so far, and it expects four thousand more before the trend has run its course." This was unprecedented, as most reissues stalled well below 1,200 playdates. Crowded theatres served to benefit still-in-production *Son of Frankenstein* as a duly impressed Universal increased expenditure for its sequel far beyond amounts previously invested in the genre. According to trades, the company had doubled its budget on *Son* to over $500,000, exclusive of large advertising appropriation. Final figures revealed exaggeration on Universal's part, as negative costs on *Son of Frankenstein* totaled $385,000, still a generous outlay for a monster pic.

As to still-playing originals, an order for 500 new prints reflected confidence that both would run well into 1939, as *Dracula* and *Frankenstein* remained in service even after *Son of Frankenstein* debuted on January 13 and, in some situations, competed with the older attractions. If nothing else, the stunning success of Universal's combo revealed the unique position these characters held in the public's imagination, for combining them formed, at least in movie-going parlance, as compelling a brand name as Coca-Cola or Kleenex tissue.

OFFICE OF *William Brandt*

Brandt Theatres
229 WEST 42ⁿᵈ STREET, NEW YORK 18, N.Y. LO. 5-3700

April 10, 1952

Mr. Jack Bellman
Realart Film Co.
630 Ninth Avenue
New York, N. Y.

Dear Jack:

I thought you would like to know that your show, "Frankenstein and Dracula, has broken every record for our Victory Theatre on 42 Street.

If ever there was a natural sleeper, this show certainly is it and in these days when sleepers are rare, it gives me great pleasure to pass the news along to you and exhibitors who need attractions badly.

This show is great—it lends itself to novel exploitation and advertising stunts which pay off. Apparently there is a brand new audience which has heard of these attractions but has never seen them. They are like nationally advertised brands of merchandise—well known and accepted.

We are still breathless over our first week's business, and our second week (Holy Week) is on its way towards duplicating this smash business. Dig up some more attractions of this kind. We will gladly use them.

Kindest personal regards.

Cordially and sincerely yours,

William Brandt

Above: Realart pays off big for the Brandt Theatre circuit. Below: The Victory, a historic Brandt Manhattan property, used the classic dare to lure in patrons and shatter records.

4th RECORD-BREAKING **WEEK!**
WE DARE YOU TO SEE IT! IT WILL SCARE THE YELL OUT OF YOU!

See—THE WEIRDEST BLOOD-CURDLING MYSTERY THRILLERS OF ALL TIME!

starring BELA LUGOSI

DRACULA
THE VAMPIRE BAT THAT LIVES ON HUMAN BLOOD!

THE ORIGINAL UNCUT VERSIONS!

FRANKENSTEIN

A MONSTER SCIENCE CREATED But Could Not Destroy!

starring BORIS KARLOFF *as The Monster*

BRANDT'S **VICTORY-42 St.**
BETWEEN B'WAY & 8ᵗʰ AVE. · LO. 5-2330
LATE SHOW TONITE! CONTINUOUS TO 4 A. M.

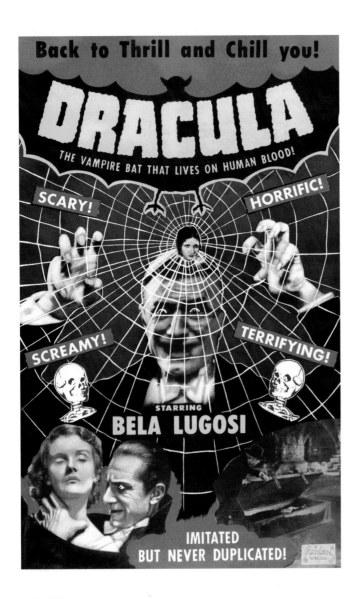

The exhibition strategy for Realart, self-styled as the world's largest reissue company, included all new, full-color lobby display campaigns.

Certainly it was *Dracula* and *Franken-stein* together that ushered in the second major horror film cycle at Universal. Sequels continued unabated through the war as monsters became more and more the exclusive province of kid and teen audiences. The bleak austerity of early-'30s incarnations seemed all the more so beside mid-'40s monster rallies with their nonstop action and wall-to-wall musical scores, yet *Dracula* and *Frankenstein* maintained caché right through succeeding decades and generations of fans. When time came for Universal to again try a thriller combo in 1947, their pick was, not surprisingly, those standbys that had delivered so well nine years earlier. The "Horror Boys" had long since been declared the safest bet for filling midnight tandem bills. *Dracula* and *Frankenstein* would go on delivering as a start-up distributor called Realart leased rights for both after the 1947 run.

Classic bally, including life-size standees on the marquee, work for Realart's 1952 run of *Frankenstein* and *Dracula*, "together in one show."

This killer couple was, and remains, a value pack that keeps on selling. Witness Universal's continual repackaging of both on DVD and Blu-ray. Fans have been special-editioned to death seeking perfect delivery of these two. Who dreamed of such commercial mileage, let alone box-office longevity, when virtually any film carried a box-office expiration tag? Universal figured on having strip-mined *Dracula* and *Frankenstein* in revivals (1938 and 1947) spread far enough apart to exhaust whatever audience might be interested. By war's end, the company sought bigger-money markets as formulas tried and true were banished from studio rosters. Budget westerns, serials, "B" musicals—all discontinued, as was identification with the sort of cheap monster movies that Universal now sought to expunge.

Three-million dollars from Realart loosened ties on inventory going back to the beginning of talkies, with Universal signing an unprecedented deal to let the smaller company reissue its studio wares for 10 theatrical (but no television) years. "Selling films is like selling anything else, for instance, sport shirts," said Paul Broder, who'd bulked out the latter and run Detroit theatres besides with enterprising brother Jack. These boys knew their onions for having handled bushels of discarded product in houses too often marginalized by circuit competitors and peanut operating budgets. They also knew oldies were still goodies, especially when paired.

With hundreds of Universal vaults now socked away in Realart exchanges, the little distributing engine that could declared itself unequivocally "the largest reissue company in the world," as if others vied for said distinction. Neighborhood houses that waited a year or more for new releases realized better gains with Realart pics they could rent cheaper and sell harder. Many were using reissues to fill 80 percent of their schedules.

Thematic combos became a Broder specialty. Jack tested them at leisure among five L.A. venues he still operated while serving as VP for Realart, and 34 Universals they shipped, profitably, for

1947–48 were bumped to 48 in 1948–49. The monster shows became, not unexpectedly, a Broder natural, as they were ideally suited for "dualers." Two mummies here, a couple of invisible men there, and before you knew it, towns were overrun with Universal, no, make that Realart, horrors.

I had a friend who grew up in Columbus, Ohio. Around 1950 he would catch the bus Saturday mornings for a weekly Realart chase through grinders for miles around, scoring up five or six per weekend of what we now call classics. For our NC backwood drive-ins, there'd be all-nighters with a quartet at least twixt dusk and dawn, ads for which cause latter day fans to salivate still.

So what of *Dracula* and *Frankenstein* in this roving encore madhouse? For these specials (and they knew it), Realart waited until 1951. As before, *D* and *F* rented singly but scored best when teamed. New York's Victory Theatre, a stone's throw up 42nd Street from the legendary Rialto, harnessed lightning in April 1952 not unlike that which galvanized their rival back in 1938. "Apparently, there is a brand new audience which has heard of these attractions but has never seen them," said Victory chief William Brandt. "They are like nationally advertised brands of merchandise—well known and accepted."

His 982-seat barn dated back to 1900 when it opened as a legit house, skidded down to burlesque in the '30s, then rose out of the ashes to become a sub-runner. The Victory's front saw the fiendish pair hovering from marquees and dressing entrance areas, touted as well in newspaper ads little changed from those appearing 14 years before. Realart put fresh coats of paint on campaigns they inherited from Universal. Poster art was sometimes more arresting than the originals. These greeted audiences at the Victory and other places where *Frankenstein* and *Dracula* bade them enter via displays that have since become "Most Wanted" collectables from the '50s.

A turning point—and after all, one had to come—was June 1957. That's when Frankenstein was finally reinvented. Ground so fertile must be freshly tilled, and red-meat, preferably blood-red, appetites could not be sated forever on the subdued sensation oldster parents had quaked over since 1931. *The Curse of Frankenstein* threw out the instruction manuals written by Universal and added that most crucial of equalizers to combat old movies and the TV sets that ran them: color. Floating eyeballs and blood-spattered lab jackets led the way for a new kind of explicit screen mayhem that fans had long anticipated via live spook shows far more direct than the timidity so far projected on

Frankenstein rebranded: *The Curse of Frankenstein* brings both color and gore to the famous monster and his maker. *Curse*, a summer release, scores big with a new generation.

screens. *The Curse of Frankenstein* showed for a first time the horrific possibilities of monsters laid face up and genuinely repulsive.

Here was science creating something like the aftermath of a car wreck you drove by coming to the theatre, a sort of full-color exclamation point to gross-out gymnatorium showings of *The Last Prom*. It was the same with *I Was a Teenage Frankenstein*, only that monster began as a crash victim and pretty much entered his Hell through a windshield. The essential fright of both films was unmistakable if subliminal. Drag race or go chicken running and this may be *your* dead end. No wonder kids got all shook up. Bally stunting as old as the hills on one hand slammed home likely unintended but hard-hitting safety warnings on the other; thus, girls planted in the auditorium would "faint," and cooperative ambulance services would roll up for showy rescues and siren-accompanied pullouts. Hopefully, real emergencies weren't unfolding elsewhere that required their services. Victims would be driven

Teen-oriented AIP product made on the super-cheap scores best when sold as a two-for one package.

around the corner and let out to repeat their stunt for next-arriving crowds. To showmen and most parents, increased gore quotients of a so-called "super deluxe model thriller"—*The Curse of Franken-stein*'s merchandising tag—were at least palatable for being attached to a name comfortably familiar from their own youth. That accepted brand again.

Jim Nicholson was formerly with Realart and knew packaging. He'd grown up loving genre pics and especially monstrous ones. Having teamed with Sam Arkoff to form American-International Pictures, Jim felt that teenagers needed a Frankenstein to call their own, and a Dracula too for that matter. The old tag team was good for a new matchup on the heels of summer 1957 grosses that *The Curse of Frankenstein* scored ($1.418 million in domestic rentals); thus, *I Was a Teenage Frankenstein* went out with *Blood of Dracula* for autumn playdates. AIP's two-for-one policy supplied theatres with black-and-white programs totaling two-and-a-half-or-so hours, enough to keep audiences turning over and make them feel they were getting value for admissions paid.

"Ninety-five percent of our bookings are for double-bills, but the pictures can later be bought singly," said Nicholson, whose product received road-testing at a trio of venues in San Diego, including two drive-ins. These helped finalize selling strategies for the wider pitch. Teens were targeted, and if critics didn't like it, and those who noticed razzed in unison…well, they could just get over it.

Was AIP straining credulity so much to imagine vampires in a girls' school, as in *Blood of Dracula*? And why not Frankenstein's creation so inflamed by recently installed hormones as to tear off heads at Lovers' Lane? These were new faces for old monsters, and kids were grooving with them. AIP got 5,000 to 7,000 bookings for such combos and often on percentage. Total domestic rentals for the *Teenage/Blood* package was $686,000, admittedly less than half of what Warners realized on *The Curse of Frankenstein*, but remarkable for ultra-cheapies that cost less combined than most anyone else's B.

AIP's junior varsity *Frankenstein* and *Dracula* helped usher Realart's vintage combination off theatre schedules, notwithstanding the fact that the reissue company's lease with Universal had expired, but in the cases of Karloff's and Lugosi's originals, it was merely a matter of relocating to smaller screens. A "Shock" package of 52 Universal thrillers went into TV syndication for 1957–58, and being they were free on home screens, seized viewing numbers beyond the wildest dreams of showmen hustling retooled monsters at drive-ins and struggling hard-tops.

The real *Dracula* and *Frankenstein* reasserted dominance on late shows in 142 broadcast markets as the Shocks took off like few other feature groups so far made available. With many more kids seeing Karloff's interpretation(s) repeated over horror-hosted TV weekends, his remained the definitive Frankenstein monster, Christopher Lee's scrambled egg visage trailing a distant second. It would be the same with Lugosi's Dracula, despite Lee's forceful debut with fangs-a-dripping in Universal's summer 1958 steamroller, *Horror of Dracula*. As both characters resided in the public domain, anyone could sully their names with merchandise unworthy of either, thus there was *Frankenstein's Daughter* and *Frankenstein–1970*, as well as bush-league vampires reflecting badly upon Dracula. Teens went for these primarily to get out of the house—"…for their kicks," said Jim Nicholson—and to make mischief with peers.

Summer 1964 ushered in a fresh wave of monster madness that had in any case been percolating at store and newsstand counters for a long time. Universal awoke to exploitation possibilities in its protected images and licensed Karloff/Lugosi likenesses to Frankenstein/Dracula models, billfolds, toys—I can't remember them all now, but I sure kept tallies then. Aurora models had box art more compelling than the plastic monsters kids built, often badly, from contents inside, but hours of struggle with glue and labyrinthine instructions merely reinforced the embrace of Boris Karloff and Bela Lugosi as the only legitimate incarnations of favorite monsters. *Look* magazine analyzed fandom in its September 8, 1964 issue, but could as easily have reprinted the New York *Times'* coverage of 1938 reissues to put the establishment's condescending message across.

The Castle Films 8mm reel of *Dracula* highlights appeared in 1963; a similar cutdown of *Frankenstein* didn't surface until 1971.

Kids deep into the life combed backs of monster magazines that were everywhere and dreamed of owning 8mm highlights of *Dracula*, released by Castle Films in 1963; its Frankenstein reel was strangely absent until late in the day 1971. I joined with a cousin and another neighbor boy to invest in *Dracula* plus Official Films' *A Lost World*, the latter made up of scenes culled from the 1925 dinosaur classic. We put on basement shows for a dime's admission and even made lobby cards from Lugosi photos unforgivably cut out of *Famous Monsters* magazine. Castle abridgements were the only way you'd play host to *Frankenstein* or *Dracula* at your own discretion. Who born of home video convenience could imagine the novelty of threading up favorites at will, let alone projecting them on bedroom walls at a time when possessing movies was a near unheard of concept?

Seven Arts' equivalent of Universal's parlay was a summer 1964 reissue of *The Curse of Frankenstein* with *Horror of Dracula*, both negatives having reverted to that company. These saturated marquees, together and apart, right into the '70s, as *Horror of Dracula* wouldn't be syndicated to television until 1966, and *The Curse of Frankenstein* showed up finally on June 28, 1974, when CBS played it as a weeknight late movie. Put an aerial on your roof in those days, and soon enough you'd be tripping over broadcasts of the originals, so much so as to make likelihood of their appearing again in theatres remote at best. Few exhibitors were so adventurous as to book features now decades old and likely broadcast in homes that very night. My ad search yielded *Frankenstein* playing our local Starlight Drive-in as late as 1959, while a more distant ozoner rounded out its 1967 dusk-to-dawn offering of *Ghidrah, the Three-Headed Monster* and *Planet of the Vampires* with "original classics" *Dracula* and *Frankenstein*. A Charlotte theatre tried the vintage combo around 1970, though it's unlikely that lines formed as in years past.

How might these "monster boys" perform in revival situations today? I tried them for a university run, and that audience was responsive. Universal horror carries a certain mystique among younger viewers, maybe owing to an increasing sense of unearthliness these films personify as they retreat further toward antiquity. For whatever outmoded techniques that modern audiences detect, the essential creep factor in play since 1931 has been, at the least, enhanced by the ripening vintage of *Dracula* and *Frankenstein*.

The classic Pair That Curled Your Hair plus the Wolf Man live on for a new generation through Aurora's plastic model kits. These monsters will share many a darkened baby-boomer bedroom.

Tyrone Power and Nancy Kelly in a scene from *Jesse James*.

CHAPTER 8

THE GREAT JESSE JAMES BOX-OFFICE RAID

My truest definition of a hit movie is one that draws people who don't ordinarily go to movies. *Jesse James* in 1939 flushed patrons out of the hills who had never been in a theatre before. It was a hit the whole country wanted to see, and by far the biggest of a western revival that included *Dodge City*, *Stagecoach*, and *Union Pacific*.

JJ was an old west *Grapes of Wrath* with Okies that fought back, its late '30s timing ideal. Jesse and Frank taking on railroads—code for banks, which they also robbed—made contemporary heroes of both from opening credits. "For good or ill," said an intro with regards Jesse and Frank, though it was clear where sympathies lay.

The biggest period-set hits are ones that evoke modern concerns. *Jesse James* did in ways peculiar to 1939, and maybe to here-and-now's economy as well. For dramatizing an austere west, it's far more the genuine article than even *Stagecoach*. I'd place *Jesse James* nearest to purity of a silent outdoor show than any a major studio tendered through the whole Classic Era, a western remarkably stripped of artifice that characterized most genre offerings.

Henry King directed, having been at picture helms since 1915. He routinely cut dialogue as first order of business, hewing to the conviction that pictures were better seen than heard. King's were rural sensibilities for having grown up in Virginia. Backwoods was his preferred location and one he made the most of, never so capably as here. *Jesse James* is countrified in the best and most evocative sense of that background, all too often simulated badly in films. King went far off beaten location paths as well and found nature's last preserve of a nineteenth century he'd only barely have to re-dress.

They filmed *Jesse James* in and around Pineville, Missouri, a town beyond small that had never seen moviemakers in its midst. Director King found Pineville after scouting landscapes in his private plane. 1939 wasn't too late to uncover Civil War-era trains discarded rail side, as these were backwoods where, among myriad artifacts, horse buggies the James brothers might have ridden still saw practical use. Fox artisans modified Pineville's main street to a past-century glow that came of having the real thing as foundation, which in this time capsule of a town, they did. Local folks played extras and a few of them spoke; you'll not mistake these for Central Casting.

King had made *Tol'able David* and others deep in the sticks and had an unerring bead on natural settings. He'd be rewarded for such instinct with hectoring wires from Fox chief Darryl Zanuck, who

Above: Stars Nancy Kelly and Tyrone Power with director Henry King. Below: Think how many faces familiar to Pineville residents are seen in the mob surrounding Ty Power and Henry Fonda during a filming break, this further evidence of the effect that stars had on a movie-mad public.

maintained *Jesse James'* crew should come home and fake remaining exteriors on backlots with process screen assist.

King must have called in plentiful markers to complete the shoot his way, and thanks be to posterity he did, for *Jesse James* would not be half the show it is had DFZ's edict been observed (none of *JJ*'s outdooring looks short-cutted, and I detect little rear projection). With regard creative and natural use of sound, *Jesse James* subs bird song and rivers running for music scored, a major lick for putting across a primitive backdrop that once upon a time shielded outlaws. There are chases over field and wood that look like home movies the real-life James boys might have shot, given cameras, and a train robbery by night, a major advance, said King, in the progress of Technicolor lensing, is marred only by Eastman processing done since and loss of three-strip elements that render impossible a true restoration for *Jesse James*.

Stars Ty Power and Randolph Scott take a break from filming in Pineville.

Pineville still celebrates Jesse James Days during each year's August. The filming there remains uppermost of town events even after 70 years and counting. Attendance tends to around 2,500 for the four days they revel, and proceeds go to local volunteer firemen. Outdoor showing of the movie is a highlight. Fewer remain who stood before 1939 cameras, but sighting of grandparents and mostly gone neighbors persists.

Pineville residents since may have forgotten Ty Power and Henry Fonda, but what fun to have had a major feature shot in your backyard, even if it's one folks way back thrilled to. The closest my locality came was *Thunder Road*, several counties away, but it seemed like home, and a silent called *Stark Love*, directed by Griffith disciple Karl Brown and shot amidst North Carolina hills back in 1927. I attended a screening at Appalachian State University in the early 1990s, where many in the audience yelled out names of locals they recognized upon that flickering, voiceless screen. Good thing *Stark Love* was run mute, for any mood accompaniment would surely have been drowned by who's who-ing from the audience along the lines of, "There's Great-Grandma!"

As to Jesse James Days, I'm sad for that time certain when no one will be left to spot kin among long-ago Pineville extras. A nice book written by Larry C. Bradley and published in 1980, *Jesse James: The Making of a Legend*, detailed the impact filming had on locals and preserved many anecdotes they passed down.

Not that *Jesse James* was any textbook of the badman's actual life. Liberties they took were many and varied, despite director King's consultation with James family members, including Frank's

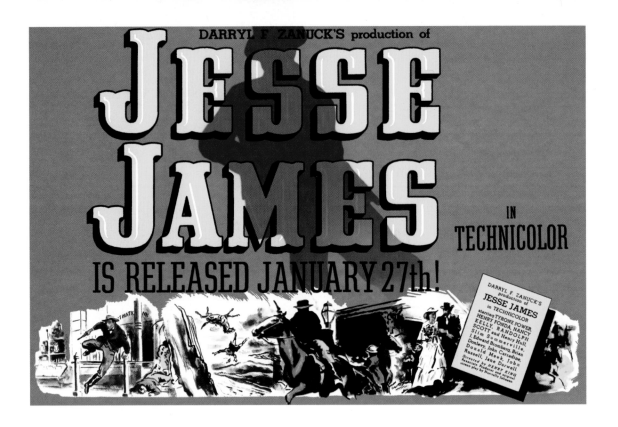

Above: It's evident from pre-release ads to exhibitors that they're to expect big things from *Jesse James*.
Below: Showmen are advised to concentrate on lavish fronts and sell big for *Jesse James*.

74

still-living son. There was no denying Hollywood convention even among remote environs, and who cared then about strict adherence to fact? Zanuck even considered alternate ends where Jesse survives; two such finishes were made, tested, then discarded.

Tyrone Power was soon to be 1939's King of Hollywood, succeeding Clark Gable, and few relished Ty back-shot by craven John Carradine. Drat history for its bummer ending imposed on a great yarn. *Jesse James* came out in a rich film-going year, and its $3.1 million worldwide rentals on $1.1 million spent made Fox that much richer.

Jesse James had appeal across boundaries of class and mass. Social/Political barbs went down smoother for a half-century's distance from events depicted, though few missed *JJ*'s ongoing relevance. The film's thumping success probably gave Zanuck surer footing for *The Grapes of Wrath* ahead, which substituted autos and banks for horses and trains. Patrons viewing one within months of the other would recognize midwesterner lives changed, but remaining pretty much a depreciated same. And in case parallels were missed, Henry Fonda's there to update Frank James as wronged-man-turned-outlaw Tom Joad, with Jane Darwell again as enduring Ma.

King Tyrone of 20th Century Fox and his queen, Jeanette MacDonald of MGM, succeed Clark Gable and Myrna Loy as Hollywood's reigning stars in the eyes of adoring fans.

Sad fact is, most old movies went to television because few had commercial life beyond initial release. There were exceptions, remarkable ones, like *Gone With The Wind, Snow White, King Kong*, etc., but the majority of studio output, being bound to years they were made, became less useful in seasons to come. Each company had evergreens, however limited. For Fox, number one of these was definitely *Jesse James*, among most lucrative of library titles sent back into theatres. Many exhibitors kept a standing order for *Jesse* and follow-up, *The Return of Frank James*, telling Fox exchangers, "Whenever there are prints, send them." The company mounted two official revivals—called "Encore Triumphs"—of which first was *Jesse*'s 1946 pairing with *Frank*, a natural combo, since the latter was a direct sequel and continuation from the first. These yielded a wondrous $1.34 million in domestic rentals, better even than some new releases Fox had that year, and several times what TCF generally realized with oldies.

A 1951 *Jesse/Frank* tandem put another $600,000 in domestic Fox coffers, with more than one exhibitor declaring both were good for at least an every other year's booking. What renewed these money markets was the timeless nature of the subject matter—westerns old were nearly as reliable as ones new—plus the fact *Jesse* and *Frank* boasted Technicolor, a surest hedge against obsolescence. Helping too was Randolph Scott, prominent among *Jesse*'s supporting cast as he'd become a most trusted western brand after the war. By 1965 both *Jesse James* and *The Return of Frank James* were on syndicated television, and paying admission days seemed over, but there would be a final roar for the 1939 favorite, a resounding one even if limited to theatres in our South-land.

Fox had got back in the outlaw business in 1969 via smash receipts from *Butch Cassidy and the Sundance Kid*, a sort of flower-child western with gentle badmen and bumptious comedy re-

Above: A life-size cutout of Ty Power provides scale for this relief map designed by Homer H. Harman, head of advertising at the New York Roxy, where the map appears. Locations in America's heartland are marked with scene stills from the film. The word WANTED flashes above the title on top. Below: Father and son collectors display 200 firearms and other items at the Palace Theatre in Canton, Ohio.

"You're a hero now, Jesse!" proclaims Nancy Kelly in this ad for the Palace Theatre run of *Jesse James*. The show promises "epic drama of a lawless and turbulent era." And delivers.

placing action highlights of Jesse James and kin. Butch just kept playing...coming back...playing again. I considered it then not a patch on rugged *The Wild Bunch*, *True Grit*, and others of more traditional bent, and maybe nearby showmen thought the same, for lo and behold, there came bookings of long-ago *Jesse James*, a had-to-see-it-to-believe-it event that sent me packing to Winston-Salem's Carolina Theatre for proof that this seeming apparition was for real. Indeed it was, a brand-new print in three-strip Technicolor, and such richness as I'd seldom encounter in theatres. I sat through *Jesse James* twice to properly burn images onto my youthful consciousness and wondered how *Butch Cassidy* followers might respond to this blast from their parents' past. There was a limited number of prints, as would be revealed later, but I'd follow them through subruns, drive-ins, and Saturday plays for what remained of the '70s and life left in these dye-transferred treasures.

By 1981 and my last sitting, *Jesse James*, at least what tatters I saw, was past need of discarding, yet small showmen wouldn't let it go. As late as 1989, a booker friend was still dispatching *JJ* to cow pasture screens in eastern North Carolina where demand was undiminished, even as the last one or two prints became increasingly banged. Details of *Jesse James'* rebirth was for me a curiosity finally satisfied by good friend and former exhibitor Robert Cline, who, as a theatre manager was very much in the thick of *Jesse's* comeback while working for ABC Southeastern Theatres, a division of the American Broadcasting Company. Robert provides an insider's account of how it all came down:

"Two or three times per year, the brass would book for us what they referred to as project pictures. The company could book these movies cheaply (usually a flat rate), develop its own advertising campaign, saturation-book into geographical areas, and, hopefully, drum up enough business to pay bills for that week. In spring of 1972, the suits reached way back and decided to go with Tyrone Power in the Fox version of *Jesse James*, then a 33-year-old western. Anti-hero westerns were a hot commodity at the time due to the success of *Butch Cassidy and the Sundance Kid*, *The Wild Bunch*, and *The Professionals*.

"I never knew all the specifics of the deal between ABC and 20th Century Fox, but a deal was struck, as were new prints, probably the first 35mm of *Jesse James* since the 1950s. The ad campaign

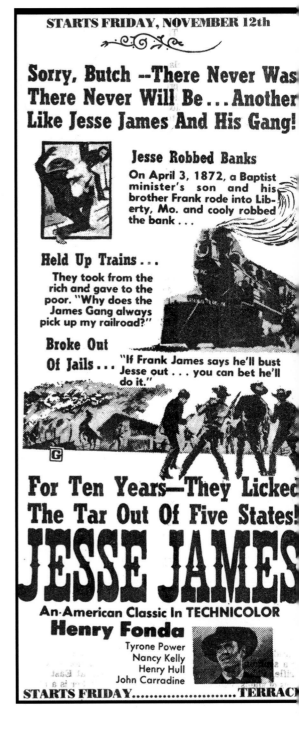

Above: Stout returns for *Jesse James*, combined with a surviving brother Frank, played by up-and-comer Henry Fonda, lead to an inevitable, and highly durable, sequel. Right: In the 1972 reissue of *Jesse James*, ads do not call out the vintage nature of the picture. Instead, links are made to the recent *Butch Cassidy and the Sundance Kid* and headlines tout the last remaining box-office draw, still-reliable Henry Fonda, instead of the traditional and long-dead Tyrone Power.

for ABC Southeastern was designed by Jack Jordan, the advertising director for our division. Jack had a pretty good knowledge of movies and did a nice job cutting and pasting artwork from a number of westerns to create a new look for Jesse; he borrowed key art with Robert Wagner from *The True Story of Jesse James*, among others. Jack knew moviegoers of 1972 had less familiarity with Tyrone Power, so he concentrated on Henry Fonda, the one star from *Jesse James* still active. Then he compared Frank and Jesse to Butch and Sundance, proclaiming the James boys the rowdier outlaw duo, at least until we played the Newman/Redford picture one more time.

"My theatre (Salisbury, North Carolina) was grouped with Winston-Salem, Lexington, and High Point. Fox delivered to ABC four sparkling IB Technicolor prints for our engagements. Then the Charlotte bookers set playdates and bought extensive radio spots through the region. My theatre paid $100 rental for the week's booking (larger cities were charged $250), this a bargain compared with prevailing rates. My share of the radio campaign was more than I paid for the feature itself. We played *Jesse James* for one week and did pretty well. With that flat rental, *Jesse* certainly performed beyond what we'd have realized with percentage shows far less likely to do comparable business."

Here then was *Jesse James*, still on the loose and seemingly to remain so for as long as the name continues to resonate, up to and including DVD availability and High-Def streaming. The champ western grosser of 1939 won't have auteurist standing of *Stagecoach* or others of like pedigree, but it hung on longer in theatres than any that surpassed it in critic estimation, and would be recalled most fondly by showmen who measured success in terms of tickets sold and audiences pleased.

I troll theatre ads, a habit ingrained since kindergarten. Each tells a story, no two are alike, and there's not a better indicator of selling policy in towns small or big. One such, the Midwest Mystic, wish-fulfilled 1935 patrons by hosting the alleged still-living badman Jesse James 4 times daily at 15 cents tops. Bob Ford having back-shot him was the bunk. Would you pay a nickel times three to see Jesse finally emerge after hiding out 51 years? I'll say I would! Depression rurals revered bandits among them, finding much to admire in Dillinger, Bonnie and Clyde, and others. No telling how many ersatz Jesses toured through the first half of the century, each answering a need folks felt to reclaim the bandit that made chumps of still-hated banks and railroads.

CHAPTER 9

JOHN FORD'S EVERGREEN STAGECOACH

Stagecoach is one done to death by revisitors, the apprehension for any writer being repetition of what others have observed. What with Criterion's Blu-ray in welcome circulation, there's been redoubling of words devoted to John Ford's signature western. Is it maybe time to give this one a rest? Could be. Only not just yet.

Stagecoach is among the most democratic of sacred texts. It has been, from 1939, a western easy for a general public to like, perhaps more so than *The Searchers*. Once it was familiar as raindrops. Television got all over *Stagecoach* early on, as did screaming exhibitors incensed by the film's free tube access from the early '50s onward. Anyone setting up a 16mm rental outlet in their basement could license prints for nontheatrical dates. Rights flew in all directions. The camera negative was pillaged for action footage that cheaper westerns could recycle. Prints bore consequent scars by the '60s and *Stagecoach* became difficult to see in quality approaching that of first-run 35mm prints.

There's less of John Ford's original in general circulation today. If ever *Stagecoach* lists anyplace other than TCM, get prepared for Fox's punk remake of 1966, or worse, a TV movie with country warblers aspiring to roles immortalized by John Ford's ensemble, such as Kris Kristofferson playing Ringo at age 50. Imagine the possibilities! The real *Stagecoach* was a saddle-buster folks remembered for giving John Wayne an early boost and putting him to shootin' Injuns for a near nine-minute chase talked about for decades to come. What Ford did with stunt riders and wagon wheels was not to be approached until counterparts paid (knowing?) homage using souped-up autos for remarkably similar pursuits in *Bullitt* and *The French Connection*.

By all means print the legends, for the plain truth of how *Stagecoach* ended up being made is largely lost to time. Did filmmakers of John Ford's generation ever consider that accuracy would one day matter so much? Imagine Ford under the microscope of exacting present-day film scholars. He'd appreciate more the many interviewers willing to kiss his rear-Admiralty before deeper researching gave the lie to yarns he spun. Was Ford really a cowpuncher during his youth, stealing off on a horse when a rancher's daughter set her cap for him? Probably not, but I'll groove with it all the same. Ford anecdotes are better taken as extensions of the movies he made, neither strictly based in fact, but both yielding much to enjoy. After all, what's the good of accuracy checking where larger-than-life personalities like Ford are concerned?

The ensemble cast poses in character. From left, Claire Trevor, John Wayne, Andy Devine, John Carradine, Louise Platt, Thomas Mitchell, Burton Churchill, Donald Meek, and George Bancroft.

The fact that John Ford didn't altogether discover John Wayne was undoubtedly a rock in the old man's shoe. Encounters with Raoul Walsh at Guild gatherings must have been awkward. Ford took credit for Wayne everywhere they'd listen, but Walsh knew different. The latter's *Big Trail* wasn't circulating much after 1930 to bear witness, unlike ubiquitous *Stagecoach*, but those in the know recognized it was Walsh who gave Wayne his first big chance.

Ford liked to tell about rescuing Duke from crummy westerns at Republic, forgetting or choosing to ignore the fact that these were, by 1939, shining Cadillacs among "B" cowboy models. Yes, Wayne spent the '30s, and most of his 20s, on programmer horseback, but he was by no means obscure, as *Stagecoach* producer Walter Wanger learned when time came to talk loan-out terms with Republic. "Like borrowing Garbo," according to Matthew Bernstein's excellent Wanger book. Wayne in fact had a major following, and that wasn't limited to nickel-ticket kids. At least in the South and points farther west, grown-ups filled Saturday seats and made that top earning day at houses for whom Republic stars were among the most popular. Ten years serving said patronage accumulated a fan base heading toward a next generation for John Wayne. By *Stagecoach* time, he promised value to marquees that small town showmen understood, even if higher-up food chain Wanger and Ford remained blinkered to Wayne's matinee following.

John Ford had more filming past invested in westerns than Wayne in any case. So what made him spend the late '20s and all of the '30s avoiding them? Ford's silent output was three-fourths cowboy-centric. He guided Buck Jones, Tom Mix, Hoot Gibson, and, most famously, Harry Carey. Did the influence of F.W. Murnau render Ford stuck-up toward westerns? Most of the dozens he made pre-sound are lost. One surfaced recently in France and became a *Stagecoach* DVD extra. *Bucking Broadway* makes me weep for others we'll never see, being perhaps more valuable to the Ford scheme of things than further *Stagecoach* excavation. A perfect world would yield Cheyenne Harry, the character Carey essayed for Ford, box sets as opposed to the mere three Ford/Careys in present-day circulation. Imagine all the echoes from Ford silents we'd find in *Stagecoach*, given rediscovery and access to them. Tag Gallagher tells a story of Harry Carey, Jr., going with his father to see *Stagecoach* in 1939 and the older man exclaiming over and over, "We did that! We did that!" Too bad the rest of us can't scrutinize the crib sheets that Ford consulted in making his first sound western, not to mention bumps from way back he'd reuse in ones to come.

John Ford seems to have developed projects along lines aspiring filmmakers could only dream of, he and creative pals lounging aboard yachts, conjuring movie magic as they brandished fish poles and cocktail glasses—this revealed in home movie DVD extras. Many a Ford script came to fruition aboard his *Araner* with passengers in party mode. Did inspiration also flow from potables downed in Mexican cantinas, such as Ford frequented with John Wayne and Ward Bond? Kodachrome glimpses suggest it did. Amidst such convivial setting was born *Stagecoach* and Fords that followed, along with our romantic concept of how this band of brothers devised westerns better than anyone else's.

Above: Quotes from showmen legitimize an atypical, character-driven western. Below: There is proof on at least *this* marquee that John Wayne is not yet a mainstream star in 1939, though Saturday matinee attendees know better.

Stagecoach bally, clockwise from top left: The trip to Lordsburg is compared to other strange journeys; the owner of the Kiowa Theatre in Hobart, Oklahoma, outfits his cashier in "full squaw regalia"; a fever pitch of excitement is promised, along with Clyde McCoy and his Orchestra and a Merrie Melody; the Boy Scouts of Breckenridge, Texas, take jamboree Indian props out of mothballs for the picture's run and stand guard with bows and arrows at the ready outside the Palace Theatre; a print of Stagecoach arrives by DC-3 and a nineteenth century Deadwood coach drives it to the Indianapolis Loew's Theatre.

The *Stagecoach* herald, handed out by showmen to patrons in advance of the playdate, is one of few ad accessories to prominently feature John Wayne.

Did *Stagecoach* bring outdoor drama back to life in 1939? Based on its reputation since, you'd think so, but this was a banner year for westerns that really didn't need *Stagecoach* one way or the other, being crowded with hits like *Dodge City*, *Union Pacific*, *The Oklahoma Kid*, and frontier monarch of the lot, *Jesse James*, which grossed more than twice what *Stagecoach* brought and was more influential besides for giving birth to a badman cycle that other studios copied.

Much of 1939's "A" lot outperformed *Stagecoach* at ticket selling, as this was a year crowded with feature product from both major and minor studios. *Stagecoach* was successful, but not a smash, earning a million in domestic rentals, which was all the better for its negative cost being approximately half that. Foreign rentals would enhance with an additional $736,000, but didn't such a pleaser deserve more? I delved into the Liberty's 1939 account ledger for a possible, if only partial, explanation.

Our Liberty Theatre has been around a long time and is still operating, and yes, ran *Stagecoach* often through the years, as witness stills for varied bookings I found during storeroom searches. The Liberty first played *Stagecoach* on Monday and Tuesday of the last week of April, 1939, a short wait for a film that had premiered in Arizona, and then opened in L.A. and New York but a couple of months before.

United Artists placed stiffer terms on its features than any other company the Liberty dealt with. *Stagecoach* carried a flat rental of $120.00, way more than Paramount charged for *Union Pacific* five weeks later ($83.47), and certainly beyond Metro's price for the "A" *Idiot's Delight* ($71.50), which preceded Ford's film at the Liberty by days.

Did UA price *Stagecoach* out of territories that might otherwise have used it? For those two days hosting Ford's western, plus *Love Taps*, a Metro musical short at $7.00 rental, and a Paramount newsreel for $3.00, the Liberty collected $147.10 in ticket sales. Combined rental expense of $130.00 for this program, plus overhead factors, wouldn't have yielded much profit from *Stagecoach*, especially in comparison to a later-in-the-week run of *The Hardys Ride High*, for which MGM charged $46.50 flat and from which the Liberty collected $177.85 for its Thursday/Friday play-off. Did other small venues yield similarly low surplus for having run *Stagecoach* in 1939?

The impact of *Stagecoach* would be felt longer than that of westerns that out-grossed it. John Wayne shot to higher rungs of stardom, even as he was obliged to report back to Republic for continuation of Three Mesquiteer "B" westerns. Warner Bros. got out trade ads trumpeting reissue of its six Wayne programmers from the early '30s in hopes of bringing back *Stagecoach* riders curious to see what a newly-minted "A" star was doing before lightning struck.

Industry folk recognized qualities of *Stagecoach* unknown to previous westerns, even epic ones, including DeMille's. The film entered a public's memory bank as one of the Great Westerns, deposits made regularly as reissues and revivals kept it in near constant theatrical circulation for a remarkable 25 years.

Advertising in the form of handbills like the two shown below detail each of the six main characters and the actors portraying them.

CLAIRE TREVOR as Dallas .. a dance hall girl run out of town. She wasn't good enough for a respectable woman to ride with but before the journey's end, she had clutched the woman's baby to her breast and saved it's life.

WALTER WANGER *presents*

STAGECOACH
Directed by John Ford • Released thru United Artists

JOHN WAYNE as the Ringo Kid .. escaped convict, hurrying to Lordsburg although he knew three men were waiting there to plug him full of bullets. Yet he surrendered to the U.S. Marshall in order to be taken along.

WALTER WANGER *presents*

STAGECOACH
Directed by John Ford • Released thru United Artists

WE'RE RINGING HIM BACK!

...Because NOW He Means More Than Ever Before!

John Wayne

IN THOSE **6** ACTION-JAMMED WARNER WESTERNS

'THE TELEGRAPH TRAIL' · 'RIDE HIM COWBOY'
'THE MAN FROM MONTEREY' · 'HAUNTED GOLD'
'SOMEWHERE IN SONORA' · 'THE BIG STAMPEDE'

New Posters New Displays New Pressbooks
A New Opportunity for a Big-Scale Western Draw!

Write 'em all in TODAY!

Warner Bros. dusts off its old John Wayne "B" westerns in the wake of *Stagecoach* success.

United Artists reissued *Stagecoach* in April 1944, and this was followed by a 1948 double-bill revival with John Ford's *The Long Voyage Home. Stagecoach* and *The Long Voyage Home* were Walter Wanger/John Ford collaborations in which the two had percentages. The combo program benefited from intersection with a post-war reissue boom that earned first-run bookings in spacious houses.

John Ford received $50,000 versus 20 percent of the producer's net income from *Stagecoach* for seven-and-a-half years, and nothing after that. My own microfilm search found *Stagecoach* continuing to play North Carolina drive-ins right through the '50s, an evergreen that showed up often. Winston-Salem's Lincoln Theatre, a scratch-house with three program changes per week, used *Stagecoach* at least once per year right through 1965 and might have continued doing so but for that site going dark the following year. Interesting here is the fact they weren't booking it as any sort of classic or repertory piece; indeed, *Stagecoach* ran August 26, 1965 at the Lincoln with co-features *Half-Human* and *The Monster from Green Hell.*

Writers have lamented bad prints of *Stagecoach* since original elements disappeared. Actually, there were and still are a handful of stunning 16mm printdowns out there. These were generated within 10 years of the film's initial release and derived from the camera negative itself. The one I used to own had a 1948 edge-code, the year of *Stagecoach*'s second reissue.

These printdowns were done for nontheatrical rental, and there were lots of them. Problematic was the fact that, being a popular favorite, *Stagecoach* picked up wear and tear not visited upon lesser 16mm titles, and finding one in clean condition posed a daunting task for collectors—mine had splicy sections. But wow, did they look a million. Contrast was richer than ever it would be again, including on DVD, and blacks registered deep as pitch, especially during the Lordsburg finish. These initial prints would unfortunately be replaced with ones softer and obviously cobbled from elements far afield of the lost original.

Stagecoach was among first "A" westerns sold to television, and there its reputation continued soaring despite by-now cloudy transmission. By the early '70s when my college had it for a run, *Stagecoach* was a long-diminished shadow of what had so impressed 1939 audiences. It was around this time that John Wayne's personal 35mm print became the source, at least in part, for preservation and circulating prints that followed. I'd assume JW's was among elements consulted by Criterion for the Blu-ray release, although it was primarily a found 35mm nitrate negative from 1942 that was used, according to sources in the know. Certainly Criterion's version represents the best *Stagecoach* has looked for many years, and combined with a bounty of extras, the most extravagant Ford package since Fox's massive box set, dedicated to the director, which was issued in 2007.

Surrealism down to a witch's hand paper-
weight helped to make *The Wizard of Oz*
a classic unmatched in the annals of Hollywood, although initially it failed to turn
a profit for its sheer weight.

CHAPTER 10

THE THREE MILLION DOLLAR SPLURGE

Every detail about *The Wizard of Oz* has been much written about, being among a group of classics to which entire books have been devoted. The fact of *Oz* having lost money from its initial 1939–40 release is well known to followers. That seems inconceivable to fans who have made a TV (and later home-video) ritual of viewing a timeless favorite. Some have even misread the first-run loss as an outright flop, a then public having rejected a film that generations since have treasured, when the simple fact is that *The Wizard of Oz* cost more than it could (then) bring back. It was, in fact, a hit from the outset, just not *enough* of one to cover an astronomical $2.8 million negative cost, plus distribution, print, and advertising expense.

MGM went into this venture with hopes of matching the fantastic success of 1937's *Snow White and the Seven Dwarfs*, the Disney/RKO phenomenon that brought $8.5 million in domestic plus foreign rentals (this including receipts through 1940). Notable from this comparison is that *Snow White* had a final negative cost of $1,488,423, around half the amount required to finish *The Wizard of Oz*. The latter's worldwide rentals came to $3 million, with a final deficit of $1,137,230.

It's odd, perhaps, to speculate on what went *wrong* for any 1939 release that earned $3 million, few movies doing so well during this era of shorter runs and lower admissions. What wasn't met by *The Wizard of Oz* was MGM's expectation of a hit to equal, if not surpass, *Snow White and the Seven Dwarfs*. The $2.8 million spent was looked upon as investment toward another record setter after Disney's example.

Metro was, in fact, set upon exhibiting *Oz* as a roadshow attraction, with two-a-day showings at advanced admission and extended playing time. This had worked before, not lately though, as evidenced by roadshow engagements for 1938's *Marie Antoinette* that were tried then put aside in favor of a general release. Roadshow was favored as a means by which expensive shows could break even sooner, but exhibitors resented product withheld from them as select theatres scooped off gravy. MGM would reconsider by July 1939 and decide not only to release *Oz* for ordinarily slower August dates, but to put it in hundreds of theatres nationwide while interest, and the weather, were hot.

A trade ad published July 22, 1939, put the question thus: **What Company But MGM Would Give You a Multi-Million Show in August Like This Technicolor Sensation?** Part of the head start was strategic, as competing Paramount had made noise to the effect that *Gulliver's Travels*, its own animated feature-length answer to *Snow White*, would be roadshown during 1939's fourth quarter. Did Metro want to avoid going head-to-head with *Gulliver*?

Metro's summer assault would place *Oz* among the company of *Andy Hardy Gets Spring Fever*, *Goodbye Mr. Chips* (which would outgross *Oz*), *These Glamour Girls*, and *Lady of the Tropics*, all solid attractions. One could argue in hindsight that this was a defining mistake on distribution's part. Shouldn't *The Wizard of Oz* have been held for a gala Christmas opening? But wait, Metro had its biggest-ever premiere set for December—*Gone With the Wind*.

The company wanted extended playdates for *Oz* and other features they regarded as special. The problem, said trades, was that *many* features in 1939 were considered special, not a few of them more so than *The Wizard of Oz*. "Too many pictures are being delivered now to make it possible for the theatres to provide much extra time for the better ones," said *Variety*, "leaving it squarely up to the producers to do something about the matter."

Early reviews meanwhile branded *The Wizard of Oz* as a kid's show, pretty but lacking in adult appeal. Toward enticement of both youth and elders and to position *Oz* as a Broadway hit, Metro sent juve stars Judy Garland and Mickey Rooney to headline stage shows at its flagship Capitol Theatre where *The Wizard of Oz* opened in New York. *Oz* was already playing key dates across the country per Loew's pledge to exhibitors, and reportage from the field were so far encouraging. The Garland/Rooney Capitol stand was record-smashing, as might have been expected. These two were approaching a peak of audience popularity, and seeing them perform on stage was, if anything, a greater lure than *The Wizard of Oz*. It was a killing pace for Judy and Mick, however—seven performances daily, nine on Saturday and Sunday, but the Capitol was averaging 40,000 tickets sold per day, and MGM had the impetus to tell a show-world that theirs was the outstanding hit for a late-summer season.

Headlines, meanwhile, touted *Oz* (with some exaggeration) as "a three million dollar splurge," a trade's way of shining light on Metro extravagance and putting forth the question as to whether the company could get all of that money back. Sub-

Metro sets the stage for a big summer 1939 that includes several "A" pictures, clearing the decks for the December premiere of *Gone With the Wind*.

NO MORE WRINKLES!

Leo's hot-weather parade of hits is the talk of the Industry!

ISN'T IT WONDERFUL!

M-G-M's Summer releases electrify every Film Row! Grateful showmen say "M-G-M's ready when a feller needs a friend!" Here are a few of the Summer Big Ones! It's all M-G-M as usual!

"ANDY HARDY GETS SPRING FEVER" The Lucky Seventh Hardy Hit! A Summer life-saver!	**ROBERT TAYLOR HEDY LAMARR** in **"LADY OF THE TROPICS"** Call out the cops!
"GOODBYE MR. CHIPS" National Release of the Extended-Run Record Holder!	And what company but M-G-M would give you a multi-million-dollar show in August like this Technicolor sensation!
"THESE GLAMOUR GIRLS" Lew Ayres, Lana Turner, Anita Louise, etc. Youth and beauty in sure-fire hit!	**"THE WIZARD OF OZ"** Watch for details of the Giant Ad Campaign in national magazines synchronized with simultaneous release in hundreds of theatres!

THE FRIENDLY COMPANY all year around!

sequent dates brought estimates closer to earth. *The Wizard of Oz* was doing well, topping all but *Babes in Arms* for domestic rentals among 1939 MGM releases, but it wasn't going near what *Snow White and the Seven Dwarfs* achieved. That one was a bona fide cultural phenomenon and *Oz* was not.

A major scorch was lowered foreign receipts brought on by war conditions and the resulting closed markets over much of Europe. This was a handicap suffered by all studio output as of the late '30s and onward through World War II. Walt Disney's own follow-up to *Snow White*, *Pinocchio*, would be similarly affected. Salvation for both *Oz* and Disney's mishap lay in evergreen status they'd acquire, both gaining in public esteem as years passed.

January of 1940 would see Metro licking wounds of *Oz*'s loss but newly determined to produce its own feature-length cartoon via staff animators Hugh Harmon and Rudolf Ising, this a result of "heavy returns" collected by Paramount on recently released *Gulliver's Travels*. Studio consensus, according to *Variety*, was that *The Wizard of Oz* "would have been more successful, both artistically and financially, if it had been made as a cartoon." But the point was moot, and the proposed MGM Harmon/Ising animated feature did not materialize.

A first major reissue for *The Wizard of Oz* came in March 1949. Metro had put its Masterpiece Reprint series into effect several years previous and realized neat profits from elderly product put back in circulation.

The Tampa Theatre urges patrons to see a show "unmatched since *Snow White*."

There was by now a subsidiary, MGM Records, to further exploit songs/music from *The Wizard of Oz* and tie in with its reissue, but the album would not be culled from *Oz*'s original soundtrack. Arrangement would instead be made for the Joel Herron Orchestra and vocal group in New York to create a two-disc package with new recordings from the score.

The Wizard of Oz circulated as part of a 1949 reissue group that included *Blossoms in the Dust* and *Sequoia*. It was here that *The Wizard of Oz* finally broke even, thanks to profits of $1,148,396 from this first revival. Indeed, 1949 showmen treated *Oz* as very much a special event. Trades featured elaborate bally campaigns on the film's behalf, *The Wizard of Oz* leading an opener week in Chicago where competing first-run shows fell before its impressive tally. MGM demanded, and was getting, percentage terms comparable to what new features drew. Ideal timing for the reissue was noted, as 1949 proved to be a more receptive than usual season for musicals.

A public's response to any movie was based on moods of the moment. A *Wizard of Oz* comeback that clicked in 1949 might find a cooler reception its next time around. MGM's next reissue

THE MIGHTY MIRACLE SHOW THAT IS THE TALK OF AMERICA!

AT LAST IT'S HERE
BIGGEST SENSATION SINCE "SNOW WHITE"!

M-G-M's TECHNICOLOR Triumph!

THE WIZARD OF OZ

How would you like to live in the merry old land of Oz?

Oz! Where you go to work at noon, take an hour for lunch, and at one you're done! *Oz!* Where the trees pelt you with fruit if you won't pick it! *Oz!* Where troubles of this world are unknown because it's east of the rainbow's trail! *Oz!* Where a mighty wizard grants every wish closest to your heart's desire! *Oz!* Where nights are gay with love and laughter and music fills the air! All aboard—for the wonderful, wonderful Land of Oz!

AMAZING SIGHTS TO SEE!

THE TORNADO
Be among the first to experience a sky high journey in a flying house!

MUNCHKINLAND
Watch the wonders whiz by as these happy folk take you to their hearts!

HORSE OF DIFFERENT COLOR

Startling **BALLOON ASCENT**

THE Flying MONKEYS

THE TREE THAT THROWS APPLES

JUDY GARLAND
as DOROTHY, the young lady who is whirled away to strange adventures by a Kansas cyclone! Your singing darling grander than *ever* before!

FRANK MORGAN
your hilarious ("Good News") favorite in his most riotous role. He's a whiz of a wiz...as "THE WIZARD OF OZ"!

RAY BOLGER
Ziegfeld's most famed dancing star as the fantastic, dancing, eccentric STRAW MAN!

MAGIC MUSIC! GLORIOUS SONGS!
by Harold Arlen and E. Y. Harburg

Over The Rainbow
We're Off To See The Wizard
Ding-dong! The Witch Is Dead
If I Only Had A Brain
The Merry Old Land Of Oz

TOTO ... he's the grandest little dog you've ever seen you'll howl too!

JACK HALEY
laugh star of screen and radio...and the merriest man in the merry old land of Oz ...as the TIN MAN!

Also in the Cast of Thousands
BILLIE BURKE • MARGARET HAMILTON
CHARLEY GRAPEWIN • AND THE MUNCHKINS
Produced by MERVYN LeROY
Directed by VICTOR FLEMING
Screen Play by
Noel Langley, Florence Ryerson and Edgar Allen Woolf
From the Book by L. Frank Baum
A VICTOR FLEMING PRODUCTION
A METRO-GOLDWYN-MAYER PICTURE

BERT LAHR
Broadway's famed comedian hits a new high in laughs as the singing COWARDLY LION!

Opposite page: The 1939 fold-out herald given by exhibitors to patrons in advance of the picture's release. This page, clockwise from top left: a color rotogravure image; strong numbers from the Mickey-Judy personal appearances in New York City; a cast shot atop the Baum hardcover; and street bally in Worcester, Massachusetts, enticing patrons to the Loew-Poli Theatre.

for 1955 saw receipts lowered from 1949, but this was well into ongoing decline for theatres as a whole, much of that brought on by television, with its ever-increasing availability of free entertainment. Against this circumstance, *The Wizard of Oz* still rung up a most impressive $930,776 in worldwide rentals for the 1955 run, a figure way in excess of what other MGM reissues from the same year realized. As example, *Anchors Aweigh*, a musical originally released in 1945, took only $289,000 from its 1955 encore.

A still-active *Wizard of Oz* cast was linked to their current film and stage successes for '55 ads, Ray Bolger with *Where's Charley?*, Bert Lahr and *Make Mine Manhattan*, and Jack Haley for *Inside USA*. Such was the means by which Metro could posit *The Wizard of Oz* as an attraction with contemporary patron appeal.

Below: Artwork for the 1949 Masterpiece Reprint lobby displays, like this title lobby card, stick to period depictions of Judy Garland. Opposite page: By the next reissue in 1955, a contemporary Judy is featured on all displays due to changes in her appearance over 16 years that had passed. Also note that the 1955 campaign calls out this "wide screen" version of the picture, meaning that the top and bottom of the 4 x 3 frame have been cropped to suit '50s demand for expanded vistas.

M-G-M's ENTERTAINMENT OF 1000 DELIGHTS!

TWO YEARS TO PLAN IT!
NOTHING TO EQUAL
THE JOY, THE MAGIC,
THE FUN AND SONGS...
ALL IN WONDROUS
COLOR BY
TECHNICOLOR
GREAT ON THE
WIDE SCREEN!

AMAZING SIGHTS TO SEE!

THE TORNADO
Actual photographs of the inside of the tornado that whirled Dorothy to a land more excitingly real than life itself!

MUNCHKINLAND
A whole city in miniature populated entirely by hundreds of midgets gathered from 42 cities in 29 states!

HORSE OF A DIFFERENT COLOR
Ever see a blue horse? Ever see a green horse? You will— when you see this magic "horse of a different color"!

Startling BALLOON ASCENT
Up in the stratosphere! What lies beyond the stars? See the glistening Emerald City . . . the wonderful Palace of Glass!

FLYING MONKEYS

TREES THAT TALK AND THROW APPLES

MORE! MORE!! MORE!!!
9200 LIVING ACTORS THRILL YOU!

starring
JUDY GARLAND

Hear beloved Judy sing
"OVER THE RAINBOW"
and many others

The WIZARD of OZ

with **FRANK MORGAN** · **RAY BOLGER**
BERT LAHR · **JACK HALEY**
BILLIE BURKE · MARGARET HAMILTON · CHARLEY GRAPEWIN
and the Munchkins · Screen Play by Noel Langley,
Florence Ryerson and Edgar Allan Woolf · From the book by
L. Frank Baum · A VICTOR FLEMING Production · Produced by
MERVYN LE.ROY · Directed by VICTOR FLEMING
AN M-G-M MASTERPIECE REPRINT

Songs
to Make You Sing and Dance by
Harold Arlen and E. Y. Harburg
"Over the Rainbow"
"If I Only Had a Brain"
"We're Off to See the Wizard"
"The Merry Old Land of Oz"
"Ding Dong"
"If I Were King of the Forest"

A by-1955 preoccupation with wider viewing saw *The Wizard of Oz* in many instances cropped at top and bottom so as to fill expanded screens. Record tie-ins also widened to include a Decca LP featuring Judy Garland performing *Oz* songs to the accompaniment of Victor Young and Orchestra, in addition to repressing of the 1949 Joel Herron album.

An actual soundtrack would wait until following year 1956 and a transitional event that saw *The Wizard of Oz* premiering on television as a Ford Star Jubilee special. This was the result of an MGM deal with CBS that called for the network to pay $450,000 for two runs of *Oz*, plus an option for two further repeats.

Toward publicizing a November 3 telecast, Ford and Metro arranged to place the new record with special displays in auto showrooms nationwide. Noting that there had never been an album based on actual music and songs from the film, *Variety* cited "serious artistic and mechanical problems in assembling the package, since the film was made in the days before separate tracks were used for music." To fill out its LP, Metro would include dialogue and "dramatic highlights" in addition to the songs.

Part of what greased the CBS *Oz* deal were discussions ongoing of a possible merger between the network and MGM. Loew's had tried to interest CBS in continued broadcasts from the studio's pre-'48 feature library, but *The Wizard of Oz* was all the network wanted. By the November 3, 1956 play date for *Oz*, there were Metro pics on TV stations across the country via syndicated release.

In addition to a modern-day Judy, the R-55 campaign also avoids the "vintage" tag by tying into current appearances by the Scarecrow, Lion, and Tin Woodsman on stage and screen.

CBS had hit a snag with Ford as to Star Jubilee and what the sponsor expected in terms of program content. Initial agreement had called for star-studded extravaganzas to provide backdrop to 1957 models being offered by the auto manufacturer. The original plan was for ten specials, which was reduced to eight. A first, *You're the Top*, was tribute to the career of Cole Porter, featuring name performers, but that ended up costing CBS $100,000 beyond what Ford approved for a budget. The sponsor was not particularly keen on CBS falling back on an old movie, even if it was *The Wizard of Oz*, to fill a second Jubilee night. As things turned out, *Oz* would be the final Ford Star Jubilee.

November 3 fell on a Saturday, observers noting that CBS telecast *The Wizard of Oz* in a surprisingly late time slot (9–11 P.M.), considering *Oz's* appeal to children, most of whom would be well tucked in before Dorothy started down the yellow brick road. As prologue to the feature, CBS arranged for Judy Garland's daughter, Liza Minnelli, to chat on camera with former Cowardly Lion Bert Lahr about the making of the 1939 classic. This, along with 12 minutes of Ford commercials and station breaks, supplemented the 101 minutes that was the running time of *The Wizard of Oz*, and filled the network's two-hour time slot. Ford's Star Jubilee was broadcast in color, but few homes had sets to receive it as such, so a vast viewership saw *The Wizard of Oz*, many for a first time, in black-and-white.

Trendex ratings reflected "a surprisingly high average" for the two hours taken up by *The Wizard of Oz*, as CBS defeated rivals Lawrence Welk, Sid Caesar, and George Gobel. *Oz* actually had its highest viewer number during a final half-hour that competed with a televised speech by Vice President Richard Nixon.

Ongoing exhibitor hostility toward film companies for selling off backlog to TV was expressed by an announcement that *The Wizard of Oz* had cost theatres $2 million in lost revenue for the Saturday night it played CBS, the 7.7 percent decline in attendance reported by film biz analysts Sindlinger & Company. Showmen would never forgive MGM and other film distributors for handing television their backlog. To exhibition's mind, any showing of *The Wizard of Oz* other than in theatres was a betrayal, pure and simple.

CBS repeated *Oz* in 1959 and for years thereafter. The film remained a home-set perennial that invariably earned ratings among the top ten programs of weeks it was broadcast. MGM would put *The Wizard of Oz* back in theatrical circulation among a "Children's Matinees" group of family-oriented oldies to play early '70s dates. These were generally new prints that ran on Saturday mornings and afternoons at participating venues. Other titles in the series included *Lassie Come Home*, *Kim*, *The Yearling*, and numerous others of child-aimed appeal. Heavy TV-ad saturation accompanied each film as it went from territory to territory. For many, these matinees would be a first opportunity to see *The Wizard of Oz* in a theatre, as opposed to television, where an increasing number of commercial interruptions necessitated minor cuts to the feature, and even worse, time compression of its 101 minutes.

The Wizard of Oz is today ubiquitous both on television and DVD/Blu-ray. There is still revival in theatres from time to time, this likely to increase thanks to digital projection that avoids the necessity and expense of 35mm printing. Expanding technology has also enabled *Oz* to stream online as well as accommodate on-demand viewership, all of which generates a continual stream of revenue that a 1939-era MGM could not have imagined.

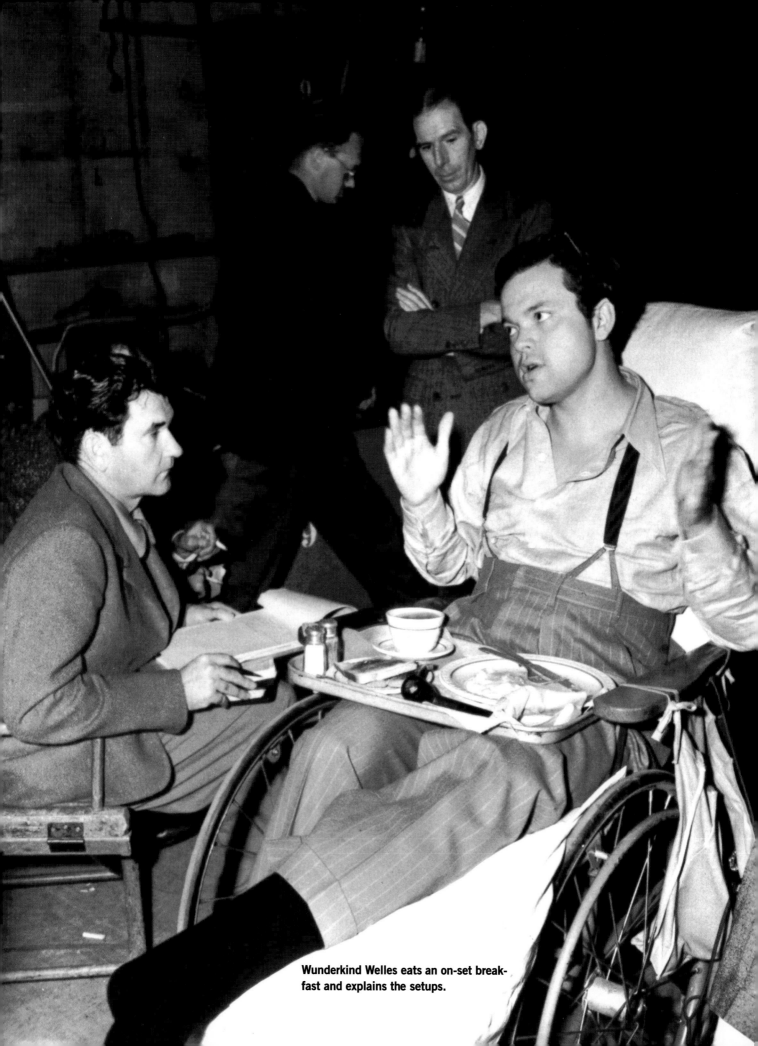

Wunderkind Welles eats an on-set breakfast and explains the setups.

CHAPTER 11

CAMPAIGNING FOR KANE

Citizen Kane lost $160,000. Historians recall both the film and its star as having gotten a raw deal, with opinions differing as to how much grief Orson Welles brought upon himself. The controversy he invited did hobble the box office; first-run bookings as well as profits *Kane* might otherwise have earned were lost as a result of RKO's war with William Randolph Hearst. It was hard enough for this company to score hits even in the best of times. Dealing with MGM rather than RKO might have meant a hit for Welles, but Metro would never have given untried talent such carte blanche nor backed him in a showdown with Hearst.

RKO president George Schaefer hungered for and was willing to gamble on prestige names that would help RKO grab a bigger market share. *The Hunchback of Notre Dame* had pointed the way two years earlier with $3.1 million in worldwide rentals. Could Orson Welles deliver the unique product RKO needed to compete with powerful majors like Paramount, Fox, and MGM?

Welles promised something new in screen entertainment, plus longer lines of customers and runs in the kind of downtown palaces that Schaefer coveted. But big companies owning said temples had little reason to court unpredictable talent like Welles, despite the remarkable strides he'd made on stage and in radio. RKO's production machinery was not so well oiled as these monoliths in control of all the best theatres. Orson Welles would team with a studio that had lost money on the following 1939–40 releases—*Vigil in the Night*; *Swiss Family Robinson*; *Abe Lincoln in Illinois*; *Dance, Girl, Dance*. Their sole money star was Ginger Rogers; she and bandleader Kay Kyser supplied most of the black ink on company ledgers.

The 1940–41 RKO product annual called for two Welles productions, the first of which would be *John Citizen, U.S.A.*, among those several preliminary titles for *Citizen Kane*. It should have been released early in 1941 but for sundry threats, legal and otherwise, made by Hearst once it was discovered that he was the inspiration for Kane's character. This was where RKO's express toward greater prestige and profit jumped the track.

As winter 1941 dragged into spring, *Citizen Kane* missed scheduled opening dates and bestirred much speculation as to whether it would be shown at all. RKO was sufficiently intimidated by Hearst interests as to delay public exhibition, though ongoing press previews assured a kettle boiling as corporate heads dithered. Orson Welles suggested they show it "in circus tents" and volunteered to take

John Citizen, U.S.A.: **One of several working titles for** ***Citizen Kane.***

Kane on the road like an old-fashioned medicine show. He'd even buy the negative! Welles went the rest of a lifetime convinced that ownership of *Kane* and control of its exhibition would have made him rich.

At least Welles had a role model in Charlie Chaplin, who'd threatened to hire halls, if not tents, to show *The Great Dictator* when circuits refused to come to his terms the previous year. Was Welles just posturing here? The practical realities of trying to seat audiences in makeshift auditoriums for jerry-built movie presentations was all right if you were running 16mm for school groups, but well-intentioned filmmakers doing battle with theatre monopolies stood little chance playing first-run, million-dollar investments in venues with sawdust for floors. Samuel Goldwyn actually tried it a few years after *Kane* when he opened *Up in Arms* with wooden chairs and telegrams from independents applauding his quixotic gesture, though audiences for that Reno, Nevada "premiere" still preferred the comfort of plush theatre seats.

Welles finally went public and threatened to sue RKO unless the studio released *Citizen Kane* forthwith. Radio City Music Hall backed out of a prior agreement to host the premiere, necessitating the quick overhaul of an old two-a-day vaudeville house that RKO had owned since the '20s. The Palace Theatre was dressed out in a wall of light four stories high. A lavish front cost $26,000 to dress, while other advertising and ballyhoo expenses stood RKO $53,000 before the doors opened on May 1, 1941.

For such confidence on display at the Palace, RKO remained tentative as to playdates for *Citizen Kane* elsewhere. "A few test showings" were all they'd promise; these would include Chicago, Los Angeles, San Francisco, and Washington, DC. They called it a roadshow, and surely *Citizen Kane* was that in terms of limited bookings and a long, hot summer in which to lose momentum before the belated general release set for September 5, 1941.

100

Citizen Kane topped an indifferent slate RKO identified as the first block for 1941–42, the trade ads colorful and replete with critical plaudits. Runners-up on the schedule included *Parachute Battalion*, *Father Takes a Wife* (remembered, if at all, as Gloria Swanson's pre-*Sunset Boulevard* attempt at a comeback), *All That Money Can Buy* (stylistically similar to *Kane*), and *Lady Scarface*. Block-booking obliged small and independent exhibitors to play all of these. *Parachute Battalion* (eventual profit $128,000) held far greater promise for showmen than *Citizen Kane*. It was as close as they could get to Warner's *Sergeant York*, the blockbuster everyone wanted, which would go into general release September 27.

Kane got a black eye from theatremen hearing crickets and fielding patron complaints as it wound through small towns. Negative comment in the trades was virulent. You'd think Anna Sten was back making pictures. There was a "World Premiere at Popular Prices" in Reading, Pennsylvania, complete with parade and baton twirlers, as fresh ad art sexed up *Citizen Kane* and assured customers they'd not pay the $2.00 asked of roadshow attendees. A revised pressbook abandoned cartoonish ad art and deemphasized the banal tagline, **It's Terrific!** New one-sheets at last suggested quality product, but they came too late; major circuits had already refused to play the film. Fox West Coast Theatres at first contracted for *Citizen Kane*, then opted not to exhibit it, effectively shutting out runs in areas they controlled.

Welles had indeed underestimated the enemy he'd made in Hearst. A deluxe trailer for *Citizen Kane* was a production in itself, but as much as it delights us today, chances are Welles' confection baffled viewers unfamiliar with the screen newcomer and whatever he was selling. RKO's season was thus a sinking ship, and George Schaefer would go down with it. *Father Takes a Wife* lost $104,000. Excellent though it was, *All That Money Can Buy* (now known as *The Devil and Daniel Webster*) was down by $53,000. *Citizen Kane* took $990,000 in domestic rentals and $300,000 foreign. That loss of $160,000 was not so egregious in comparison with other RKO features bleeding as much every year, and surely it was dwarfed by the blow Welles would take with his next, *The Magnificent Ambersons*, a loser to the tune of $620,000 and one of the worst lickings RKO sustained that decade.

One critic described *Citizen Kane* as "the picture of a man who is not really worth depicting, and here is the film's weakness." But was it Kane he rejected or the actor playing him? Welles was, at the least, unfamiliar as a screen presence.

The *Citizen Kane* ad blitz included an uninspired tagline, "It's Terrific!" and cartoon artwork more befitting the recently introduced Superman.

Above: RKO artwork reflects the Welles vision of selling his picture from the grass roots up. Below: Modest sets of bleachers allow fans to get up close and personal for a red-carpet premiere.

Audiences knew that voice, but was it too overpowering, or even intimidating, when combined with Welles' looming physicality? He's surely no leading man in the conventional sense. Rubber-necked masks and skull caps do not a romantic leading man make, and what of those not ready for prime-time Mercury players? Joseph Cotten alone would break into romantic leads. The rest were at best character support, and few fulfilled the bright promise Welles foresaw in his *Citizen Kane* trailer.

I could suggest revisionist casting that might have turned the commercial tide had the picture been made but months later. Consider the young man among reporters wandering amidst Xanadu treasures in the final sequence. Attentive listeners will identify that unmistakable Alan Ladd voice as it's heard several times.

What if Ladd had played Kane, just after *This Gun for Hire*? Imagine following the sensation of his breakout role in that Paramount thriller with Alan Ladd as Charles Foster Kane! Welles would have had an unqualified hit and juice enough to stay on and direct no telling how many more RKO projects. At the very least, Welles and Mankiewicz might have rewritten *Citizen Kane* to accommodate a shared lead with Ladd. Consider this for instance: two-fisted enforcer Ladd for Big Jim (more sinned against than sinning) Gettys goes after C.F. Kane/Welles but falls for Emily just as he's closing in on that love nest his quarry shares with "singer" Susan Alexander. For Emily's sake, Ladd lets Kane off with a warning, exacts his promise to lay off Gettys and stay out of politics, then decamps with Emily, who's decided she prefers this bantam with the heart her venal husband lacks. Think they'd have bought *that* in 1941?

Following its general release during the 1941–42 season, *Citizen Kane* went into hibernation that would last nearly 15 years. While Orson Welles struggled to resurrect a Hollywood career, exhibitors with bitter memories of *Kane* in first-run shunned it like a plague. Despite maintaining one of the industry's heaviest reissue schedules, RKO couldn't be bothered with this one. European audiences discovered *Citizen Kane* after the war, but hosannas published in foreign language publications were not enough to revive interest stateside.

Further impediments arose when nitrate-based film was phased out in favor of safety stock. This had been a major safety issue largely ignored during interims between disastrous booth fires, wherein projectionists sometimes lost their lives.

An economic alternative was needed, and industry heads worked together toward finding it: by mid-1950, there would be an 85 percent

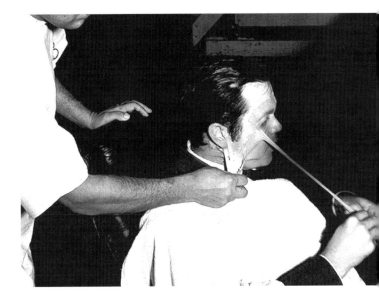

Top: The Palace Theatre in New York City stands in for Radio City as *Citizen Kane* premieres. RKO dresses out the Palace in a $26,000 wall of light four stories high and spends a total of $53,000 to launch its "terrific" picture. Center: For the unconventional Welles, rubber-necked masks and skull caps do not a romantic leading man make. Bottom: Could bit player Alan Ladd (center, with hands on hips) have played Kane and made the Welles picture an unqualified hit in first-run?

industry conversion to safety stock. The phasing out of nitrate also made obsolete thousands of features and shorts previously printed on the unstable stock. Extant prints of *Citizen Kane* would be cleared from RKO exchanges along with discards now considered hazardous. Safety printing of library titles on 35mm would be limited to proven past hits scheduled for reissue. *Cat People* was back in 1952 to earn a $65,000 profit, over and above $183,000 it garnered in black ink during the original release 10 years earlier. Favorites like *Suspicion* and *Top Hat* would also return on safety stock.

Citizen Kane made a reappearance finally in 1956, shortly after RKO announced the sale of its film library to television, sending shock waves through exhibition corridors, even as this was not an altogether unexpected move. Studios had been hinting at possibilities of a TV sale for several years. Howard Hughes let go RKO's caboodle (742 features) to General Teleradio, who quickly firmed a deal with the C&C Super Corporation. Paying $15.2 million for rights, C&C soon had 75 percent of existing television sets within range of RKO movies, many dating back to the early days of sound, and broadcasts began as of March 1, 1956.

THE BIG ROAD-SHOW SENSATION ...NOW AVAILABLE FOR POPULAR-PRICE SHOWING! At the crest of the wave the highest praise and the widest public ever given a motion picture . . . Ready the millions who have been pre-sold a who are waiting for a chance to see it . Red-hot for YOU— and the biggest crow in your community!

ORSON WELLES *CITIZEN KANE*

The Mercury Actors

JOSEPH COTTEN   DOROTHY COMINGORE
EVERETT SLOANE   RAY COLLINS
GEORGE COULOURIS   AGNES MOOREHEAD
PAUL STEWART   RUTH WARRICK
ERSKINE SANFORD   WILLIAM ALLAND

EVERYBODY'S TALKING ABOUT IT! *It's Terrific!*

Sexed-up advertising finally replaces the cartoon art of the original campaign, but by now it's too late.

C&C sweetened its deal by licensing the group in perpetuity. Member stations could run RKO forevermore, with no limit as to number of airings. I wonder how many present-day station managements are even aware of that ongoing privilege after 50 years? A number of stations could be running *Citizen Kane* right now, as those 1956 contracts would presumably remain in effect, despite Turner's eventual purchase of the library.

Exhibitors in 1956 felt betrayed by RKO and said so loudly in print, stopping just short of a boycott against the company's product. A handful of big-screen reissues nevertheless emerged that year. Showmen asked why they should book RKO product that might show up on free television the very night of their engagement. C&C included a rider with TV contracts in which listed titles were withheld from the initial group sold, including ones designated for 1956 theatrical release—*King Kong, She Wore a Yellow Ribbon*, and *Citizen Kane*, among others. New campaigns were prepared for these films, RKO reasoning perhaps that fresh posters might lessen hostility among theatremen. Availability for TV was promised no sooner than July 31, 1956, and no later than December 22, 1957, a pretty indefinite window for exhibitors already taking grief from patrons asked to pay for shows they'd just seen at home.

Citizen Kane was thus back in exhibition news when Bryant Haliday and Cyrus Harvey, Jr., former operators of Harvard's Brattle Theatre, acquired the 55th Street Playhouse in New York and booked *Kane* there for an "exclusive" revival in February 1956. The renovated art house had been the setting for a benefit performance of the 1941 release, with proceeds going to the Film Preservation Fund of the Museum of Modern Art. Their effort raised $500 for MOMA and favorable publicity for a newly viable *Kane* in theatres. RKO announced a limited art-house re-release for March, with engagements "carefully selected," said vice president in charge of worldwide distribution Walter Branson. "We are satisfied that there is public acceptance of this unusual picture in the proper theatres, and we feel that by continued careful handling on a very selective basis, appreciative revenue can be realized by exhibitors."

Would theatres other than art houses be considered? "Drawing power, location, or policy would determine that," said the RKO executive. One mainstream house did break records with *Citizen Kane* in 1957 by preceding its run with four days of radio saturation and commercial copy emphasizing the Hearst/Kane link—W.R. having died in 1951. The Casa Linda in Dallas was rewarded with triple the theatre's best receipts since opening. As with any attraction, exploitation was everything.

RKO closed its exchanges in 1957, with remaining prints going to independents. These small depots scrounged for whatever coin was left in pictures now heavily saturated on television. RKO titles continued playing kid shows and grind schedules well into the '60s. My examination of theatre ads for the Winston-Salem/Greensboro territory found many turning up years after late-night TV would have presumably wrung them dry. *Mighty Joe Young* was an evergreen for triple features at Greensboro's National Theatre; I found three bookings for it there in 1964–65. Winston-Salem's Carolina Theatre regaled youngsters with rock 'n' roll on stage and *Gunga Din* on screen in 1965. WBTV's horror host Dr. Evil popped in at the Lincoln a few blocks down, and *I*

Citizen Kane certainly is talked about...as the picture that reached out and poked a bear named W. R. Hearst. Not among Orson Welles' best or smartest career moves.

105

Walked with a Zombie accompanied his live show. All these would have been booked for no more than $15 to $20 flat.

The situation overall was much the same as it had been 10 years earlier. *Citizen Kane* was for art houses and television—action and monsters jingled the cash register. With its running time of 119 minutes, *Kane* came in for particularly brutal treatment by TV station editors. Two-hour slots were as much time as movies got for daytime or early evening telecasts. Imagine whittling 20 or so minutes out of *Citizen Kane* for a Saturday afternoon run. Its "News on the March" opening was usually first to go, being self-contained and easily snipped.

The mutilation inflicted on *Citizen Kane*'s syndicated placement in a 90-minute time frame amounts to frightful prospect, yet this is how many viewers saw the film between 1956 and the 1990s. Its placement on various 10-best lists assured pride of place among revival house booking sheets, but for distributors, it was hardly worth the shipping cost of a 35mm print. Manhattan repertories were paying just $50 flat to play *Citizen Kane* for three days in 1965. "Rentals earned have barely covered the cost of handling," said the New York *Times*.

The tide turned in March 1966 when Janus Films acquired theatrical rights for *Citizen Kane* along with *King Kong* from RKO General, Inc. Withdrawing the two from theatres, Janus partner Saul J. Turell promised "their reappearance will be backed by a promotion campaign aimed at the growing audience of what the trade calls film buffs. A fresh campaign might obtain higher prices from exhibitors as well," said Turell. "The existence of this audience is reflected by...theatres devoted almost exclusively to the showing of film classics, as well as in the proliferation of university courses and film societies."

Citizen Kane would now command $175 against 50 percent of all gross receipts, whichever was higher. Janus control did not extend to free showings. These were still handled by Films, Inc., the 16mm distributor supplying nontheatrical ven-

Nothing deleted? Exhibitors are not happy to hear such news about a picture that had them hearing crickets. And about a man many thought not worth depicting in the first place.

ues. Its 1971 *Rediscovering the American Cinema* catalogue labeled *Citizen Kane* a "special," with prices on a sliding scale: $50 to $100 for schools and convents, $65 to $250 for colleges, universities, museums, and film societies, depending on audience size. Thanks to these, *Citizen Kane* would at last get back some of its lost prestige.

Digital magic has spoiled twenty-first century *Kane* watchers. For a cold splash of what patrons settled for during the '60s and '70s, check out the grisly frame blow-ups from 16mm that Pauline Kael offered in her controversial *The Citizen Kane Book* in 1971. Revisionist as to text, her illustrations only emphasized the film's appalling state of

ALL *NEW* POSTERS AND ACCESSORIES

New poster designs for a 1956 reissue could not offset the fact that *Kane* would soon be had for free on television sets across the country.

preservation. Still years away from restoration efforts and DVD near-perfection, audiences for *Kane* took what they could get, and often what they got were prints as murky as those images Kael relied upon for her book.

The fact we can now enjoy home-theatre presentations far superior to anything 1970s patrons had in public spaces is something none of us should take for granted. Of course, it was video that would once again banish *Citizen Kane* from theatres. Why drive across town and pay an admission when you could stay home and watch your Nostalgia Merchant VHS tape, even if it was poorly mastered from 16mm? These began appearing in the late '70s.

As had been the case in 1956 with television, RKO's library would be among those first available to cassette collectors. Having succeeded to theatrical rights in *Citizen Kane*, Paramount tried another reissue in May 1991. Their box-office gross was a rewarding $1.585 million, unusually good for *any* library title in our age of video. Projection TV has largely overtaken film as the format of choice for institutions and groups lacking equipment and resources to book 35mm. Swank Motion Pictures, Inc., licenses titles for most of the film companies. Virtually all the other rental houses have gone by the wayside. Television runs of *Kane* are limited mostly to TCM, a good thing as they're always complete, uninterrupted, and look wonderful—not so good, however, if your cable service doesn't offer TCM, or you don't have cable at all. Minimal effort can put us all by way of a now-available Blu-ray disc. Past days of watching *Citizen Kane* chopped in syndication, of riding subways to distant art houses or pursuing worn 16mm costing hundreds of dollars—all these seem remote indeed. Orson Welles lived long enough to see the beginning of this transition. Would he be pleased by its culmination?

Simone Simon in one of many haunting scenes in *Curse of the Cat People.*

CHAPTER 12

THE THINKING MAN'S EXPLOITATION SHOCKERS

The frustrated career of Val Lewton served as both inspiration and cautionary fable for Hollywood insiders long before horror fans and writers began taking up his cause in the late 1960s. There's no better evidence of this fact than 1952's *The Bad and the Beautiful*, shooting within a year of Lewton's death and basing its protagonist's rise specifically, if not accurately, on *Cat People* lore and a "B" producer scavenging the lot for props to make his thrillers.

Industry folk must have talked lots about Lewton and why he rose and fell. There were few better object lessons on the peril of seeking art over commerce, nor a more effective argument favoring team play and sucking up to supervisors when necessary. Val Lewton kept his integrity, but little else. He was a talent to admire, but forget about emulating him if you wanted a future in pictures. Sad stories like his were best told in eulogies.

Those nine chillers (but were they *really*?) that Lewton made for RKO became scholarship bait long before we seriously embraced other Hollywood horrors. Like so many hard-luck cases, Lewton achieved immortality too late to do him good, as he died at 46, but at least his family enjoyed bows that VL wouldn't live to take. My recollection is of Carlos Clarens getting there first, though *An Illustrated History of the Horror Film* was merely the initial Lewton celebration of a second wave starting in 1967. Bigger names recognized him earlier, but I wonder if James Agee and Manny Farber's laudatory reviews during the '40s benefited Lewton or helped in bringing him down at RKO.

Agee wrote, "I think that few people in Hollywood show in their work that they know or care half as much about movies or human beings as he does." That critic and others praised Lewton as a remarkable exception to prevailing philistine standards. Former boss David O. Selznick may have done more hurt than benefit when his post-*Cat People* congratulatory wire crossed RKO chief Charles Koerner's desk: IS IN EVERY WAY A MUCH BETTER PICTURE THAN NINETY PERCENT OF THE 'A' PRODUCT THAT I HAVE SEEN IN RECENT MONTHS. OTHER STUDIOS HOPEFULLY HAVE EXTENDED SUCH OPPORTUNITIES TO WOULD-BE PRODUCERS BY THE SCORE WITHOUT GETTING A RESULT SUCH AS YOU HAVE DELIVERED.

We know corporate intrigues and politics proved Lewton's undoing. Were jealousies inflamed by these and other plaudits? Koerner was a supporter, but lesser RKO brass sniffed "too arty" when Lewton's name and accomplishments entered commissary chat. The fact he kept to himself and avoided studio camaraderie raised hackles further; Lewton disliked shaking hands—imagine how that played among vice presidents. Lesser talent had but to wait for things to go south. In Lewton's case, that wouldn't take very long.

Val Lewton's charge was, at a budget ceiling of $150,000 each, to dream up stories for pre-fab titles that RKO execs had consumer tested. *Cat People* initiated the series of cut-rate horrors. It became what they called in those days a "sleeper." Writer DeWitt Bodeen once estimated a $4 million gross. Modern historians took him up on that tall tale, and further credited this modest show with saving RKO itself, calling it "their biggest hit of that period." No, those would be *Once Upon a Honeymoon*, *Hitler's Children*, and *Mr. Lucky*.

It's tempting to propagate such myths when we admire the man and his films so much. *Cat People* did earn $360,000 in domestic rentals. $175,000 came back from foreign. There was $183,000 in profit, an excellent return for a "B." The comparable *The Falcon in Danger* ended $91,000 in the black, while *The Saint Meets the Tiger* actually lost $25,000.

Studios could realize only so much on pictures that generally played the bottom of tandem bills. *Cat People* opened on Broadway as a single, though the Rialto Theatre was not otherwise the sort of venue majors sought for prestige bookings. With a modest 600 seats and no balcony, the Rialto prided itself on ballyhoo techniques otherwise abandoned on the Great White Way. Front displays looked like Grand Guignol. Thriller engagements called for all-out chamber of horror enticement for passers-by willing to enter and be horrified.

Owner and operator Arthur Mayer was a well-respected industry veteran whose career dated back to silents. He thrived on low-down exploitation. Having shepherded Paramount's nationwide Panther Woman search for *Island of Lost Souls* a decade earlier, he knew how to beat publicity drums.

Above: The RKO horror formula tests audience reaction to phrases-as-concepts, approves the best of these, then develops advertising for the trades before a foot of film is shot. Above is concept art for *Cat People*. Below: *Cat People* as conceived by Val Lewton: RKO leading man Tom Conway romances tortured Irina (Simone Simon) amidst the shadows, with a slinky Simon also seen in the border art of this lobby card.

Mayer balked at the expense of print ads in the New York *Times*: "With my limited budget, I had little money to spend on newspaper advertising, so I was forced to use the theatre front and the lobby for my major shilling." Replacing objects of art with gargoyles and displays of torture instruments, Mayer proudly trumpeted the "Rialto's strictly masculine fare policy," reflecting his wish "to satisfy the ancient and unquenchable male thirst for mystery, menace and manslaughter."

Critics enjoyed slumming at the Rialto to a point where the theatre itself became a running joke in their columns: "Like a flower of evil, the Rialto Theatre has endeared itself to a little coterie of necrophiles that haunt the area as a perfect rendezvous for Witches' Sabbath and Walpurgis Eve celebrations."

Admissions were the cheapest around for first-runs. *Cat People* played in December 1942 for 25 cents before noon, 40 cents until 5 P.M., and 65 cents to closing. Sometimes they didn't clear the house till 4 in the morning. Patrons could even smoke in either of two side sections in the auditorium. Pretty punk for a Broadway engagement, but RKO could at least boast of having opened there when time came to sell *Cat People* among block-books to independent exhibitors.

Larger audiences for Val Lewton's understated chiller found it bringing up the rear behind big-ticket crowd-pleasers like *Springtime in the Rockies*, with which *Cat People* played in multiple New York City theatres on the RKO circuit starting January 7, 1943. Though Betty Grable's musical is barely remembered today, hers was the kind of show that actually got those $4 million grosses. In fact, *Springtime in the Rockies* took $4.4 million in worldwide rentals, making its estimated gross nearly twice that.

The Hollywood host for *Cat People* was the Hawaii Theatre, whose box office was redressed with a sign reading "Feed the Kitty Here." A presumably uncomfortable ticket seller sat inside an enormous cat head that covered the window, sliding both ducats and change along a feline "tongue" that draped toward the sidewalk. *Cat People* shared this first L.A. run with Warner's *The Gorilla Man*.

Despite critics' applause, Val Lewton got little in the way of recognition from bosses at RKO, and his compensation remained minimal. Koerner tossed a wet blanket when Lewton reminded him of *Cat People*'s success. "The only people who saw that film," Koerner said, "were negroes and defense workers." All RKO wanted from the Lewton unit was horror movies, preferably conventional ones. Fortunately for Lewton, *I Walked with a Zombie*, his second for the company, maintained *Cat People* profits and extended his creative autonomy.

Sophisticated chiller-man Val Lewton maintains a serious mien in this RKO office pose.

Above: *Cat People* opens at the Rialto Theatre on Broadway, where audiences run a spooky gauntlet to reach the chamber or horrors within; showman Arthur Mayer chooses to spend on dressing his own high-traffic storefront rather than investing in expensive print ads. Below left: Redressing of the box office at the Hawaii Theatre in Hollywood forces ticket buyers to "feed the kitty." Below right: A generic cat suit used for street bally favors Felix more than Irina.

O.E. Simon's trenchant commentary followed his Menno, South Dakota, booking of Val Lewton's follow-up to *Cat People*: "In the picture, the nurse walked with a zombie. The patrons walked out of the theatre, and the exhibitor walked around in circles trying to think what to do to make up for the loss."

Was Lewton determined to work against horror expectations as his series went on? *I Walked with a Zombie* and *The Leopard Man* suggested he was. Said the showman at Dewey, Oklahoma's Paramount Theatre of *The Leopard Man*, "People said they didn't understand this so-called horror picture. Business was light."

Zombie's negative cost crept $6,000 beyond the $150,000 limit RKO had set, and its worldwide rentals of $496,000 slipped below those of *Cat People*, though profits of $181,000 insulated Lewton for the present, as he now earned press recognition as a "Merchant of Menace," "Sultan of Shock," or whatever lamebrain tag they chose to hang on him. While Lewton dismissed the recipe as pure formula, profilers wondered what made those chillers tick. The last thing this producer needed was a perception that he took horror movies seriously. Ingredients required were plenty of dark patches and three bumps per show; easy as plugging in a waffle iron so it would seem, though Lewton's creative team knew well the efforts he'd made to distinguish his thrillers from the rest.

Always the last RKO employee to leave the lot at night, Lewton assumed final responsibility for script pages going before a camera. As with mentor Selznick, each setup bore Lewton's signature. Despite the disappointment his films sometimes yield on first viewing these many decades later, hanged if they don't mesmerize upon further acquaintance.

The problem in 1943 was impatience on the part of showmen accustomed to brightly lit mummies and wolf men chasing girls up trees. *I Walked with a Zombie* transplanted Jane Eyre to the tropics, just months before Fox did the latter with "A" money and bigger stars. *The Leopard Man* would belie its title, being devoid of man-into-mankiller technics, and in fact, those apparent leopard murders were a red herring for human villainy. Lewton kept snatching rugs from under horror fans, and numbers began to reflect an awareness of same. *The Leopard Man* cost $155,000 against domestic rentals of $303,000, with foreign at $100,000. Final profits of $104,000 represented a steep fall from the first two entries. The Lewtons now were running even with, if not behind, the Falcon series. A serious, if inevitable, drop-off would begin with *The Seventh Victim*. Soon it would become a challenge staying even with returns from RKO's Tim Holt westerns.

Insofar as artistic pretensions went, Val Lewton made Orson Welles look like a piker, so how did VL survive for eleven

Playing the Big Apple circuit, *Cat People* supports, and benefits from, song-and-dance sensation Betty Grable.

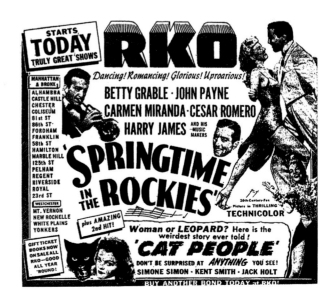

pictures as opposed to Welles' measly three? Possibly it was due to far less noise he made. Lewton didn't seek press; newspapers and popular mags paid little attention to horror producers in any case. Treading lightly below the radar served him well, but there was slippage evident by late 1943 and *The Seventh Victim.* "We must have been the eighth victim; patrons walked out," said N.C. Hillburn of the State Theatre in Inman, South Carolina. "Business poor. Some of the kids would not sit through it."

A lot of exhibitors avoided chillers when they could. Too many complaints of kiddie nightmares and headaches all around. Others limited genre stuff to every third month or so. What they hated most were horrors failing utterly to deliver on the promise of poster art. Said A.C. Edwards of Scotia, California, of *The Seventh Victim,* "This is without doubt the most unsatisfactory picture we have any recollection of."

Diminished profits reflected exhibitor hostility. A mere $59,000 in black ink was a long way down from *Cat People,* this despite reduced negative costs of $130,000 for *The Seventh Victim.* The problem arose from domestic rentals reduced by a third from *The Leopard Man,* itself a drop from numbers scored by *Cat People* and *I Walked with a Zombie.* Marquees trumpeted star Tom Conway and little else.

For all their moronic scripts and, by now, pedestrian sequels, Universal could at least boast of pre-sold horror names in its stables. Often as not, Lewton films were serving as rear guard for rival studio "B" pictures. Meanwhile, the producer was mapping out an "A" comedy to spotlight Tom Conway as Casanova(!). But like any number of proposed projects, it came to naught. Could this have been the point where RKO began negotiating its multi-picture deal with Boris Karloff?

"Lewton's masterpiece may well be *The Seventh Victim,*" declared Carlos Clarens in *An Illustrated History of the Horror Film.* "Rarely has a film succeeded so well in capturing the nocturnal menace of a large city, the terror underneath the everyday, the suggestion of hidden evil."

Not having seen the film upon acquiring the book, I breathlessly awaited coming TV broadcasts. My bafflement after watching was seeming proof I didn't breathe the same rarified air as Clarens. Was I was too

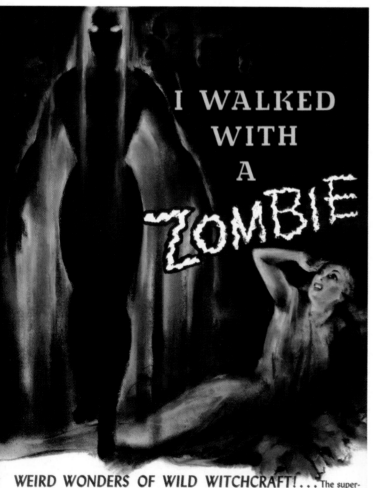

Teaser art for the *Cat People* follow-up features a sexy hour-glass spectre menacing a sexy damsel. Lewton's execution of the concept leaves some exhibitors, who are used to well-lit mummies and wolf men, cold.

WEIRD WONDERS OF WILD WITCHCRAFT! . . . The super-startling story of a beautiful American girl who flung aside the forbidden veil of voodoo and saw the secret world of the Zombies — The Walking Dead . . . on a green and purple island in the Caribbean. Based on the experiences set forth in the widely-discussed "American Weekly Magazine" story by Inez Wallace.

For Lewton, art trumps horror, but exhibitors lured by pre-production trade ads feel increasingly cheated by returns. At around the time that Frankenstein is meeting the Wolf Man to surefire business, one showman calls *The Leopard Man* "a so-called horror picture," while another pronounces himself the Eighth Victim because "patrons walked out" on *The Seventh Victim*. To an exhib, *this* is true horror.

obtuse to get it? Forty years later, I'm still wondering. Is *The Seventh Victim* a picture we're supposed to like as a way of demonstrating our grasp of Lewton's deeper meanings? Play it to general audiences at your peril. Carlos Clarens referred to *The Seventh Victim* as "a hauntingly oppressive work." Exhibitors in 1943 might have agreed with him, though for entirely different reasons.

Val Lewton used lots of second-hand props. This much I knew from multiple references to that *Magnificent Ambersons* staircase in *Cat People*. Good Lewton sets usually have their origins in someone else's movie. RKO's *The Hunchback of Notre Dame* was cannibalized for a number of them. It was the producer's policy to dress up one or two backgrounds for maximum effect and stage much of the key action therein. *The Ghost Ship* borrowed a vessel built for *Pacific Liner*, a modest-to-begin-with actioner released in 1939. This show as much as any demonstrates the miracles Lewton wrought with low budgets. It may be the only contemporary sea story produced in 1943 without a single wartime reference.

The Ghost Ship made me long for a film noir unit Lewton should have eventually helmed. What magic he might have made piloting Robert Mitchum, Jane Greer, Robert Ryan, and the rest.

As it is, we have the Lewton imprint on noirs his directing pupils gave us: Jacques Tourneur and *Out of the Past*, Robert Wise with *Born to Kill* and *The Set-Up*, and so on. Much of the look and mood of these can be traced to lessons taught by Lewton. *The Ghost Ship* provides proof positive of his expertise with subjects other than horror, despite a title promising more of the same. You'd not go far afield calling it the tightest and most efficient in the series. I found those 69 minutes mighty taut going and wondered if anyone could surpass Richard Dix as the deranged captain.

Profits for *The Ghost Ship* were actually up, as its negative came in the lowest of any Lewton production at $116,000. Profits of $105,000 resulted from domestic rentals of $272,000 and foreign receipts of $130,000—clear sailing but for a lawsuit brought by a writing pair who'd submitted a remarkably similar play supposedly received, but not read, by Lewton's office. The mess could have been settled for $700, but Lewton stood on principle and insisted upon litigating the thing out. Twelve men good and true came back with $25,000 for the plaintiffs, which appeals courts let stand despite Lewton's disavowal of allegations made because the claimants were, by his account, "charlatans and extortionists."

The fallout was serious, and I suspect that this, as much as anything, helped put skids under Lewton. Sadder still was the fact that his excellent movie had to be withdrawn and buried for generations to come. *The Ghost Ship* became itself a wraith largely unseen. It was in the C&C Movietime package of RKO features from 1956 into the early '60s, but someone in legal must have eventually checked the file, for by the time United Artists repackaged the Lewtons into a 58-title horror group for May 1963 syndicated release, *The Ghost Ship* was out.

A very few 16mm prints from older packages floated amongst collectors during this period. Harris Films out of England was the U.K. rights holder for RKO, and a number of *Ghost Ship*s ventured our way when Harris cleared its shelves in the late '80s. The issue became moot in any case when an early '90s clearance of rights permitted Turner to finally put it back in circulation. Purchasers of the Lewton DVD box set are likely unaware of what a scarce collectable this once was.

The Ghost Ship, an effective chiller made economically, becomes a Flying Dutchman after a writing duo claim Lewton stole the story. It will not be seen for decades.

Every appreciation of Lewton's next, *Curse of the Cat People*, begins with an apology for its title. Were it not for that baleful thing heralding the credits, this might be regarded as one of the 1940s' permanent film classics. Lewton wanted to call it *Amy and Her Friend*, which might only have hastened his departure from RKO premises, but surely then he'd have gotten recognition richly deserved for what many, myself included, consider his finest work. The child's dream world depicted here is much like one a lot of us occupied and shared with this movie during late-night views. The spell it cast was something special after den lights were down and parents abed. Were Amy's spectral companions so different from those we welcomed on Shock Theatre each week?

The killer-cat woman who clawed her rivals to shreds is dead—but her vengeful ghost is stalking the night for new victims!

It's money in the bank . . . this NEW horror-thriller, because it's even more terrific, more spine-chilling, more amazing, astounding and out-of-this-world than the startling sensation it so successfully succeeds!

"THE CURSE OF THE CAT PEOPLE"
with SIMON SIMONE · KENT SMITH · JANE RANDOLPH
Produced by Val Lewton

Above: Pre-production art for the trades sells *The Curse of the Cat People* as a continuation of blood-dripped horror featuring the same cast that had brought us *Cat People*. (Note the misspelling of Simone Simon's name.) Below: Upon release, RKO sells its new picture with the line, THE BLACK MENACE CREEPS AGAIN, even though *Curse of the Cat People* as envisioned by Val Lewton tells the charming and innocent story of a melancholy little girl visited by the spirit of a woman who seeks only redemption.

"THE *screaming* SKULL"

Dead men DO tell tales—and what a tale this one has to tell! . . . of ghosts, of murder, of death in the dark and life in the grave! Sheer scare sensation to make you shiver—and we do mean you, and you—AND YOU!

Favorable audience reaction to tantalizing titles leads to announcements for Lewton features to come. The two above will be scrapped when box office for *The Seventh Victim* and *The Ghost Ship* is soft.

No other Lewton, indeed no other fantasy film, calls up such intense emotion. I cried with it at 13 and again more recently. It's impossible to imagine such delicate and, yes, poetic filmmaking coming from any other major studio—and during World War II. RKO may have mutilated *The Magnificent Ambersons* two years before, but surely redress was had for enabling a small masterpiece like *Curse of the Cat People*. DeWitt Bodeen maintained that the producer junked his writer's ending due to front-office pressures, but from what I've read of said finish, it would seem Lewton came to the rescue of what might have been a botched and melodramatic original as conceived by Bodeen. It was the last time these two would work together.

James Agee again sang Lewton's praises, claiming to have sat among hardened Rialto patrons through what he expected would be a film disappointing to them, only to be relieved by a burst of applause at the end. Who says horror fans have no sensitivity? I can't help believing MGM was watching as well, for what is *Meet Me in St. Louis'* Halloween segment but a glossier recap of Ann

The ghost of the greatest lover of all time returns to earth for twelve night hours—and what a terror thrill for the women he encounters!... Shriek-and-scream amazement blended with comedy to give the utmost in unusual entertainment!

The "AMOROUS GHOST"

Produced by Val Lewton

Carter's frightful walk through the night? Atmospheric, set-bound parallels between the two features are striking. For the record, *Curse of the Cat People* was shot during August and September of 1943. *Meet Me in St. Louis* followed with production beginning November 1943 and extending into spring of the next year. Did someone at RKO give Vincente Minnelli a peek at Lewton's handiwork? Judging by evidence at hand, I'd say they did.

Curse of the Cat People was the sixth release in Lewton's RKO horror group. It also performed the poorest of any thus far. The first of the chillers to pass a negative cost of $200,000, this required $212,000 to finish, a figure not likely to endear Lewton to his employers. Domestic rentals of $268,000 surpassed *The Seventh Victim* and *The Ghost Ship*, but profits added up to a paltry $35,000. All six entries in RKO's contemporaneous Tim Holt "B" western season did better. New directions were clearly needed if Lewton's series was to continue.

RKO got ambitious for Lewton as its 1943–44 product annual to exhibitors announced flamboyant projects that didn't come to fruition. A "Twin Horror Bill" of *The Screaming Skull* and *The Amorous Ghost* demonstrated the company's customary flair with exploitable titles, and unmistakable was RKO's intent to copy Universal's all-star monster rallies with *They Creep by Night*, which proposed cat people, zombies, leopard folk, and whatever other scraps could be gotten off Lewton's floor. Latter-day fans can only imagine what such potpourri might have amounted to.

Not one, not two, not three . . . but ALL of the famous creeper characters you ever heard of, plus some new ones, in the wildest nightmare of terror thrills that mind can imagine! . . Cat People, Zombies, Leopard Men, beast-women and bat-men, blood-curdlers by the dozen . . . all in a merger of monsters that will make anything else in this line look like a Sunday School picnic!

"THEY CREEP BY NIGHT"

Influenced by Universal's all-star monster spooktacular, *House of Frankenstein*, RKO conceives *They Creep by Night*, bringing together "Cat People, Zombies, Leopard Men, beast-women and bat-men." Like *The Screaming Skull* and *The Amorous Ghost*, *They Creep* will not be produced.

Lewton longed to produce "A" pictures, but sadly got only so far as a pair of oddball non-horrors that lost money for RKO and likely ended any dreams of graduation from low-budgeters. Ironic that directors he mentored would move up prestige ladders while Lewton ran in place. Jacques Tourneur's *Experiment Perilous* was reward for that director's fine work on *Cat People, I Walked with a Zombie*, and *The Leopard Man*, and the studio's borrowing of MGM star Hedy Lamarr assured concentrated effort toward bookings better than any of Lewton's offerings might receive. Trade support for *Experiment Perilous* confirmed its position as one of RKO's top 1944 releases.

Lewton's *Youth Runs Wild* meanwhile fell into line with juvenile delinquency melodramas being turned out en masse by not only the mini-majors, but straight-out exploitation producers as well. Columbia offered *Youth on Trial*. State's Rights distributors peddled *Youth Aflame* for those who preferred teen issues more explicitly dissected; minus a Code seal, such cheapies delivered on baser promises. *Where Are Our Children?* and *Are These Our Parents?* would seem to have answered similar lines of inquiry. Why see them both? Indeed, why engage *Youth Runs Wild*, especially with a title that would, by comparison, confer dignity even upon *I Walked with a Zombie*?

RKO took the post-production scissors route to *Youth Runs Wild*. Lewton called the remnants "a stinker." The prospect of an audience beyond kids loosened RKO purse strings, and as a result, *Youth Runs Wild* had a negative cost of $291,000. But JD problem pictures made little impression on foreign markets already hobbled by the war; thus, overseas rentals were a low $50,000. A final loss of $45,000 couldn't be blamed on Lewton, for the market was nearly as glutted with teenage troublemakers as theatres themselves would be by the mid '50s.

Worse to come was Lewton's non-genre *Mademoiselle Fifi*, with rentals of $150,000 domestic and $48,000 foreign against a negative cost of $228,000. The loss this time, $110,000, justified RKO's lack of confidence in *Fifi*. Judging by so little mention in the trades, you'd hardly know it was out there.

Accustomed lower berths did not bode well for Lewton's effort at a more sophisticated product, so it was back to the horror grind, but now with a twist. If Lewton wouldn't look to Universal for inspiration, RKO would bring Universal to him.

Jack Gross was a producing vet at the latter who liked his monsters straight up and uncomplicated. Now he'd come aboard as Lewton's boss at RKO and bring commercial lure Boris Karloff along to resuscitate the box office. Lewton adamantly opposed Gross and Karloff, at least at the beginning. How could he know that this partnership would result in the biggest grosser of his RKO sojourn, indeed the only one of the bunch that would give showmen and their customers precisely what they wanted in the way of horror?

We can sit home with our DVDs and think we've seen *The Body Snatcher*, but that's like steak without garnishment compared to banquets 1945 audiences reveled in. A St. Louis premiere was the biggest launch yet on behalf of a Lewton film. The sales department must have recognized a winner early on, because they ran with gusto on *The Body Snatcher* like no other in the series. Trade ads were lavish and plentiful. That St. Louis opening at a 3,600 seater became the centerpiece of campaigns suggested in the pressbook. Showmen this time really had something they could latch onto.

RKO gives Lewton a new production boss and a big horror name in Boris Karloff. The result: monster returns at the box office.

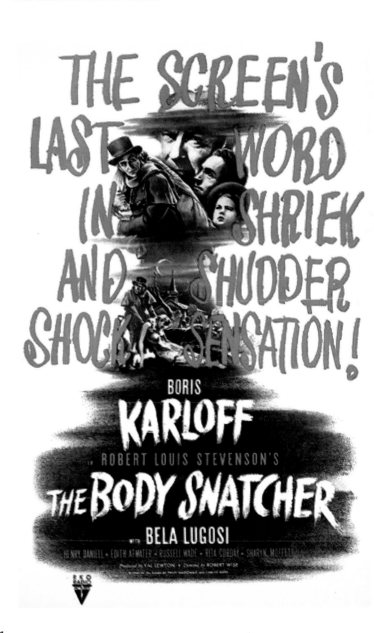

121

Clockwise from above: Dr. Neff menaces Bela Lugosi in a stage show; a killer premiere in St. Louis at the Missouri Theatre, and at regular prices! Macabre lobby displays show corpses and ghouls; and a decked-out theatre, '40s-style.

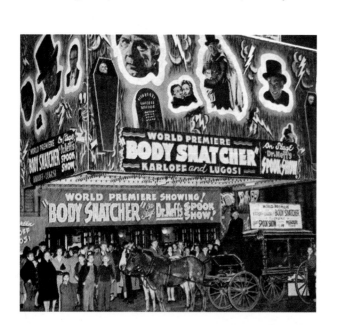

The name Dr. Neff may not ring a lot of bells today, but in his glory years, this was the absolute dean of spookmeisters. As if a world premiere of *The Body Snatcher* wasn't enough, St. Louis also got Neff's live act that served as vanguard for the new movement toward all-out audience participation screamers, a format he mastered. Bill Neff began doing teenage magic acts with Indiana, Pennsylvania hometown pal James Stewart (yes, *that* Stewart). Their lives took divergent paths, though crowds might have said in the late '40s that Bill achieved at least as much glory in his field as did Jim thesping.

Neff carried sets worthy of DeMille. Nobody came away from his shows with less than exultant praise. Bela Lugosi sought Bill for a stage partner when the vampire king took his show on the road in 1947. Those sad stories we've heard of Bela sharing degradation with guys in tattered gorilla skins didn't apply here, as Neff's act went beyond mere stage illusion. He dragged girls planted in the audience out of their seats and buzz-sawed off their heads. Bloodthirsty teens blew a gasket when his crew came to town. The thought of getting all this plus *The Body Snatcher* first-run amounted to nirvana in any fan's language. I checked St. Louis archives for press accorded the world premiere. Guess they were more sanguine about such things then, for Dr. Neff and *The Body Snatcher* received but one multi-column display ad, on Valentine's Day, plus holdover into a second week. Ah, the stuff they took for granted then.

There were complications. Manager Harry Crawford had a warrant served on him for disturbing the peace. Seems his ideas for a scare exhibit to adorn the top of the Missouri's marquee unsettled nearby tenants and otherwise sedate passers-by. "Why should a mechanical dog howling at one-second intervals annoy anyone?" asked Harry. Gendarmes advised him to tell it to the judge. A 15-foot square lobby display featured a motorized Karloff figure dragging a female corpse out of its tomb, while a "hundred-year-old hearse" carried dummy cadavers thither and yon with the assist of what were described as "two decrepit horses."

Boris Karloff brings his prestige name to *Isle of the Dead* as he had for *The Body Snatcher*. Ads for showmen promise a carpet of corpses but the picture disappoints with its slow pace and only an occasional chill.

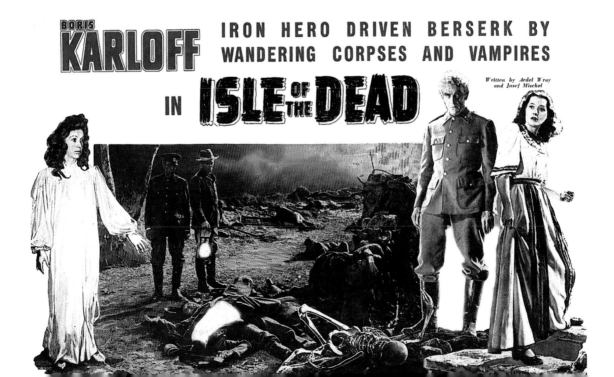

As *The Body Snatcher* opened on February 14, valentines were dispatched about town showing Boris strangling Bela with the caption, "Please Give Me a Piece of Your Heart." RKO's New York office supervised the campaign. There were horrors staged live at the Missouri Theatre that Lewton pictures, denuded by the Code, couldn't begin to duplicate. Kids doubtlessly got more genuine scares out of Neff's pageant and accompanying front displays than *The Body Snatcher* would deliver, yet here at last was a solid hit that demonstrated what Val Lewton could do when he turned his hand toward baser shocks.

The Body Snatcher's negative was on the high end at $221,000, but domestic rentals rang up a satisfying $317,000, with foreign money the best ever for this series at $230,000. RKO's net amounted to $118,000, the most since *I Walked with a Zombie*. Were it not for a higher cost, *The Body Snatcher* would have been the most profitable of all Lewtons. As it is, the film stands as the biggest single grosser of the nine.

You'd have thought Universal producer Jack Gross would ride herd over Val Lewton once he assumed supervisory duties at RKO, but the man behind Universal's recent monster sequels seems to have pretty much left VL alone. Gross is credited as executive producer on Lewton's next, *Isle of the Dead*, although Lewton portrayed Gross as another of those studio troglodytes with a cigar in one hand and his racing form in the other. Evidence of the last two entries in Lewton's series belie such an image. They are, in fact, among the artiest of the group.

Isle of the Dead took its inspiration from a painting of the same name by one Arnold Bocklin, who set

Above: Patron of the arts Karloff poses beside one of five original Bocklin paintings. Below: Art of a different kind is on display in a theatre front dressed for *Isle of the Dead*. Numbers will still be off from those achieved by *The Body Snatcher*.

his gothic scene to canvas *five* different times. That's right, five near-identical "originals" are hanging in galleries worldwide. Boris Karloff assumed patron-of-the-arts duty for a field trip to New York's Metropolitan Museum, where he was photographed standing alongside one of them. It flattered Karloff to keep company like this. He was a cultivated man and appreciated that quality in others. Whatever misgivings Lewton had about using this actor dissolved once they met.

The producer frequently called upon memories of creepy art he'd been exposed to as a child— that generation's equivalent of our monster magazines, perhaps—and *Isle of the Dead* would emerge as very much a tribute to things that went bump during Lewton's boyhood nights.

Karloff was the first real star to do a Lewton picture. Fans could wish he'd been in more than just three, but did RKO really pay him a mere $600 per week as I've read?

Serious *Isle of the Dead* delay ensued when BK fell out due to back problems. A spinal operation laid him up for months; time enough for the project to lose momentum and Lewton's interest to wane. "A complete mess," he now called it, but *Isle of the Dead* always rang the bell for this viewer. Slow it is, but isn't that the case with most Lewton merchandise? Amazing how all nine of his features have their adherents. I've read passionate arguments crediting each as best in the series.

Life was simpler when they were new. Showmen thought *Isle of the Dead* dragged at first, but relished patron screams when a woman gets buried alive in the second half. Even that may not have been enough to offset continuing inertia at ticket windows, as *Isle of the Dead* was way down from the stellar numbers recorded by *The Body Snatcher*. A $246,000 negative cost was the highest yet for a Lewton horror and way more than RKO spent for other "B" pictures, although costs after the war were generally up throughout the industry. Domestic rentals amounted to $266,000, with foreign $117,000. RKO's profit was the lowest so far: $13,000. These were slim pickings during a year when expectations ran high, as one couldn't help making money off movies in 1945. Was the public tiring of horror films or just Lewton's horror films?

His next, *Bedlam*, was the first to actually go into the hole. It mattered no longer that Lewton's was an eccentric approach to the genre. Pictures like these had headed south. Maybe folks were just waiting for someone to spoof excesses endured with recent Universal monster rallies. *Abbott and Costello Meet Frankenstein* would answer that call, but not for another two years. In the meantime, there was ongoing tepidity of Uni's *She-Wolf of London* and *The Spider Woman Strikes Back*. Was Universal surrendering the field to rivals? If so, RKO wasn't taking the bait.

A fortune in lobby cards, oversized posters, and banners (as judged by today's value to collectors) welcome the pairing of RKO's *Isle of the Dead* and Universal's latest, *House of Dracula*, in a 1945 double bill.

Kids wanted screen shows as gruesome as Dr. Neff with his tossed heads. They instead got extravagant promises and timid fulfillment of same, but that was the Production Code Administration, not producers, who applied the brakes. Lewton had no end to censor problems with *The Body Snatcher*. Indeed, his career might have better flourished had he come along in the '60s. *The Innocents* from 1961 plays like one of his, and certainly *The Haunting*, directed by Robert Wise, was nothing if not a homage to Lewton's technique.

Film noir reflected a new toughness in crime thrillers. Horror films could do with a bit less reading between the lines as well. It would seem that audiences were ready for Hammer Films 10 years before Hammer Films were ready for them. Had these two gotten together sooner, we might well have had a post-war horror boom.

But *Bedlam*, like other late-in-the-day chillers, was a tough sell. Neither fish nor fowl was this. A problem picture about lunatic asylums sounds fine when Olivia de Havilland's your inmate, but Boris Karloff presiding could mean only one thing, and therein lay the disconnect. *Bedlam*'s star didn't help when he insisted it wasn't a horror film at all. "A historical picture," corrected Karloff.

Negative cost reflected a steady rise in expense that these shows generated. Modern writers claim Lewton had a budget of $350,000 plus extended pre-production time, but RKO ledgers indicate $264,000. Domestic rentals of $257,000 and $98,000 foreign were sufficiently eroded as to result in $40,000 lost on *Bedlam*.

It's no disgrace to any filmmaker when his series winnows out. The fact that Lewton managed nine horror features of such enduring quality within the confines of a formula-driven system like RKO's, is some kind of miracle. His standards remained high, even if the box office didn't. No one else in Hollywood made chillers so intelligent and stimulating as Lewton's. You can pick at any and find minor fault, but who even bothers over most of the stuff Universal was doing after 1942—*Captive Wild Woman*, anyone? Looking at this series again made me realize anew what a unique talent his was.

Lewton might have taken solace over the evergreen status his films achieved were it not for his premature death in 1951. RKO kept the series in circulation for as long as that company re-

Bedlam is Val Lewton's swan song as a surrealistic horror overlord of the mid-1940s. Karloff doesn't do Lewton any favors by calling *Bedlam* "a historical picture" at a time when Universal is still selling its big three of Frankenstein, Dracula, and the Wolf Man.

mained afloat, reissues a constant well into the '50s. Even after RKO closure, Lewton horrors made theatrical rounds via independent franchisees renting them even during the 1960s. *Cat People* had a 1952 reissue that scored domestic rentals of $125,000 and resulting profits of $65,000. Most of the others were back as units in double-feature packages. *Isle of the Dead* returned with *Mighty Joe Young* in 1953; *I Walked with a Zombie* supported *King Kong* in 1956.

The only two not reissued were *The Ghost Ship* and *Bedlam*. Circulation of Lewton features in the 1950s meant safety prints in 35mm. If you grew up then, chances are you saw some of them theatrically. Television lumped the series into enormous packages of RKO features, which meant that stations purchasing smaller groups might get two or three Lewtons, but seldom all, unless they sprung for C&C's bulging library of 741 titles.

This time the promise of FIRST TIME ON ANY SCREEN won't work, and despite elaborate front-of-house displays, *Bedlam* goes on to lose $40,000.

That May 1963 syndicated release referenced earlier was the first opportunity many stations had to unspool all the available Lewtons on respective late-night horror shows. United Artists' package of 58 features combined sci-fi and monster offerings from backlogs controlled by UA at the time, thus we had Warner's *Doctor X*, *Beast with Five Fingers*, and *The Walking Dead*, UA's own *Beast of Hollow Mountain*, Hammer's *Hound of the Baskervilles*, along with the Lewtons and other RKO favorites, including *King Kong* and *The Thing*. This was a next best to having Screen Gems' Shock and Son of Shock groups. Nontheatrical rental went through Films, Inc., whose daily rates reflected critical hierarchy within the series. *Rediscovering the American Cinema* catalogue devoted a page to the Lewtons, and promised to add still-in-limbo *The Ghost Ship* to future listings. Worth noting is the fact that *Bedlam*, *The Seventh Victim*, and *The Leopard Man* were available at lower rates than the rest. Could these, then, have been regarded weakest by opinion makers of the day?

Val Lewton stands tall among screen immortals, his films in frequent rotation on TCM and some even streaming elsewhere in High Definition. We pick and choose less today among the group; all are valued, if not revered—ask six fans to name a favorite and you'd probably get six different choices. Lewton's was exemplary work rewarded more than a half-century too late to do him good, but so long as there is demand for subtle gradations of horror, this producer's legacy, and his library, will thrive.

127

Humphrey Bogart ascends to romantic lead in *Across the Pacific*, here with Mary Astor and the spectre of the Rising Sun.

CHAPTER 13

STATESIDE THEATRES OF WAR

There's nothing like the urgency you get from World War II films made during that conflict. Imagine how they played to audiences still in doubt as to its outcome. Whatever tension was generated on screen was redoubled by real-life anxiety over who'd win or lose. Were the likes of *Flying Tigers* and *Across the Pacific* there as much for reassurance as escape? Looking back from our comfortable distance makes it easy to wax superior over clichés and wrong-then and wrong-now attitudes, but how many films since have confronted such an imperative, with the very survival of democracy hanging in the balance?

I'd sure have looked to Humphrey Bogart, Clark Gable, or John Wayne as counterweight to headlines appearing in 1942, a year mostly bleak for the Allies. Theatres were a refuge that promised ultimate victory with a necessary caution that getting there would be rough and demand sacrifice. Unlike dreamscapes of the '30s, wartime movie houses were recruitment and basic-training sites for home-fronters eager (or not) to do their civilian part. Patrons ran a gauntlet of war-bond-selling booths positioned in most lobbies. Kids rolled discarded tires to scrap drives that showmen sponsored. There was no more prominent community center than a theatre in small towns, and no experience so intense as attending with stakes this high.

A first year's wake of Pearl Harbor found theatre lobbies dressed out with every conceivable lure for patrons to aid in the war effort. The Victory Booth was a common sight, as showmen were among the most effective bond salesmen. Those patriotic features, shorts, and newsreels didn't go for naught. Audiences were besieged with solicitations before they even got through the front entrance. Scrap collection displays on a sidewalk could overwhelm prosaic marquees in back of them, priorities writ large in this time of national emergency.

The idea of tossing refuse into the open mouths of our enemies seems to have been effective, as one can envision parents lugging discard into theatres, then letting their kids have fun playing ring toss with Adolf. Day-and-night service at Victory Bond counters was no idle promise. Many houses maintained round-the-clock schedules to accommodate third-shift war workers anxious to catch the latest Andy Hardy before heading home for A.M. shuteye.

Patrons often got the fish eye for walking past a bond booth without purchasing. Civilian slackers were no more to be tolerated than able-bodied men out of uniform, and the pressure to buy bonds and kick in on scrap drives must have been enormous. Imagine contemptuous looks from expectant

Above: Audiences flock to see John Wayne's birds-eye view of the Japs before and after Pearl Harbor. Below: Wayne, here with Anna Lee, establishes his essential screen character in *Flying Tigers*.

managers, ushers, and corn poppers, each conveying silent disapproval as you arrive sans scrap and leave minus bonds. I'll bet they even took names in some of the smaller towns.

War years were boom years for theatres. Whatever lingered of the Depression would dissipate as record patronage put even weak attractions into profit. Never had there been such appetite for escape as now. One among ancillary benefits was a boom in concession sales. That, however, was affected by wartime rationing, sugar being a rare and hotly desired commodity.

How then to measure observance of restrictions versus cash so readily made? Insight as to that dilemma came via a local old-timer who'd served in the uniform of usher and concession salesman. "Back when I worked at the theatre...," I heard him say one morning at a local diner. The fact it was a long-gone site piqued my interest even more.

Wesley Clark's job had been hustling popcorn. He couldn't be bothered about the movies they ran, but his memories of that corn were sufficiently vivid to permeate my imagination with the smell of molten butter. Seems business was a little slow in '42 when Wesley initially took charge of the counter—popcorn was all they had for concessions, by the way, no candy at all, and a single cola machine in the lobby. He made do with sluggish sales until the fateful day he added extra seasoning to the mix.

Connoisseurs of theatre popcorn know that the matter of seasoning can often draw the line of demarcation between a culinary treat and tepid negation of one's entire movie-going experience. Wesley's enhanced popcorn was an immediate sensation, and sales rocketed. The boss was delighted. Only problem lay in the fact that there was a war on, and popcorn seasoning was a rationed item. His theatre could get only one 450-pound barrel every four months. Wes had used up his barrel in six weeks. Not to worry, said senior management, and then, in a hushed aside, "I'll get that seasoning…" Maybe there was a war out there somewhere, but selling 1,500 bags of popcorn every Saturday, and at a nickel a bag, amounted to $75. For this kind of windfall, rationing be damned!

Wesley wouldn't speculate as to just how the boss got his extra barrels. All he knows is they were got. Speculation runs riot at the prospect of a small-town exhibitor dealing in black-market popcorn seasoning. Just how did he acquire it? Was our little community honeycombed with dealers in wartime contraband? Were patrons eating popcorn at the expense of our boys in uniform? Moral and ethical questions abound, along with speculation as to the scale (nationwide?) of popcorn condiment hoarding.

Salty treats were but one stimulant to wartime movie going. There was new adrenalin pumped into shows America went to see. Cartoons got faster and louder. Progress of the war was daily aired on large screens in crowded auditoriums. It was not unusual for patronage to cheer or weep openly over the content of newsreels. These, in fact, were promoted as must-sees in newspaper ads. *Captured Jap Footage* and *The Fall of Corregidor* were as alluring as features, even double ones. It was vital in those early days of the war to give the impression we were whipping the Japanese even as they were in actuality creaming us.

For whatever pleasures are had watching *Flying Tigers*, *Across the Pacific*, and *Somewhere I'll Find You*, all released during height-of-emotion 1942, it's worth

Top Right: Local showman Lester Pollock creates an "Avenge Dec. 7" display featuring a one sheet of the Pearl Harbor Flag in his Rochester, New York theatre. Center: James McKillip, manager of the Wisconsin Theatre in LaCrosse, watches as patrons drive nails in Hitler's coffin, which is then burned. Bottom: Rags, metal, and rubber are shoved into the villainous mouths of Hitler, Mussolini, and Tojo in Macon, Georgia during a run of *Wake Island*.

SLAP THE JAP!

Rig up a punching bag in lobby with caricatures of Hirohito on each side of the bag, as shown below. Sign invites patrons to "slap the Jap — Across The Pacific".

Above: Showmen are urged to let patrons get physical. Below: A lobby display and matching 4 x 7" handouts keep crosshairs fixed on the enemy in Atlanta.

remembering that the excitement and encouragement they generated would answer a need more critical in those uncertain days than for future generations who'd dismiss such films as crudest propaganda.

Calendars are the stuff of high drama in both *Flying Tigers* and *Across the Pacific*. A December 7 close-up assured gasps of recognition and grim foreknowledge of dreadful things about to happen. Timeliness was an advantage for war stories. Set the action in months that had just passed, and features became an extension of the newsreels preceding them, a kind of seamless narrative lots more realistic than movies had been before.

Flying Tigers was shot from April to June 1942 and released in October. It told of Americans volunteering to help the Chinese rout Japanese oppressors in the air. Their war becomes ours when a *Flying Tigers* third-act highlight shows John Wayne and others listening to President Roosevelt declare war just after Pearl Harbor. Action stops for this, and we linger over troubled expressions as the speech is heard in its near entirety. I'm betting very little popcorn went into mouths as the president spoke and Wayne reacted.

Flying Tigers was barely rejiggered from aerial dramas Howard Hawks (*Only Angels Have Wings* and *Ceiling Zero*) and others had done, though they lacked impact furnished by a real-life war. Familiar narrative devices of reckless pilots and cowardice aloft were buttressed by opponents foreign, sinister, and—since Pearl Harbor—easy to hate. Never had the "other" exhibited such otherness.

Japanese pilots in *Flying Tigers* are subhuman and lethal. They wear caps with mangy fur linings. When shot down, which is often, they clutch their throats and upchuck blood; imagine post-December 7 cheering at that. Ads for *Flying Tigers* minced few words as to the propaganda mission: **To Blast to Bloody, Burning Hell the Sneaking Japs Who Unleashed Their Terror on the World.** Patrons might indeed have benefited from issuance of Valium tablets with their concessions for appeals so forceful as this.

Flying Tigers was the only feature in 1942's top 20 not produced by a major studio. Small-timer Republic had never had product so grand or timely as this to sell. Budget was set at $264,384, but negative costs ran to $397,690. The company, accustomed to flat rental rates for its westerns and serials, now demanded 35 percent for booking *Flying Tigers*. They'd not have gotten such terms but for John Wayne, now a bona fide "A" star and bound by a Republic contract. You can look at this show and those he did before it and know that Wayne's essential screen character was born in *Fly-*

ing Tigers. He's fully formed at last after years in rough draft. No longer is he the uncertain youth of *Stagecoach*, but a leader of men and warrior of unquestioned judgment.

Wayne from this point would remain the sober alternative to recruits brash and green, exemplified in *Flying Tigers* by John Carroll as a go-it-alone hotshot pilot based on the old Cagney model, discredited now in a war demanding team effort. To be exemplary in battle meant pitching in for the good of all. One-man bands played mostly in graveyards. Wayne was fortunate for age advantage promoting him to onscreen officer status and roles better suited to the sort of underplaying he did best. It's efforts of a John Carroll, all smirk and acrobatic eyebrows, that emphasize Wayne's cooler hand. As an actor, he benefitted for doing less.

While Wayne developed his soundstage combatant, ambitious players like Carroll and James Craig over at MGM followed examples soon to be outmoded, patterning themselves on pre-war first-teamers who were themselves service bound. Wayne knew his career turned upon opportunities he might seize while these rivals served. A decision to stay out of the war probably spared him the afterward fate of many who'd enlisted short of firming up stardom.

Across the Pacific, if not heralding the arrival of Humphrey Bogart as romantic leading man, at least gave him recognition as such after years of varied service to criminal enterprise and "B" leads onscreen. Jack Warner saw *ATP* and wired home that his studio finally had its own Clark Gable in Bogart, little realizing that his asset was one of greater longevity than he'd suspect.

Bogart was like Wayne in shaping a hero for the war that would sustain beyond

Above: The Victory Booth at the Broadway Theatre in Norwich, Connecticut, includes the next generation and another Pearl Harbor flag one-sheet. Below: *Across the Pacific* sells heavy doses of "yellow peril."

133

SO Glad When People Don't Buy War Bond—Thank You

FOR the month of September, the Motion Picture Industry will lead the drive for intensification of the sale of WAR BONDS and STAMPS . . . September is our BILLION DOLLAR BABY . . . September's the month we're going OVER THE TOP . . . Come on and join up with your Uncle Sam's Home Front Forces. BUY A BOND TODAY . . . and keep on buying them as often as you can . . . BUY A BOND to honor every Mother's Son In The Service . . . Let's all join in making this the Biggest BIG PARADE of ALL . . . let's make it the parade that'll give the axe to the axis . . . right where it'll do the most good!

Buy Your War Bonds from Cincinnati's "Minute Maids" in Bond Booths of Downtown Theatres . . . or from the Service Staffs in many of your Neighborhood Movie Houses.

(This advertisement sponsored by RKO Cincinnati Theatres.)

its conclusion and help redefine masculine codes for a generation to come. He's more believable for being less fully committed than others who laid down sacrifice without question.

Bogart cashiered from the service in *Across the Pacific* seems not an unlikely premise, but the fact that he turns out to be working undercover is frankly less plausible. Despite the several war-themed films they did together, the characters of Bogart and Sydney Greenstreet seem always to function as men without countries—at most, figures minus loyalty except to themselves. The template established by *The Maltese Falcon* died hard, but the conversion of self-server Bogart to an Allied calling made hits like *Casablanca* possible. His patriotic fervor seemed more an informed choice than those of guileless leading men suiting up at the bugle's first call, but again, it was Bogart's age and presumed maturity that made his character's choices more reasoned ones.

Across the Pacific combines that equivocation with a playful undermining of the straightforward know-your-enemy message put forth by *Flying Tigers* and simpler-minded Jap-slappers. Here we have Sydney Greenstreet as a jovial, if untrustworthy, proponent of oriental culture given legitimacy by his appreciation of it. A judo exhibition in *Across the Pacific* amounts to endorsement of that art as superior to defense tactics of our own.

For all the film's recognition of a cunning and formidable enemy, *Across the Pacific's* promotion relied on Yellow Peril devices and a by-now familiar revenge theme (**I've Been Hoarding This Sock Since December 7**, says Bogart in poster art). Its September release brought domestic rentals of $1.3 million against negative costs of $576,000, with foreign an additional $994,000. Final profits of $1,005,250 were the largest yet for a Bogart vehicle.

Certain star images conferred foresight with regards World War II that make you wish they'd been in charge around pre-war Washington rather than having such clairvoyant talents go to waste in Hollywood. These guys knew all along we couldn't trust the Japanese. Assurances of peace out

Opposite page, clockwise from top left: The Warner Bros. one-sheet for *Across the Pacific* promises a Jap-boffing Bogart; E.V. Dinerman of RKO Theatres places this ad in Cincinnati papers and distributes a matching handout to patrons; a theatre depicts Axis leaders as rats with opened mouths ripe for taking scrap metal. Right: Mere weeks after the death of wife Carole Lombard on a lonely Nevada mountaintop, Clark Gable poses for stills with Lana Turner. His tortured eyes say it all.

135

of Tokyo were the bunk. Clark Gable says as much in opening scenes of MGM's *Somewhere I'll Find You*, the latter taking place during weeks preceding Pearl Harbor. His assurance of Nippon perfidy makes chumps of those who censored Gable's news dispatches out of China, here depicted as just another backdrop for soldiering for fortune and incidental fortune-telling re America's naïveté. When Gable says wake up, we best call off peace conferences and prepare for combat.

Somewhere I'll Find You was one of those with a script near dry before bombs dropped on December 7, so rewriters got hasty putting Gable's hero wise before that surprise attack. The pic began shooting January 15, 1942. Events made it timely and far more than a kissing marathon's encore to *Honky Tonk* of the previous year for Gable and co-star Lana Turner. Gable's image gained stature for parallels it drew with Rhett Butler and that character's pre-Civil War awareness of battlefield realities. There was a sense of his knowing our enemy long before we woke up to recognition of same.

We'll never know what opportunity Gable, and his public, missed for the star's enlistment in the wake of wife Carole Lombard's death in an air crash the very day after *Somewhere I'll Find You* production began. Combat actioners with him through this war would have been a rewarding lot for the credibility Gable accumulated over 10 years of onscreen leadership. Wisdom attained through that would have made him an ideal man at the head of a fictional fighting column. Roosevelt's advice to the actor and a studio's plea should have been honored: Stay home and do battle where civilians' morale and potential recruits could best use it. To put an aging Gable—41 and having smoked/imbibed to the brim of it—in Army uniform and behind a real machine gun was waste of a resource far more needed in theatres. *Somewhere I'll Find You* shows what a next three years might have yielded toward better winning a war on Metro soundstages.

The pre- and post-Pearl Harbor elements of *Somewhere I'll Find You* make for a kooky mix. Here's a story that needed more revision than they evidently had time for. Its hot-off-the-press advantage mitigates lumpiness of a narrative that began as mere parlor setting for innumerable clinches with Gable and Lana Turner. They were **The Team That Generates Steam** and no war, not even a world-encompassing one, was going to get in the way of that. Was MGM aware of the serious conflict we'd gotten into, or did they figure their public wasn't?

Kiss scenes were permissible, but only just, as sex stimulus for Code-shackled audiences. Close-up smooching timed on a stopwatch was socially accepted pornography for folks denied, or ashamed to go out in pursuit of, the real thing. The women that MGM presented in trade ads weren't fantasy. Millions lined up to see Lana crushed in Gable's arms. No telling how many *Honky Tonk* babies were conceived in 1941, and more would go into pipelines thanks to *Somewhere I'll Find You*. Sex figures like Gable and Turner generated manpower production for future wars and did so with probable greater efficiency than those working swing shifts at ball-bearing plants. They were, for good or ill, a then-patron's most accessible models for lovemaking and courtship ritual.

When Gable and his women collided, Metro cameras rolled up to face profiles so close the audience risked getting sprayed, and said formatting rule was inflexible—even director John Ford was obliged to assume the position in 1953's *Mogambo*. Imagine three-ways in theatres, viewer plus screen lovers, with the voyeur's object(s) blown 30 feet high. Such erotica could be but fully absorbed

Opposite page: MGM knows that sex sells, so they go all out to infer fantastic lovemaking in *Somewhere I'll Find You*. Millions of women dutifully queue up to see Clark Gable crush Lana Turner in passionate embraces.

"And there's a hundred million others like me"

"OH, MR. GABLE"

You've got that gleam in your eye again!

GABLE · TURNER

Somewhere I'll find You

HELD OVER 2nd BIG WEEK! LOEW'S

SIZZLING TEST ENGAGEMENTS TELL THE TRADE!

*The First BIG New Season Hit is from Metro-*GOLDMINE-*Mayer*

CLARK GABLE · LANA TURNER in "SOMEWHERE I'LL FIND YOU" with Robert Sterling · Patricia Dane · Reginald Owen · Lee Patrick · Charles Dingle · Screen Play by Marguerite Roberts · Adaptation by Walter Reisch · Based upon a Cosmopolitan Magazine Story by Charles Hoffman · Directed by WESLEY RUGGLES · Produced by PANDRO S. BERMAN · A Metro-Goldwyn-Mayer Picture

SEPTEMBER BOND AND STAMP SALE · The Motion Picture Industry's SECOND FRONT!

in dark auditoriums with overpowering images that concealed ragged breathing and beads of sweat forming on watchers drawn into shared embrace with idols they could nearly touch. And don't ignore the yawning chasm between generations-removed DVDs and the glistening nitrate 35mm prints these folks reveled in. Based on the way Gable and Turner go at it in *Somewhere I'll Find You*, I wonder how couples delayed their own consummations till at least getting out to parked cars.

At a halfway point where story gears shift abruptly right after Pearl Harbor, Lana Turner and Gable decamp to a soundstage labeled Indo-China, represented by Tarzan foliage and dry ice fog. Movies are most magical when they're confined to facilities close at hand where artisans improvise with what they've got. Metro often used layers of process screening to make you think 3-D's come early to features.

Gable, clad in suit and tie but loosened slightly, searches an easily penetrable jungle only briefly before greeting Lana Turner's picturesque arrival in what looks like a Chinese touring gon-dola. It's just outrageously silly enough to be completely endearing, the sort of experience you might find if sites at Disney World permitted romps backstage. People nowadays imagine that 1942 onlookers were childish enough to take all this for the truth of foreign climes and conditions. I don't think for a minute they did.

Somewhere I'll Find You makes winning this war look so easy that you'd wonder why we weren't all back home before the picture could be released. There's a climactic battle sequence almost balletic in its absurdity. Japanese invaders appear like insects at a distance toward which flit bombs are tossed with stunning accuracy. They are blown up and/or buried alive by MGM juveniles hopeful of a wartime contract and paying off for Pearl; starting-out Van Johnson is among them, as is Keenan Wynn.

Did boys turning 18 or just out of high school watch this and make for recruiting stations? I wonder how much enlistment could be traced to 1942's first brace of war-themed shows girding our loins for a fight. No one took polls measuring the true influence of movies during those years. How could they? But I'd venture this one had affects we'd not imagine for watching it so casually and from such distance of time.

The real drama connected with *SIFY*, and the one for which it's remembered, if at all, is the industry's, and Gable's, loss of Carole Lombard

Relentless selling of Clark and Lana as erotica works like a charm for Metro-*Goldmine*-Mayer.

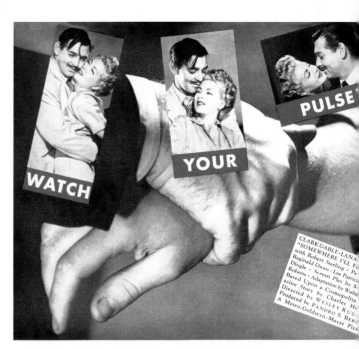

MR. GABLE AND MISS TURNE ARE KISSING AGAIN!

And pulses are popping in ⟶
And lovers are sighing in ⟶
And turnstiles are turning in ⟶
And money is flowing in ⟶
So watch those test runs in ⟶

Baltimore, Norfolk, Richmond, Wilmington, Harrisburg, Reading, Dayton, Atlanta, New Orleans
and other hot spots

"SOMEWHERE I'LL FIND YOU
is a New Season Hit from
Metro-GOLDMINE-Mayer!

going in. There's been lots written about how he finished the picture in mourning. In fact, it was almost all shot after her death—although production began on January 15, it wouldn't wrap until April 22. By then, Gable had made up his mind to enlist (*Send me where the going's roughest*, he said), so maybe by chance but likelier intent, his concluding scene in *SIFY* plays like a valedictory not unlike Joel McCrea's close in 1940's *Foreign Correspondent*. Gable's monologue, dictated to furiously typing Lana Turner, is, in effect, telling us he'll be gone for the next few years but to keep lamps burning and maintain the fight. It's one of the actor's all-time blockbusting speeches.

No wonder they missed him so much afterward. *Somewhere I'll Find You* stayed in circulation longer than most off MGM's fast assembly line. Our Liberty Theatre brought it back after year one of Gable deprivation. Audience hunger was such as to allow even Fox to cash its own ration ticket by reissuing *Call of the Wild* to $730,000 in fresh domestic rentals for eventual profits of $502,000. *Somewhere I'll Find You*, released September 1942, had a negative cost of $1,060,000, scored $2.8 million in domestic rentals, with $1.1 foreign, and ended with profits of $1.7 million.

Leading men gone to fight left a civilian force short of heroes to win the war on screens, but knowing that stars were part of the actual struggle conferred respect and appreciation upon Hollywood for its patriotic works. The industry never enjoyed so positive an image as generated by this struggle, which movies would share with audiences. Stateside theatres of war supplied therapy over a four-year, ongoing exchange of reassurance and can-do that helped assure victory.

Above: Sweat-covered and lusty—that's the way MGM preferred to present Clark Gable and Lana Turner in *Somewhere I'll Find You*. Below: The Loew's Regent in Harrisburg, Pennsylvania, boasts a striking front to sell Gable and Turner.

A candid moment with Gloria Swanson, William Holden, and the "waxworks."

CHAPTER 14

PARAMOUNT'S ROAD TO SUNSET BOULEVARD

For Paramount, *Sunset Boulevard* was an idea whose time had come, but no one expected such a poisoned pen house of horrors a mere three years after the studio's bouncy 1947 *The Perils of Pauline*, its nostalgic optimism personifying a town proud for having taken care of its own. Who was Billy Wilder to dredge up ugliness that could bring only embarrassment, if not discredit, to an industry reeling from the court-ordered disposal of affiliated theatres and an oncoming locomotive of television? Louis Mayer summed up thus: "How dare this young man, Wilder, bite the hand that feeds him?"

If indeed the director replied as he'd later claim, to wit: "I am Mr. Wilder, and go fuck yourself," then I'd not argue Mayer's justification in attacking him. I don't believe, however, that Wilder said any such thing. Long-dead ogres like L.B. made easy marks for self-serving anecdoters bragging of how they stuck it to hidebound Hollywood way back when—this we got often from those who lived long enough to get the last word.

Wilder's lucky that his movie turned out as well as it did. Otherwise, he may have been unceremoniously run out of the business. Taking a long chance can end in triumph when one delivers as with *Sunset Boulevard*. Fifteen years later, *Kiss Me, Stupid* would finally trip and fell the director on his own vaunted outrageousness. Luckily for us, Wilder had sufficient youth and nerve in 1949 to bring off a project that all but heaped manure in his own backyard.

Paramount's Henry Ginsberg hosted a reception for eastern and studio executives in March 1949. Notable here were special guests representing old Hollywood, among them Mack Sennett, Adolph Zukor, and Cecil B. DeMille. Ginsberg announced Para's coming slate of releases, among them a screen bio of Mack Sennett. Comedy's Golden Era promised laughter for a new generation. Contemporary stars Betty Hutton and John Lund, reunited after the success of *The Perils of Pauline*, were set to play Mabel Normand and Sennett. It would be a nostalgic tribute to that quaint but still vital period, recalled with affection by several generations of moviegoers.

Old-timers and the flickers they'd made had long been objects of gentle mockery. All in fun were shows like *Hollywood Cavalcade* and *Glamour Boy*, wherein industry castoffs gave fleeting encores for fans who remembered. Serious attention was paid less often to those discarded. Blanche Sweet played a silent star down on her luck in Warner's 1930 *Show Girl in Hollywood*, first among pictures to recognize casualties inflicted by the microphone.

Director Robert Florey appreciated career ruin left in the talkies' wake. His 1936 *Hollywood Boulevard*, also from Paramount, portrayed in realist terms the desperation felt by those who'd been major names but a few years before. Warners would throw a twentieth anniversary screening of *Don Juan* in 1946 for cast and crew survivors, the object being less to pay tribute to their heyday than to celebrate two decades of sound that had displaced them. Betty Hutton's Pearl White in *The Perils of Pauline* had little to do with an actress by then comfortably deceased, and little ailed William Powell's curmudgeon matinee idol in 1949's *Dancing in the Dark* beyond the need of a few weeks' work in talkies.

Late '40s revival of silent films was rare outside museum screenings. There were tentative bids to relive past times while *Sunset Boulevard* was being prepared for release. Then, as now, people's interest in antique movies was limited to ones they could laugh at. Fox West Coast ad manager Seymour Peiser dug up the original Keystone Kops as ballyhoo for his November 1949 booking of *Down Memory Lane*, a Mack Sennett compilation with as many sound as silent highlights. Another Sennett staple, *Tillie's Punctured Romance*, occasioned the time-

Right out of the gate, trade ads signal something unique and different about *Sunset Boulevard*. But is it *too* different to catch on with audiences?

honored Chaplin-look-alike gag popular since grandma's day. Chaplin himself would reissue *City Lights* just ahead of *Sunset Boulevard*'s 1950 opening. Warner Bros. compiled newsreel and entertainment footage for a backward look called *50 Years Before Your Eyes*, which opened in five New York City newsreel theatres during July 1950. Producer Robert Youngson treated modern viewers to glimpses of Valentino and Ben Turpin, among many others featured in the historic hodgepodge.

It's hard to believe an era just 20 years gone could be so irretrievably lost. Silents were stone-age relics best left on scrap heaps, or worse, bonfires to which studios consigned non-talking libraries. Imagine such a yawning chasm between the screen life of today and a mere 20 years ago. Have times changed so drastically since then? I'll venture that silent films were more suppressed by the industry than forgotten by those who'd attended them. They were an affront to progress supposedly made between 1927 and 1949. Such passage of years made Wilder's gothic treatment credible to audiences who viewed pre-talking stars as things ghostly and suggestive of decay.

I can only imagine how Mary Pickford felt when Paramount's team went to read her the script. Wilder and co-writer Charles Brackett were casting about for an authentic silent name to play Norma, but Pickford's horrified reaction forced a retreat. How could she, or anyone of her generation, have responded otherwise in the face of such a lacerating depiction? Down-the-line choice Gloria Swanson had better perspective of changed times, having stayed busy at performing since a silent peak. Maybe she was less protective, too, of an image long since discarded as the Swanson career took newer direction. Norma Desmond was not a threat to this actress.

Gloria Swanson did her heaviest lifting as Paramount's roving goodwill ambassador between October 1949 and August 1950. She was on studio payrolls for, all told, more than a year. Upon completion of principal photography on *Sunset Boulevard*, GS hit the road for purpose of increasing the public's regard for an industry still vulnerable to scandal and condemnation. The Ingrid Bergman stink was hot news and so was a Senate probe into Un-American activities. Swanson combated the ramifications of both in hundreds of radio and television appearances nationwide. Emphasizing Hollywood's good works, she lectured before civic organizations, women's clubs, and charitable groups.

The thousand a week that Swanson earned obliged her to thump for *The Heiress* as well. Paramount knew it could build anticipation for William Wyler's prestige drama with assist from a well-known and articulate spokesperson. This wouldn't be the last time a silent luminary was called upon for lecture touring. Fox sent Francis X. Bushman out in support of *David and Bathsheba* two years later. Silent stars were assured of recognition among

Above right: Mack Sennett's Keystone Kops hit the road for *Down Memory Lane*. Center: An ersatz Chaplin stumps for *Tillie*. Bottom: Covering 50 years in 73 minutes seems like a bargain in New York City.

community leaders of an older generation less likely to recognize contemporary names. Gloria Swanson as keynote speaker at your Kiwanis Club carried more cache among local opinion makers than a Joan Caulfield would have.

Swanson's subsequent Academy Award nomination was well-deserved recognition for a great performance, but I wonder if she wasn't actually better off before her own image became so confused with that of Norma Desmond.

Sunset Boulevard harked to a past in movies as it looked to a future in exploitation. This would be among first features to incorporate TV spots into its advertising campaign. National Screen Service was the distributor of trailer sets made up of two 20-second spots and a pair at one minute each. The package could be rented from NSS for $35.

Television was finally recognized in 1950 as a necessary adjunct to publicity campaigns, despite studio abhorrence of the home screen. Talk and panel programs were fertile ground for

Above: A proud assemblage attends a Paramount reception in March 1949. From left to right—William Farnum, Mack Sennett, Adolph Zukor, Gloria Swanson, Cecil B. DeMille, and Hedy Lamarr. Below: Swanson cuts a cake in recognition of the 20,000 miles logged on behalf of *Sunset Boulevard*, the second wave on her cross-country schedule. Co-star William Holden and Paramount advertising-publicity director Norman Siegel flank her.

free advertising. Much of the word Gloria Swanson got out on behalf of *Sunset Boulevard* came as a result of her appearances on local chat shows across the country.

Previewing, reshooting, and extensive post-production delayed *Sunset Boulevard* for almost a year, but this provided Paramount with an opportunity to raise press and critical awareness of the exceptional product it had. This being a Hollywood story, industry screenings were numerous and a hot ticket among movie personnel eager to see their walk of life dramatized on screen. Wilder wanted authenticity and so used actual names and places. Fictional "Monarch" and "Miracle" studio references were jettisoned in favor of the real thing.

Big names agreed to lend flattering quotes for use in *Sunset Boulevard* ads. Celebrity endorsement is often suspect. When stars recommend a movie, some benefit generally accrues to them for having done so. Warner players would often rave in print over Warner pictures, one hand washing the other. Endorsement ads for *Sunset Boulevard* do reveal a few stars that were in bed with Paramount at the time, including Barbara Stanwyck, Joan Fontaine, and Loretta Young. Were they merely greasing wheels, or did they really like *Sunset Boulevard*? Joan Crawford often endorsed rival studios' product because she was generous that way. But Humphrey Bogart was nobody's shill when it came to recommending movies; this is the only time I recall seeing his name attached to an ad blurb. The columnists quoted were in the business of promoting films, so no surprises there, although I wonder if Hedda Hopper's "Great!" refers to *Sunset Boulevard* or her performance in it— probably both, and she's right.

Here was a show that got attention, particularly in the town it dissected so brilliantly. I've no doubt that everyone in the industry wanted to see *Sunset Boulevard*, and most would likely be impressed, if not made a little uneasy by it.

Norma's fate was/is one that might be visited upon any celebrity. Many a present-day washout plies his/her trade on weekends at far-flung autograph shows. The only difference is most of them don't have crumbling Hollywood mansions to go home to. Could even Norma have been reduced to peddling her signature for $15 in a hotel ballroom as modern counterparts do today?

I suspect that industry reaction to *Sunset Boulevard* cut along generational divides. Those who'd arrived and flourished with talkies no doubt saw it as accurate with regards the silent era, while survivors of that vanished period felt cruelly exploited and put upon. Mary Pickford was said to have left her screening prior to lights coming up. I'd venture that much of Louis Mayer's wrath came of having spent his own early career in silents, being a decade and a half older than Gloria Swanson. Could Mayer have sensed the Hollywood scrap heap laying in wait for him? Perhaps symbolic, if

Gloria Swanson lends her brand name to meet-and-greets on behalf of her comeback picture.

HOLLYWOOD RAVES

...about a most unusual picture !!!

"After seeing 'Sunset Boulevard,' as I have, I am sure anyone will agree that it is one of the great pictures of 1950 or any other year. Gloria Swanson's performance is brilliant and exciting."
—HUMPHREY BOGART

"Seeing 'Sunset Boulevard' is a thrilling experience which I will never forget."
—JOAN CRAWFORD

"The praise which all of Hollywood has heaped on Gloria Swanson, Billy Wilder and Charles Brackett for 'Sunset Boulevard' is richly deserved. This picture is a distinguished and engrossing product of film-making. I am sure it will be highly successful."
—JOAN FONTAINE

"Gloria Swanson and William Holden in 'Sunset Boulevard' join our all-time 'greats' of motion picture history."
—BARBARA STANWYCK

"I think it's the most wonderful picture I've ever seen. Combining the writing and direction of two of the most original men in Hollywood, 'Sunset Boulevard' is bound to be a huge success."
—GENE TIERNEY

SUNSET BOULEVARD

A HOLLYWOOD STORY!

A Paramount Picture

starring

WILLIAM HOLDEN
as Young Joe Gillis

GLORIA SWANSON
as Norma Desmond

ERICH von STROHEIM
as Max von Mayerling

with NANCY OLSON · FRED CLARK · LLOYD GOUGH · JACK WEBB
and Cecil B. DeMille · Hedda Hopper · Buster Keaton
Anna Q. Nilsson · H. B. Warner · Franklyn Farnum

Produced by Charles Brackett · Directed by BILLY WILDER
Written by Charles Brackett, Billy Wilder and D. M. Marshman, Jr

Left: Hollywood stars rave about *Sunset Boulevard*, and seem to mean it. Below: In the twenty-first century, a woman like Norma Desmond will take on the label of "cougar," but did 1950 audiences have difficulty with the sophistication, and kink, of the Desmond-Gillis relationship? Here Swanson and Holden send up their characters for the benefit of the still photographer.

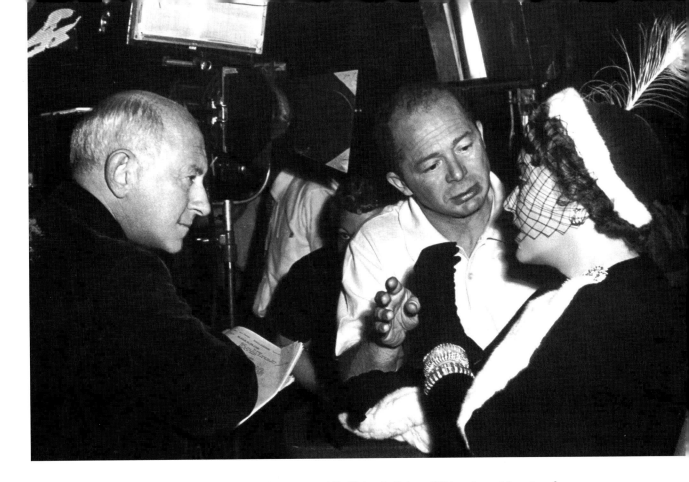

Above: DeMille, Wilder, and Swanson on CB's *Samson and Delilah* set. Below: Wilder places his actors for one of the climactic scenes in his most unusual picture.

coincidental, was the fact that *Sunset Boulevard* would be among the last major studio releases shot on nitrate negative.

Sunset Boulevard did find an audience, morbidly curious perhaps, but sufficiently large to return domestic rentals of $2.35 million against a negative cost of $1.76 million.

Paramount's bigger fish that year was gigantic hit *Samson and Delilah*. The pictures merge in *Sunset Boulevard* when Desmond visits DeMille on the *Samson* set. It's amusing to hear DeMille shun the notion of filming "that awful script" (Norma and Joe's *Salome*), yet here he is in 1949 shooting what amounts to a modern *Salome*. So entrenched was CB in silent technique and staging for his own productions that differences between *Samson* and the would-be *Salome* are negligible at best. No director was as wedded to traditional method, although DeMille remained up to the minute in terms of showman instinct. I've no doubt he could have turned the Desmond-Gillis *Salome* into another *Samson*-sized smash, given the inclination.

The "waxworks" label had to sting. Cinematographer John Seitz had been there when Rudolph Valentino did *The Four Horsemen of the Apocalypse* in 1921. He was 57 when *Sunset Boulevard* was made, having been in the business since 1916. Would this man have looked in the mirror and seen waxworks? Wilder's caustic vision consigned many a veteran, some not so much older than BW himself, to perhaps premature oblivion. "Dim figures you may still remember from the silent days," says William Holden's narration. For Buster Keaton, it was merely another (single) day's job, but this was not a man otherwise disposed to sit in a rocking chair, and hadn't H.B. Warner done fine work as Mr. Gower the druggist just a few years before in *It's a Wonderful Life*?

Above: Urbanites queue up in Manhattan. Below: Radio City affords *Sunset Boulevard* a fast start and records, albeit non-holiday records.

These Are
The Facts About

Sunset Boulevard

IN NEW YORK: 4th week of records. Radio City Music Hall opening week set all-time non-holiday high—and 2nd week topped that!

OUT OF TOWN: Held over in 12 out of its first 15 sensational test engagements—which included big and small situations!

TERRIFIC IN ALL OPENINGS": Says *Variety's* National Box-office Survey, reporting it industry's number 1 money-maker today!

"SUNSET BOULEVARD"
starring William Holden, Gloria
Swanson, Erich von Stroheim,
with Nancy Olson, Fred Clark,
Lloyd Gough, Jack Webb · and
Cecil B. DeMille, Hedda Hopper,
Buster Keaton, Anna Q. Nilsson,
H. B. Warner, Franklyn Farnum
Produced by Charles Brackett
Directed by Billy Wilder · Written
by Charles Brackett, Billy Wilder
and D. M. Marshman, Jr.

PARAMOUNT HAS THE PRODUCT PAYING OFF BIGGEST TODAY:
"Sunset Boulevard," Bob Hope's "Fancy Pants"(Technicolor), Hal Wallis' "The Furies," Hal Wallis' "My Friend Irma Goes West"—and soon "Union Station"

The complex and adult plot of *Sunset Boulevard* has aging Desmond (Swanson) after cynical, younger Gillis (Holden), while butler Max (Erich von Stroheim), Norma's former director, watches and protects.

A look at call sheets for Frank Capra, John Ford, and, yes, Cecil B. DeMille pictures, will reveal large numbers of so-called waxworks in both bit and speaking roles. These directors went way back in American film and formed numerous professional attachments along the way. Billy Wilder was a comparatively recent arrival, and had not the sentiment they felt for longtime contributors to the industry. These colleagues might have agreed with Mayer that Wilder was indeed biting the hand that fed him.

Norma Desmond's film archive appears to be better stocked than that of any silent personality I'm aware of. She and Joe Gillis watch movies three times a week according to Holden's narration, and all of them Desmond vehicles. This is one occasion where *Sunset Boulevard* departs well from reality, as few stars owned copies of their work, let alone complete libraries in 35mm.

Indeed, Gloria Swanson would lament the extinction of most of her films. The memoir she published in 1980 mentioned a then-lost pairing with Rudolph Valentino. Who'd have guessed then that *Beyond the Rocks* survived, let alone among the holdings of an eccentric loner collector in the Netherlands? Imagine excitement for UCLA archivists going through Norma Desmond's private stash! Those with home libraries generally owned the negative—thus DeMille, Mary Pickford, Harold Lloyd; each maintained storage for practical as well as sentimental purposes. Few working actors took prints home. Colleen Moore had a number of First National features in which she'd maintained some ownership. These were donated to The Museum of Modern Art in the '50s, but subsequently lost when mistakenly shipped to Warners. All those years Moore safeguarded her prints, and now they're gone. Clara Bow's family has but two of her films, that's all, and both are talkies.

These people spent old age with no more idea than we had of how to see their old pictures. Most who lived in Los Angeles drove down to John Hampton's Silent Movie Theatre to get a glimpse of themselves. Norma Desmond might have made fewer suicide attempts had she known how lucky she was to screen 35mm nitrate reels of *Queen Kelly* in her living room, and you'd think ongoing access to such viewing treasures would make Joe Gillis' gigolo status a lighter burden to bear as well, despite his professed indifference to the silent classics. The two of them watching *Queen Kelly* plays like an excursion to some Indian burial ground, yet there was a comparatively short time between that unfinished feature and *Sunset Boulevard*.

Watching *Sunset Boulevard* puts one to speculating upon real Norma Desmonds among retired screen stars in 1949. Did Wilder base his story on fact, legend, or mere imaginings he'd had? Surely there was gossip about crazy ex-movie queens alone in crumbling mansions, but who and how many? *Sunset Boulevard*'s gothic treatment seems right. Wilder had to have encountered fallen stars in their natural habitat to come up with something so authentic as this. I don't recall any interview where the writer-director actually revealed his inspiration for the character. Certainly there were actresses whose final days evoked Norma Desmond. Mae Murray was said to have engaged in ab-Norma behavior. Kenneth Anger published ghoulish stills of Nita Naldi, Alma Rubens, and others. He'd even get around to taking down Gloria Swanson in Volume Two of *Hollywood Babylon*. Some guys in a Hollywood bookstore told me once that Madge Bellamy used to come in doing a Baby Jane number, and Mary Miles Minter was said to have been cracked wide open for years.

Iconic poster art: Obsessed Norma and doomed lovers Joe and Betty—with Joe's fate revealed.

150

Movies treated former membership pretty shabbily after *Sunset Boulevard*. Either they were good for laughs, as in fictionalizations like *Singin' in the Rain* and *Dreamboat*, or bio'ed in slow-dripping acid. The waxworks melted as Hollywood lovingly dramatized their "struggles." Ones with money remained above it. Harold Lloyd could sit out the ugliness at Greenacres, but Buster Keaton needed a house and let Paramount exploit him with *The Buster Keaton Story* to get it. Artists too obscure to see their lives dissected on film were thrown to wolves via Ralph Edwards and *This Is Your Life*. Check out Frances Farmer's episode to appreciate just how lucky Norma Desmond was. There were no oil wells pumping and pumping for folks this desperate.

Increased interest in Golden Era film did bring salvation of sorts to Norma colleagues that survived. With the '60s

Will America's heartland warm to Wilder's vision of Hollywood, including bug-eyed, pistol-toting Norma Desmond?

and a boom for nostalgia, plus emerging academic focus, old-timers evolved into objects to revere. Last gasps for Wilder's mode of disrespect would include 1962's *What Ever Happened to Baby Jane*, and lesser hiccups that gave way to proper respect for those who pioneered an industry.

Screenings would be arranged to which veterans would appear as honored guests. Documentary filmmakers like Kevin Brownlow sought out Colleen Moore, Eleanor Boardman, and others who'd spent decades since stardom ignored. Yes, there were the casualties, as dissected by Hollywood Babylonians and poisonous bios, but more of a silent era's membership proved lucid and entertaining as to recount of fabled lives. Norma Desmond was fittingly seen as more caricatured fruit of Wilder's imagination than What Ever Happened to...reality.

It's just a shame these pioneers weren't consulted much sooner, when more of them were alive, to document firsthand their experiences. Brownlow, for instance, got his start interviewing silent survivors in the early '60s. Writer/Teacher/Historian William K. Everson had made contacts sooner, but was nearly alone for taking seriously the contributions of a vanishing group. Much of what we know about the silent era is the result of Brownlow, Everson, and trailblazing others bringing home proof that Norma Desmond was the exception, rather than a dispiriting rule. They would confirm *Sunset Boulevard* as far more fiction than fact and do real service toward serious appreciation of vintage film.

Fresh off his successful *Champion*, Kirk Douglas conveys toughness in the Cagney tradition

CHAPTER 15

WILDER'S ACE GOES IN THE HOLE

Ace in the Hole's re-emergence on video, satellite, and streaming was a cinematic equivalent of raising R.M.S. *Titanic*, a treasure for years that had been less lost than unwanted. Few major studio features underwent a title change *after* release, Paramount out with *Ace in the Hole* in June 1951, only to rename it *The Big Carnival* two months later. For this company's sales division, Billy Wilder's poison pill would not go down smooth.

Admittedly a bummer movie that general audiences have never been crazy about, *Ace in the Hole*'s impact has been blunted further by imitators since. Still and all, it remains a cultist's pet, an incendiary device flung by writer/director Wilder at studio convention, loved all the more by adherents for just that.

Early biographer Maurice Zolotow got balls rolling with 1977's *Billy Wilder in Hollywood*: "*Ace in the Hole* was castigated by the critics and shunned by the public. Wilder was called a cynical man. The film was denounced as an untruthful attack on the integrity of American newspapers and on the new medium of television."

Further Wilder analysts would call *Ace in the Hole* a box-office disaster, a film ahead of its time that told a 1950s public things about themselves they did not want to hear. Had Wilder's acerbic depiction of American culture and institutions cost him, and Paramount, a shot at break-even on their latest project?

Indeed, the director was eventually persuaded. "They never gave it a chance," Billy Wilder said.

I only hope Billy wasn't referring to Paramount, because evidence indicates they gave it every chance, with a campaign as aggressive as any mounted during 1951. As to its box-office disaster, *Ace in the Hole* no doubt took a loss, but no more so than a lot of other features the company was distributing that year. With $1.2 million in domestic rentals, it equaled *The Last Outpost* and *Submarine Command*, while outperforming Hal Wallis' production of *Peking Express* ($936,000) and a comedy sequel thought to be promising, *Dear Brat* ($890,000).

The thing that was killing Paramount and other majors was television. By mid-1951, millions more homes had a set than even a year before, and Hollywood movies were becoming more ubiquitous there. Republic had announced imminent sale of its backlog, and independent features were dumped on airwaves with each passing week. You had to have something really special to entice people away from all that free entertainment.

A Statement About "Ace In The Hole"

By Its Star,
KIRK
DOUGLAS

I've just returned from a trip around the country, where I attended a series of press screenings of my latest picture, "ACE IN THE HOLE."

Never in my entire career, including "CHAMPION," has a picture stirred up the heated controversial discussions that greeted this film.

Many people said it's stark and pitiless.

Even more said that "ACE IN THE HOLE" is vivid . . . exciting . . . realistic. That it portrays true-to-life *people* as they really react to a desperate situation.

You know there *are* women as greedy, as heartless, as unfaithful as Lorraine, played by Jan Sterling.

And there *are* men like Chuck Tatum, the ruthless man that I play who lets neither men, women nor morals stand in his way.

You may hate me as Chuck Tatum . . . or cheer me—but I don't think you'll be indifferent . . . and as long as it stirs you, excites you . . . as an actor I'll be satisfied.

I think American audiences are adult enough to appreciate the impact of this frank, hard-hitting picture, especially as brought to the screen by Billy Wilder, whose equally powerful pictures, "The Lost Weekend," and "Sunset Boulevard" were universally acclaimed.

Being a part of this picture has been an experience I'll never forget. I hope that seeing this picture will be an experience you'll never forget!

KIRK DOUGLAS in "ACE IN THE HOLE" with JAN STERLING · Bob Arthur · Porter Hall · Produced and Directed by BILLY WILDER · Written by Billy Wilder, Lesser Samuels and Walter Newman · A Paramount Picture

Above left: Kirk Douglas assumes a defensive posture amidst the controversy. Above right: From their chuck-wagon vantage point, Douglas and Jan Sterling sign autographs for the Albuquerque swarm.

Paramount kept a man in the field by the name of Rufus Blair. He'd been with newspapers and was a crack merchandiser. You might classify him as a Chuck Tatum with ethics. Rufus spent April and May 1951 canvassing 34 cities on behalf of *Ace in the Hole*. He had an open door with publishers, having worked with a number of them, and his mission was to target media folk—editors, reviewers, radio personalities, whatever.

Armed with a print of the feature, Blair knew *Ace* would click with newshound colleagues. Trade critics were already flipping over Wilder's trenchant drama, and Paramount brandished raves among the trades at least two months prior to release. They played it up as a tough show in the tradition of *The Public Enemy* and Kirk Douglas' previous *Champion*. News dailies swarmed over it.

Ace in the Hole's journalist was rugged and ruthless after fashions of Cagney, Bogart, and Ladd. He grabbed a story by the throat and took no guff from bosses and women-folk. Rufus Blair knew reporters would identify, at least on some levels, with Chuck Tatum, and sure enough they did. The character's ruthlessness shocked many onlookers, sure, but Tatum's tenacity flattered on-the-ground scribes having to scratch livelihoods much as he did. Was Chuck really so different from the demon reporters that Lee Tracy and others of pre-Code lineage had enacted?

Further promotion in advance of *Ace*'s open found Jan Sterling getting a New York build-up on behalf of the pic. Paramount tied in with Royal desserts for recorded ads with Sterling, all of which concluded with a pitch for *Ace*, while millions of gelatin boxes went out with her image emblazoned thereon.

154

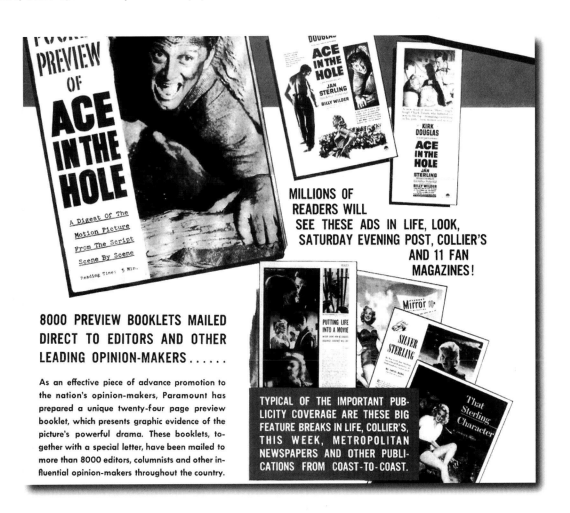

Above and below: Paramount launches "the most concentrated effort since *Samson and Delilah*" in support of *Ace in the Hole*, a picture sure to win the hearts of journalists coast to coast. Jan Sterling cheesecake graces *Life*, *Collier's*, and metropolitan newspapers.

Here's the Ace of Paramount's

MORE BETTER BIGGER PICTURES

KIRK DOUGLAS

"Socks across his role in fashion of 'Champion'"
(Daily Variety)

in

ACE IN THE HOLE

with

JAN STERLING

reaching stardom "in fine performance." — Variety

WORD IS SPREADING WITH WORDS LIKE

BOXOFFICE	SOCKING	IMPORTANT
POTENT	SHOCKING	EXCELLENT
ACE	FORCEFUL	VIVID
RUGGED	EMOTIONAL	STRONG
REALISTIC	TERRIFYING	BEST
— Exhibitor	— M. P. Daily	— Film Daily

WOMAN'S SLANT
"Gals will adore Douglas. He makes Cagney and Bogart look like sissies." —*Columnist Dorothy Kilgallen*

BOXOFFICE SLANT
"Will do strong business." —*Variety*

BOB ARTHUR · PORTER HALL
Produced and Directed by
BILLY WILDER
WRITTEN BY BILLY WILDER, LESSER SAMUELS
AND WALTER NEWMAN

And Here's the Ace Campaign of Paramount's Famed Pre-Selling

38-city advance tour by special representative in the most concentrated effort since "Samson and Delilah."

Pocket Preview booklet (stills and script excerpts) mailed to 7,500 public-opinion molders.

National ads in Life, Look, Collier's and Saturday Evening Post, plus complete fan schedule.

Kirk Douglas cross-country tour to meet the press.

Jan Sterling visit to New York for unprecedented magazine, press and radio build-up.

"Location" World Premiere in Albuquerque (where picture was filmed.)

Five months of advance screenings to set summer-long publicity breaks on coast to coast scale.

Special TV trailers.

Unusual exploitation material, now in hands of Paramount's field representatives.

—and many other ticket-selling aids set up for every type of situation.

POCKET PREVIEW OF
ACE IN THE HOLE

A Digest Of The Motion Picture From The Script Scene By Scene

Reading Time: 5 Min.

8000 PREVIEW BOOKLETS MAILED DIRECT TO EDITORS AND OTHER LEADING OPINION-MAKERS......

As an effective piece of advance promotion to the nation's opinion-makers, Paramount has prepared a unique twenty-four page preview booklet, which presents graphic evidence of the picture's powerful drama. These booklets, together with a special letter, have been mailed to more than 8000 editors, columnists and other influential opinion-makers throughout the country.

MILLIONS OF READERS WILL SEE THESE ADS IN LIFE, LOOK, SATURDAY EVENING POST, COLLIER'S AND 11 FAN MAGAZINES!

TYPICAL OF THE IMPORTANT PUBLICITY COVERAGE ARE THESE BIG FEATURE BREAKS IN LIFE, COLLIER'S, THIS WEEK, METROPOLITAN NEWSPAPERS AND OTHER PUBLICATIONS FROM COAST-TO-COAST.

KIRK DOUGLAS in ACE IN THE HOLE

with JAN STERLING

A *Paramount* PICTURE

The Hallicrafters Corporation, then one of the big three radio/television manufacturers, continued its mutual sales push with Paramount that had begun with *The Mating Season* earlier that year. Field men for both companies linked up with local dealers, and Hallicrafters' equipment was featured onscreen during *Ace in the Hole*. Billy Wilder was not above a little product placement.

The Albuquerque location premiere followed in mid-June with a simultaneous opening in three theatres, attended by Kirk Douglas and Jan Sterling, who passed out autographs from their vantage point aboard a chuck wagon. New York's opening at the Globe Theatre on June 29 would be a benefit of the Newsdealer Association's welfare fund, the 1,475-seat Globe having been chosen for its long-run potential. "Paramount execs compare *Ace* to its *Lost Weekend* in type and not suitable for linking with a stage show," said *Variety*, which also noted the company's hope for at least a six-week Broadway stay for *Ace in the Hole*. Billy Wilder was in town as well to do TV appearances and con-fabs with home office ad-press-publicity staff.

New York's business was "socko," said trades, this mirrored on the West Coast by "hefty" figures out of L.A.'s Four Star Theatre, a 900-seat house thought best for this unusual attraction. Urban runs, in fact, showed overall promise of a hit, but diminishing grosses in wider release by mid-August made it clear that Paramount had a problem.

Executives figured that a picture with Kirk Douglas in the lead and reviews as positive as *Ace in the Hole* had garnered should not be playing to tepid houses. Was the title to blame?

Eleventh-hour title changes were not uncommon prior to releasing a feature. Such an ac-

Above: The theatre in Albuquerque decked out for *Ace*'s world premiere. Below: Rufus Blair reviews publicity material with an exhibitor contact.

KIRK **DOUGLAS** in
THE BIG CARNIVAL

with **JAN STERLING**

A PARAMOUNT PICTURE

Opposite page and above: These two seven-foot banners say it all. The title *Ace in the Hole*, thought to be causing audiences to imagine a gambling story, is replaced with *The Big Carnival*. Now, will patronage regard it a story about the carny circuit? Below: Jay Emanuel's trade-ad letter to Paramount's Al Schwalberg. The "I told you so" will be short-lived.

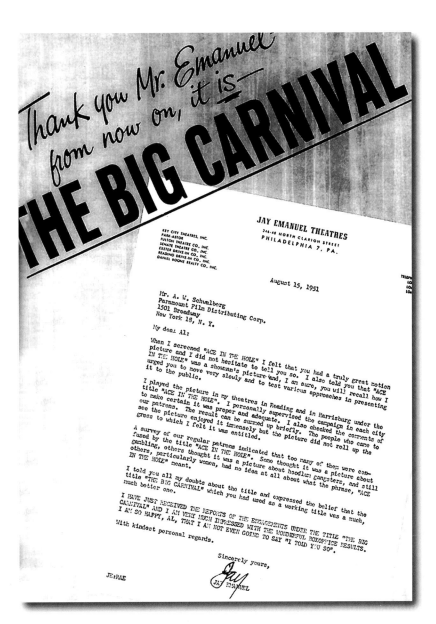

tion *post*-release was almost unheard of. An embarrassment for marketing, publicity, and distribution, it suggested a botched campaign.

"Isn't there somebody in the studio organization who can yell murder when an un-showmanship title comes through the ordinary routine of production?" asked the *Motion Picture Herald* after two Metro 1951 offerings sputtered on release. "Wouldn't it be possible to learn these facts a little earlier?"

Two Weeks with Love and *Inside Straight* represented good product badly sold. The *Herald* felt both could have benefited from exhibitor input on the front end. "*Inside Straight* fell flat on its title during Easter week on Broadway," said the trade, "because people assumed it dealt with card playing," whereas this was actually a period show about the California gold rush. *Ace in the Hole* was also adjudged misleading. Was it too about gambling? If so, women weren't interested. Many patrons had no idea as to meaning of the phrase. Would they wait until after paying admission to find out? Circuit heads thought not, and these were men charged with getting pedestrians off streets and into theatres.

Showman (as well as editor-publisher of *Motion Picture Exhibitor*) Jay Emanuel spoke to the controversy in a letter reproduced in trade ads. Latter-day cultists would consign Emanuel to the role of philistine, but I suspect he knew exactly what he was doing: "I personally supervised the campaign in each city to make certain it was proper and adequate. I also checked the comments of our patrons. The results can be summed up briefly. The people who came to see [*Ace in the Hole*] enjoyed it immensely, but the picture did not roll up the gross to which I felt it was entitled."

This sort of grassroots movement on the part of exhibitors resulted in a newly rechristened *The Big Carnival*. Paramount tested bookings with the new title and claimed business got a lift. Prints already in exchanges had to be amended to reflect the switch. Paramount found this a costly procedure.

"*Ace in the Hole* was a bit too smart a title," admitted the company to *Variety*, "despite its perfection in describing a story of a man trapped in a cave and efforts of an ace reporter to tie up the story." The tab would be $20,000 to redo pressbooks, accessories, and physical prints of what was now *The Big Carnival*. "Most important is loss of coin spent in getting audience penetration of the original title," added *Variety*. No doubt a few straggler prints titled *Ace in the Hole* continued playing through 1951, much like that last rattlesnake Chuck Tatum described as having gotten away in the feature.

Billy Wilder spoke to a still-sore topic years later: "Behind my back, because I was making a picture in Paris at the time, Mr. Freeman, head of the studio, changed the title from *Ace in the Hole* to *The Big Carnival*—like this is going to attract people. Without asking me! It was one of the reasons I left Paramount."

All well and good for a director wanting to distance himself from an event well after the fact, but Y. Frank Freeman wasn't the one to call this shot. New York would have made such marketing decisions. I'm betting too that Wilder was consulted and ultimately bowed to sales department wishes. These weren't the idiots and troglodytes he liked to portray before adoring interviewers taking his anecdotes at face value. They were capable merchandisers who knew how to campaign on behalf of their product. Wilder just handed them sour fruit this time, and neither exhibitors nor customers were sure how to digest it.

So what happened to *The Big Carnival* when it got into the general release market? "For my money, the title would not change box office," was the report from Hollister, California's State Theatre. "The picture is different, but drawing power, in spite of exploitation, is limited—the second and third day died."

Could this have been the result of bad word-of-mouth among locals? The Booth Theatre's manager in Rich Hill, Missouri, spoke to that: "Our patrons thought it a little heavy. Got a bunch of kids who did not know what the show was about."

No, it sure wasn't for kids, but really, was it for anyone? "OK picture, but did poor business," was curt appraisal from the Jackson Theatre in Flomation, Alabama.

Well, you couldn't bring them into theatres at gunpoint after all, and Wilder's line in nihilism really wouldn't come into fashion for at least another 20 years.

Paramount couldn't be bothered with a reissue, and the death march to television opened with a berth on NBC's December 4, 1965 broadcast of *Saturday Night at the Movies*. From there, *The Big Carnival* was shuffled off to syndication as part of the company's Portfolio One package, where it would share late show dates with *The Man Who Shot Liberty Valance, I Married a Monster from Outer Space, My Favorite Spy*—some 50 Paramount titles that became available to local TV markets in April 1967. You could rent it through Films, Inc. during the '70s on a sliding scale. Titles in their catalog received ranking by stars—from one, two, or three to "special" based on perceived merit. *The Big Carnival* got a one, which meant it could be rented for anywhere from $15 a day for schools and convents (!) with less than 100 in the audience, probably a cinch with this one, to a maximum $100 for colleges and film societies with more than 1,251 in the room.

Ace in the Hole got sporadic, as in seldom, play for years. TCM's January 2007 broadcast was something of an event for many who'd not had proper opportunity to see it. Resurrection on DVD via Criterion got enthusiastic response denied the film for several generations. Paramount even has *Ace in the Hole* streaming in High Definition, giving us pinpoint clarity to guide future ways into Wilder's dark cave.

Above: This unorthodox marquee display makes it difficult to understand the type of picture being shown at L.A.'s Four Star Theatre. Below: "A little heavy" is how one showman describes *Ace in the Hole/The Big Carnival*. A lobby card drives home the point. Despite the title change, *The Big Carnival* "did poor business," says one exhibitor. "The second and third day died," says another.

Helen Hayes is menaced by Van Heflin and a soon-to-depart Robert Walker.

CHAPTER 16

FORGOTTEN BUT NOT GONE
MY SON JOHN

My Son John was buried alive for more than half a century, the bastard offspring of many distinguished careers. Leo McCarey was pilloried for directing it. Helen Hayes regretted coming out of movie retirement to make it, and Robert Walker died before he could finish it. Now *MSJ* is back in circulation and there's even a Blu-ray disc available. Strange are paths of pictures we call significant.

Misinformation put out on *My Son John* months before release remains in circulation. It's been variously described as hysterical, malignant, embarrassing, McCarthyite, idiotic, and paranoid. Perhaps we should just agree on controversial and leave it there. Even today, *My Son John* remains a pariah best handled with sterilized gloves, as hot a social and political potato as ever.

Leo McCarey had been a friendly witness before the House Un-American Activities Committee. Prior to that, he'd supervised Laurel and Hardy, made screwball comedies, and produced and directed a pair of smash hits about priests and nuns, *Going My Way* and *The Bells of St. Mary's*. He was devoutly Catholic and deplored Communism's dismissal of religion.

It was only natural that McCarey would catch a wave of films attacking totalitarianism in the early '50s. Most were easily digestible spy and espionage melodramas wherein ideology took a back seat to chase action and sneaked documents. Slinky women would cast nets to ensnare otherwise loyal Americans as malcontented weaklings turned traitor in hopes of money and power. It took Yanks with the mettle of a John Wayne to overcome them; indeed, it was his *Big Jim McClain* that near alone would profit from the Red Scare cycle. Robert Ryan, John Agar, Robert Taylor, and others purloined secrets on behalf of the Party during a half-decade's run of alarmist thrillers. Virtually all of these, including *The Red Danube, Conspirator, The Iron Curtain*, and *The Woman on Pier 13*, lost money.

A heavy hand of propaganda reflected industry anxiety over public perception of Hollywood's own loyalty. The HUAC was busily ferreting out movie-making Communists even as these films strove to reassure everyone of that town's unswerving patriotism. Studios probably knew their ledger ink would end up as red as regimes they were attacking, but with Hollywood itself under siege, such gestures, even if unprofitable, had to be made. Leo McCarey departed from these by focusing on Communism's impact on the American family. He viewed the latter as unwitting incubator for youth misguided by too much education as imparted by high-browed intellectuals ready to take over from within now that we'd won the war against fascism.

Helen Hayes and Dean Jagger play parents invaded by would-be body-snatching son Robert Walker, he of suspect graduation from university and black sheep among brothers otherwise shipping off to Korea to fight for their country. Had *My Son John* been properly completed, there might have been stuff here for quite a movie, as it does reflect heartland fear of sinister and barely understood forces preparing to take over. No wonder science fiction found this a fertile ground for exploration, the American public having readily equated Communist threats with alien encroachment. Whether such fears were rational was beside the point.

Of making *My Son John* the unorthodox Leo McCarey said, "This is my first Hitchcock."

Leo McCarey was already in decline when he began *My Son John*. There'd been complications over alcohol abuse, and his one feature since *The Bells of St. Mary's* was a misfired Gary Cooper vehicle called *Good Sam*. Both these were profitable, the first immensely so.

Leo McCarey would spend a long time gestating *My Son John*. He began with anything but a completed script. "I have one point," the director told trades. "Does it matter how I arrive at it?" The story was McCarey's, but he brought on John Lee Mahin and Myles Connolly to flesh things out.

McCarey spent autumn of 1950 in pursuit of Helen Hayes to star. Getting her would be a coup, as the self-described First Lady of the American Theatre had been off movie screens since the mid-'30s save for a cameo in *Stage Door Canteen*. Hayes' participation was a major selling point for *My Son John*, as other casting followed close behind her agreement to star.

In December 1950 McCarey described his project as "highly emotional, but with much humor," this being lure that brought Hayes aboard. His films were best loved for gentle humor and heart appeal, reliable handmaidens to a sock box office as proven by McCarey with *Going My Way* and *The Bells of St. Mary's*.

My Son John's story would remain top secret even as the 40-person crew arrived in Washington, D.C., during March 1951 for location work, including principals by then in place. Several weeks were spent there, but little of what they filmed made way to the final print. McCarey admitted that his script "is in far from final shooting shape," adding that, "I knew enough of what I wanted in Washington to do some exteriors and other background shots here."

At this point the director hoped to finish *My Son John* by early June for late 1951 release, though wandering around town in search of interesting backgrounds wasn't getting the job done any faster. An entire day was spent filming Helen Hayes in a Catholic church McCarey had come across and liked, but none of this footage would be used.

"We've only shot one scene that was in the original script," observed his star actress.

Being producer, director, and busy rewriter gave McCarey authority to make whatever changes suited him, even as slow pace of production brought him closer to rendezvous with Robert Walker's unexpected passing on August 28, 1951. Walker had been a loan-out from MGM, still home lot for the actor. Bob brings all the fun of Bruno Anthony to his performance as prodigal son John, a less-privileged first cousin reduced to office droning that Bruno would have deplored in *Strangers on a Train*, with low-level treason barely a step above Anthony's dreaded catching of the 8:15 in the morning "to sell paint or something." And what of detective Van Heflin worming his way into family confidence as means of trapping one of their own, much in the same way MacDonald Carey did in *Shadow of a Doubt*?

My Son John is a clear amalgam of Bruno and Uncle Charlie, so much so as to suggest Alfred Hitchcock himself lent a guiding hand. Suspicion as to that finds confirmation in a March 1951 interview Leo McCarey gave to the New York *Times* during production on *My Son John*. "There's a lot of the suspense element in the film," read the article, "and McCarey boasts of having gone directly to the master—Alfred Hitchcock—for pointers."

McCarey added: "This is my first Hitchcock. He even ran off the first four reels of his new film for me. I'm taking a lot of kidding about how I stop before every shot and try to figure out how Hitchcock would do it. I may even put myself in one scene like he does."

Those four reels McCarey referred to were from *Strangers on a Train*, awaiting July 1951 release as he continued laboring on *My Son John*. Did Hitchcock suggest the partial recap of his own *Shadow of a Doubt*? And was Robert Walker's casting the result of McCarey's sneak peek at those reels? There's enough of Bruno in John to suggest AH lent advice as regards the characterization. Cer-

Frank McHugh, Richard Jaeckel, Dean Jagger, Helen Hayes, and James Young appear on location at a Catholic church found by Leo McCarey in Washington, D.C. The setup calls for a background procession of local parishioners, but the result is little to show for a time-consuming trip east.

tainly McCarey showed a very public willingness to be guided by the Master's counsel, though he drew a line at staging suspense of a "melodramatic chase type."

Hoping to start a new trend, according to reportage, McCarey identified his *My Son John* goal thus: "It's more a suspense of ideas in conflict."

Back in Hollywood, McCarey's approach remained highly improvisational. He'd come on the set most mornings and noodle at a piano while searching his mind for ideas. Helen Hayes said he threw out the script for *My Son John* and every day was chaos. The picture was in production through the summer of 1951 and indeed had much work still to complete when co-star Robert Walker suddenly died over the weekend of August 25.

Nothing about this was expected. Walker had been in and out of rehab over several years, but fortunes were looking up after his triumph in *Strangers on a Train*. Now he was gone, and McCarey was stuck with a picture only half finished.

Damage control necessitated white lies for the press. "I have worked closely with Bob during these past few months," said McCarey, "and learned to know him as both a fine gentleman and a great actor. We had our final working session together only last Saturday. At that time he showed no indication of being in ill health. On the contrary, he did his final recording with great zest. I had just run the rough-cut of the picture for him, and, although a modest fellow, he fairly beamed at the results."

The *Motion Picture Herald* also received assurance that Walker "had just completed work in *My Son John*." With a final negative cost of $1.8 million, this was not an investment Paramount

In retrospect, Robert Walker's puffiness may have been a sign of trouble, as Jean Harlow's had been on the *Saratoga* set 15 years earlier. Thanks to the booze, Walker looked far older than his 32 years.

could write off. Such breakdowns were not unheard of, as minor players would often be replaced due to unexpected death or disability, and most famously, there was Jean Harlow and her demise during *Saratoga*.

Disasters subsequent to *My Son John* would be covered by cast insurance. Montgomery Clift's auto crash and attendant delays on *Raintree County* were compensated, while United Artists collected for losses sustained when Tyrone Power collapsed and died more than halfway through *Solomon and Sheba*. Leo McCarey had no such out. *My Son John* would somehow *have* to be completed.

In fact, the picture should never have been released. *My Son John* plays

A lobby card shows helpless parents Helen Hayes and Dean Jagger with their son John, the Godless Communist. Only one picture with such themes will make serious money during the Red Scare, John Wayne's *Big Jim McClain*.

like a jigsaw puzzle with parts missing and others jammed into place. The crude surgery goes way beyond mere patching of Walker footage from *Strangers on a Train* to cover for an ending they needed. Truth finally willed out in 1969 when McCarey sat down with interviewer Peter Bogdanovich and gave his account of the salvaging. The director was by then near the end of his life, and *My Son John* had been out of circulation for years. He would admit what critics and viewers had to suspect in 1952, that indeed *My Son John* was far from an end to shooting when Walker died. There would be a three-month break in shooting as McCarey searched for means to cobble what footage he'd shot into a coherent film. That job would take another 12 weeks.

My Son John was not released until seven months after Walker's death. In the meantime, McCarey had to change his ending altogether using outtakes and doubling gymnastics. Vital story points play out torturously during telephone conversations between chattering cast survivors and slowed-down-to-a-crawl footage of Walker standing in booths or reacting to something other than the scene he's now been grafted onto. McCarey had become a filmmaking Baron Frankenstein attempting to breathe life into something irretrievably dead.

The referred-to-by-others finish was indeed made up of footage from *Strangers on a Train*, as are scenes of Walker taxi-riding through Washington just prior to his onscreen demise. There's even a brief shot in which he consults a pivotal lighter that caused so much trouble for Farley Granger in the Hitchcock film.

McCarey matted Walker's head and shoulders from *Strangers* into a shot of the actor's *My Son John* character dying in the back of a cab shot up by Communist assassins, going so far as to personally dub in dialogue for the deceased player. McCarey was many wonderful things as a director, but he was not a convincing vocal stand-in for Robert Walker. It had never been his intention to kill off the character in any case; the public and New York critics would see to that.

A Topeka showman breaks from Paramount and puts politics front and center, his Fox Theatre's invitation extended only to those "for America 100%." His grassroots selling proves rewarding—the house clocks top 10 in Topeka grosses for the week. Exhibs throughout the Fox-Midwest circuit follow suit, with *My Son John* scoring well above national averages, indication that Paramount's own marketing may have been off the beam.

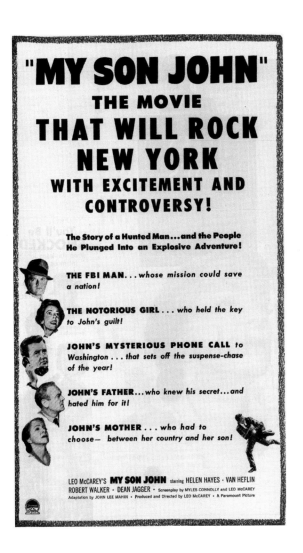

Top: Controversy over a picture does not always guarantee winning box office. Above: Leo McCarey, second from left, receives an award from the Catholic Institute in New York City. Right: Showmen are encouraged to involve the American Legion, a group far too powerful to buck.

USE AMERICAN LEGION TIE-IN TO RALLY ALL-OUT LOCAL AID!

The American Legion, the nation's largest and most powerful veteran's organization, is so overwhelmingly impressed with the importance of "MY SON JOHN" that it has instructed its thousands of posts throughout the country to cooperate, wherever possible, in bringing this motion picture to the full attention of the American people. Illustrated here is a full page ad, containing an unqualified endorsement of "MY SON JOHN," which is scheduled to appear in the June issue of the nationally circulated American Legion Magazine.

With this extremely valuable American Legion backing, plus the support of the American Legion Auxiliary and various other veteran's, religious, educational and civic groups, you can rally forth an all-out community reception for "MY SON JOHN," thus generating the large-scale interest and excitement which the newsworthy and patriotic theme of this picture so justly deserves. Outlined here is the program to be followed in undertaking a gala civic welcome for your playdate.

WHAT YOU CAN DO:

1. Well in advance of your opening, invite officials of the participating groups to attend a special screening of your picture. This affair should be well publicized with press, radio and photo releases.

2. After the screening, prominent mention of "MY SON JOHN" should be made in all publications and news mailings turned out by these organizations. This can be supplemented with photo and story items from the publicity section of this pressbook.

3. Organization bulletin board displays recommending the film and meeting house window displays should also be included in your plans.

4. Stage a full-dress parade to your theatre on opening day. This march should include the full memberships of every group involved in your civic welcome project. A parade of this sort would most probably develop into a headline affair that should result in heaps of invaluable publicity for your playdate.

5. Induce the cooperating groups to participate in a co-op ad, welcoming the film locally. Banner tie-in copy might read: *"Blanktown extends a proud and grateful welcome to 'MY SON JOHN!' "* This ad should appear a few days prior to opening, and mention of the parade should be made in its context.

Here is the enthusiastic endorsement given "MY SON JOHN" by Donald R. Wilson, National Commander of the American Legion. Use it to your best advantage by featuring it on a lobby board.

"I CALL ON ALL LEGIONNAIRES . . . and all Americans to see 'MY SON JOHN' without fail! It shows what an overwhelming force for good the motion picture industry can marshal!"

Donald R. Wilson, National Commander, American Legion.

By soon-to-be happy coincidence, Walker had made his rehearsal recording of a climactic speech two days before his death, and McCarey now added this element to a final reel as clumsily executed as it is uncomfortable to watch. Everyone at Paramount had to realize this unfinished hodgepodge would win few laurels, but an April 1952 opening date was looming. What choice but to release it and let chips fall where they may?

Reviews would be split along ideological lines. The New York *Times* excoriated *My Son John*, and an indignant McCarey flew into town for a reckoning. He'd been "slighted as a director, insulted as an artist, and libeled as a human being," according to press accounts. The same sort of high-brows that misled his benighted character John were now calling McCarey a bigot and trashing his movie all over New York tabloids.

There were champions at the ready to defend him, however, and they wielded a lot more influence. The American Legion had tied in with Paramount when advance screenings assured them this was their kind of picture. Now on board with a Legion-sponsored premiere, they generated literature to further encourage attendance.

We forget today just how powerful the Legion was at that time. This was the combined fighting force of two world wars, and now they were taking up arms against Communism. *Harrison's Reports* warned exhibitors not to cross them. Legion agitation and picketing had already sunk

Hollywood's local premiere of *My Son John* at the Fine Arts Theatre features a parade down Wilshire Boulevard with the American Legion's 50-piece Junior Boys' Band and accompanying color guard, all of whom serenade top industry celebs as they arrive.

Columbia's *Death of a Salesman,* owing to suspect political sympathies on the part of playwright Arthur Miller. Protective measures recommended by *Harrison's* included the purchase of *The Star Spangled Banner* from National Screen, a trailer that would cost $6.50 and play 70 seconds at the beginning and end of each theatre's day.

Harrison's added: "As patriotic Americans, we must take aggressive steps to obliterate any blight of *red* or *pink* that may attach itself to our theatres." Patrons in many situations were encouraged to stand and salute during the trailer.

With regards the American Legion, editors at the *Motion Picture Herald* minced no words: "You can do well to be on their side of a controversy." McCarey certainly was, and appeared to benefit by it. Legion honors were ac-

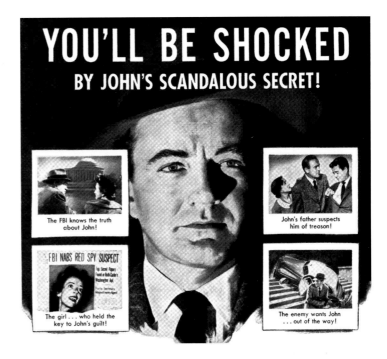

An already-complicated plot becomes impossible to resolve with the death of the leading man.

corded, and he basked in praise from the Catholic Institute as well. News photos showed him being awarded after guest speaking at a communion breakfast in the same New York where he'd so recently been vilified. You'd think a film as polarizing might catch a little box office by virtue of its controversy, but *My Son John* sunk like a stone. Domestic rentals of $895,000 were the best it could scrape up. Against that $1.8 million spent, this was plain disaster for Paramount and McCarey. *Variety* had been on record with a warning: "It faces selling difficulties because of the usual public indifference to propaganda pix."

And then there was McCarey's goal of "a suspense of ideas in conflict," which may have been the film's problem of problems, as things turned out. With Hitchcock fully in charge, we'd have had, at the least, a full-throttled espionage plot with John at its center, and perhaps a whammo finish atop the Washington Monument. AH would certainly have ditched propaganda in accordance with past policy and delivered a thriller fans might not have waited all these years to see again. Would *My Son John* be a classic today if Leo McCarey had collaborated as writer with director and final decision maker, Alfred Hitchcock?

Henceforth, anti-Communist messages would be delivered via giant ants, jet pilots, and lone cowpokes fighting totalitarianism on the plains, while *My Son John,* deemed as dated and useless as yesterday's editorial page, limped off to oblivion for generations to come.

Its more recent revival came as a result of efforts by film critic of the *New York Post* Lou Lumenick and writer/historian Farran Nehme, their push to have it shown on TCM in 2010 enabling *My Son John's* first TV exposure since an ABC network broadcast in 1974.

No actor in Hollywood was better qualified to portray conflicted Henry Fleming than real-life hero Audie Murphy, here recreating for the still camera his triumphant moment capturing the Confederate battle flag.

CHAPTER 17

METRO AND THE RED BADGE BLOW OFF

How radical was John Huston's *The Red Badge of Courage*? Some insiders who saw his proposed version were impressed, others not. It was only when preview audiences laughed and walked out that panic ensued. The story reads like a second act for *The Magnificent Ambersons*, another legendarily mutilated classic still unaccounted for in its entirety.

The Red Badge of Courage sunk amidst studio infighting as lethal as the Civil War battles it depicted. Atop this came public rejection a sales department predicted, with resulting egg on the faces of production chief Dore Schary and others who had championed Huston's effort.

Red Badge should have moved through the Metro system like dozens more literary adaptations going back to the company's inception, so I've got to figure Huston's treatment was, at the least, a major departure from the formula applied to ones that came before. Accounts of production and off-set conflict abound thanks to a remarkable series of articles published in the *New Yorker* and collected in a hardcover edition after *Red Badge* itself was dead and buried. Little time was needed for this one to evaporate out of theatres. Huston would remember it as his first film to lose money, and indeed it did, to the tune of $940,000, though a lot of other MGM releases shed skin as well during those troubled years when a public seemed to have decided en masse to stop attending movies.

For whatever good or bad reason, the studio gave *New Yorker* writer Lillian Ross total access to staff involved with *Red Badge* and received for their hospitality a primer book—the collected articles, hardbound—on corporate myopia and venality. Huston got out largely unscathed for having charmed the author, but others, including VP in charge Dore Schary, came off looking like weak sisters bent on vandalizing a talented director's work. Ross may well have been right on that account.

The Red Badge of Courage was perhaps too far ahead of 1951 to survive that year intact. Everyone seemed desperate to salvage jobs placed in perceived jeopardy for having worked on it. They all nodded yes to the scissors Schary personally applied after those disastrous previews and Huston's splitting town to do *The African Queen*. Like *Ambersons*, it's still a worthy show, but you have to decode much of *Red Badge*'s remains to divine what Huston had in mind.

The real story was a behind-scenes smack-down between pro-*Red Badge* Schary and soon-to-be-deposed Louis Mayer, who unwisely brandished this modest project (final negative cost: $1.673 million) as Exhibit A for a him-or-me ultimatum to New York studio chief, and deciding voter, Nicholas Schenck.

AUG. 14th
"THE RED BADGE OF COURAGE"

M·G·M TRADE SHOWS!

AUG. 20th
"THE PEOPLE AGAINST O'HARA"

ALBANY—8/14—2 P.M.
20th-Fox Screen Room
1052 Broadway
ATLANTA—8/14—10:30 A.M.
197 Walton St., N.W.
BOSTON—8/14—2 P.M.
M-G-M Screen Room
46 Church Street
BUFFALO—8/14—2 P.M.
20th-Fox Screen Room
290 Franklin Street
CHARLOTTE—8/14—1:30 P.M.
20th-Fox Screen Room
308 S. Church Street
CHICAGO—8/14—1:30 P.M.
H. C. Igel's Screen Room
1301 S. Wabash Avenue
CINCINNATI—8/14—8 P.M.
RKO Palace Bldg. Screen Room
16 East Sixth Street
CLEVELAND—8/14—1 P.M.
20th-Fox Screen Room
2219 Payne Avenue
DALLAS—8/14—2:30 P.M.
20th-Fox Screen Room
1803 Wood Street
DENVER—8/14—2 P.M.
Paramount Screen Room
2100 Stout Street
DES MOINES—8/14—1 P.M.
20th-Fox Screen Room
1300 High Street
DETROIT—8/14—1:30 P.M.
Max Blumenthal's Sc. Rm.
2310 Cass Avenue
INDIANAPOLIS—8/14—1 P.M.
20th-Fox Screen Room
326 North Illinois Street
JACKSONVILLE—8/14—8 P.M.
Florida State Screen Room
128 East Forsyth Street
KANSAS CITY—8/14—1:30 P.M.
20th-Fox Screen Room
1720 Wyandotte Street
LOS ANGELES—8/14—2 P.M.
United Artists' Screen Room
1851 South Westmoreland
MEMPHIS—8/14—12 Noon
20th-Fox Screen Room
151 Vance Avenue
MILWAUKEE—8/14—1:30 P.M.
Warner Screen Room
212 West Wisconsin Avenue
MINNEAPOLIS—8/14—2 P.M.
20th-Fox Screen Room
1015 Currie Avenue
NEW HAVEN—8/14—2 P.M.
20th-Fox Screen Room
40 Whiting Street
NEW ORLEANS—8/14—1:30 P.M.
200 South Liberty Street
NEW YORK-N.J.—8/14—2:30 P.M.
M-G-M Screen Room
630 Ninth Avenue
OKLAHOMA CITY—8/14—1 P.M.
20th-Fox Screen Room
10 North Lee Street
OMAHA—8/14—1 P.M.
20th-Fox Screen Room
1502 Davenport Street
PHILADELPHIA—8/14—11 A.M.
M-G-M Screen Room
1233 Summer Street
PITTSBURGH—8/14—2 P.M.
M-G-M Screen Room
1623 Boulevard of Allies
PORTLAND—8/14—2 P.M.
B. F. Shearer Screen Room
1947 N. W. Kearney Street
ST. LOUIS—8/14—1 P.M.
S'Renco Art Theatre

The best film about the War Between the States since GWTW.

◄ M-G-M presents Stephen Crane's Great American Story "THE RED BADGE OF COURAGE" · Starring Audie Murphy Bill Mauldin · A John Huston Production Screen Play by John Huston · Adaptation by Albert Band Directed by John Huston · Produced by Gottfried Reinhardt

Spencer Tracy scores again!

M-G-M presents
SPENCER TRACY
in "THE PEOPLE AGAINST O'HARA"
Co-starring
PAT O'BRIEN
DIANA LYNN
JOHN HODIAK

ALBANY—8/20—2 P.M.
20th-Fox Screen Room
1052 Broadway
ATLANTA—8/20—2 P.M.
20th-Fox Screen Room
197 Walton St., N.W.
BOSTON—8/20—2 P.M.
M-G-M Screen Room
46 Church Street
BUFFALO—8/20—2 P.M.
20th-Fox Screen Room
290 Franklin Street
CHARLOTTE—8/20—1:30 P.M.
20th-Fox Screen Room
308 S. Church Street
CHICAGO—8/20—1:30 P.M.
H. C. Igel's Screen Room
1301 S. Wabash Avenue
CINCINNATI—8/20—8 P.M.
RKO Palace Bldg. Screen Room
16 East Sixth Street
CLEVELAND—8/20—1 P.M.
20th-Fox Screen Room
2219 Payne Avenue
DALLAS—8/20—2:30 P.M.
20th-Fox Screen Room
1803 Wood Street
DENVER—8/20—2 P.M.
Paramount Screen Room
2100 Stout Street
DES MOINES—8/20—1 P.M.
20th-Fox Screen Room
1300 High Street
DETROIT—8/20—1:30 P.M.
Max Blumenthal's Sc. Rm.
2310 Cass Avenue
INDIANAPOLIS—8/20—1 P.M.
20th-Fox Screen Room
326 North Illinois Street
JACKSONVILLE—8/20—8 P.M.
Florida State Screen Room
128 East Forsyth Street
KANSAS CITY—8/20—1:30 P.M.
20th-Fox Screen Room
1720 Wyandotte Street
LOS ANGELES—8/20—2 P.M.
United Artists' Screen Room
1851 South Westmoreland
MEMPHIS—8/20—12 Noon
20th-Fox Screen Room
151 Vance Avenue
MILWAUKEE—8/20—1:30 P.M.
Warner Screen Room
212 West Wisconsin Avenue
MINNEAPOLIS—8/20—2 P.M.
20th-Fox Screen Room
1015 Currie Avenue
NEW HAVEN—8/20—2 P.M.
20th-Fox Screen Room
40 Whiting Street
NEW ORLEANS—8/20—1:30 P.M.
200 South Liberty Street
NEW YORK-N.J.—8/20—2:30 P.M.
M-G-M Screen Room
630 Ninth Avenue
OKLAHOMA CITY—8/20—1 P.M.
20th-Fox Screen Room
10 North Lee Street
OMAHA—8/20—1 P.M.
20th-Fox Screen Room
1502 Davenport Street
PHILADELPHIA—8/20—11 A.M.
M-G-M Screen Room
1233 Summer Street
PITTSBURGH—8/20—2 P.M.
M-G-M Screen Room
1623 Boulevard of Allies
PORTLAND—8/20—2 P.M.
B. F. Shearer Screen Room
1947 N. W. Kearney Street
ST. LOUIS—8/20—1 P.M.
S'Renco Art Theatre

M-G-M, the company that released "GONE WITH THE WIND", presents a new drama of the War Between the States

STEPHEN CRANE'S immortal classic

THE
RED BADGE
OF
COURAGE

"Pictorially breathtaking! The performers all first-rate!"
—LIFE

starring
AUDIE MURPHY · **BILL MAULDIN**
A JOHN HUSTON PRODUCTION · Screen Play by JOHN HUSTON
Adaptation by ALBERT BAND

Directed by **JOHN HUSTON**
Produced by GOTTFRIED REINHARDT

N. Y. PREMIERE   TRANS-LUX
THURSDAY · 52nd on LEXINGTON
                                        PL. 3-2434
LAST 4 DAYS! "KIND LADY"   IT'S MGMTIME, U.S.A.

Schary won, but blinked when the *Red Badge* pet he'd adopted grew teeth upon rejection by early crowds and threatened to become an industry joke at his expense. To avert that, he'd simply cut the print until the laughter stopped.

Red Badge seemed too inconsequential to arouse such backlot rancor, for Huston was at no time extravagant, spending inflated by post-production tinkering of others. This director was no von Stroheim challenging studio authority. Huston had recently brought profit to Metro with *The Asphalt Jungle* and was shaping up as one of postwar's first total filmmakers, worthy of rank beside experienced writer-directors prized for being so few in number. The studio indulged his wild-man ways for having delivered goods and showing a keen eye for what sold in theatres.

According to some accounts, Huston turned in *The Red Badge of Courage* at less than 90 minutes. "It was never a long picture," he later said.

I've read variously of running times at 95 and 105 minutes. Some remembered two-and-a-quarter hours of agony for patrons, half of whom jeered while others walked out. Battle scenes were alleged to have been gorier and in greater abundance. Huston presented a Civil War far more hellish than conservative Metro was willing to depict. Louis B. Mayer blanched at carnage and ruefully commented that it was typical of excess from this director; LB had heartily disapproved of *The Asphalt Jungle* as well.

Other Metro personnel who had earlier liked *Red Badge* chickened out now. Schary went to plucking, and yes-men called him a hero for a result that lasted just over an hour. The *Motion Picture Herald* announced a September 1951 release in July of that year, with the running time to be 81 minutes, though by the August 18 trade screenings for exhibitors, it was down to a final 69 minutes. *Variety* had reported back in April that MGM was delaying *Red Badge*'s release "pending addition of added scenes and some editing."

Left top: Trade screenings for showmen do not prove fruitful for *Red Badge*. **Left: A New York art-house opening portends difficulties ahead for the latest MGM orphan; it will die after a couple weeks of decent returns.**

Everyone connected with the sorry affair spent years trying to justify actions taken in mutual panic. Longtime MGM editor Margaret Booth told *Focus on Film* in 1976 that *Red Badge* was very long at first, that it was better shorter, and still managed somehow to emerge a classic. For his part, Huston pronounced the complete version perhaps the best film he ever made, yet he seems not to have held grudges. He'd even hire Booth to edit his much later *Fat City*. Narration from Stephen Crane's source book was appended to the re-cut *Red Badge* to give literary weight and essentially dare patrons to ridicule it as they previously had.

It was clear those 69 minutes had been arrived at by way of hacking. Reviews proved laudatory, but critics didn't cover house nuts ruptured by a black-and-white downer about cowardice on the battlefield. Independent film buyers charting for the *Motion Picture Herald* called it poor. MGM's New York sales division, where studio releases were made or broken, admitted indifference to investigating Lillian Ross, saying they'd known all along it would be a dog. Such candor as shared with an outsider was unprecedented.

Red Badge ended up an art film mishandled by a company unequipped and frankly resentful of that label. Metro still targeted a mass audience seated in big auditoriums, but here was a show that would reach neither. The fallback was to open, late by a month, at New York's Trans-Lux 52nd Street art house, which seated 539 and had been home to a number of Metro orphans thought unfit for wider bows.

"Opening a new picture at the Trans-Lux houses instead of on Broadway saves the major companies money for an elaborate house front," said the *Herald*. "The New York newspapers devote an equal amount of space to reviews of pictures at the art houses. Thus the art spots, which formerly played British, Italian, or French product exclusively, are now getting offbeat pictures from the majors and giving them long runs, which gives favorable word-of-mouth a chance to build business."

Below left: MGM production boss Dore Schary with Leo the Lion; does Leo smell a dog in *Red Badge*? Below right: Huston's just-previous *The Asphalt Jungle* features an important early role for Marilyn Monroe.

Said *Boxoffice*, "The Trans-Lux was good for a six-to-eight week engagement of Metro peculiars like *Teresa*, *Kind Lady*, and *The Man with a Cloak*, far more than they would have played at a large Broadway house." *The Red Badge of Courage* did have a good couple of weeks at the Trans-Lux, but then came the fade as it seemed even the art crowd couldn't be bothered.

Red Badge would be offered up as another *Gone With the Wind* for purposes of wider advertising, while its trailer promised a latter-day *Birth of a Nation*. Columnists at the time, most notably widely syndicated James Bacon, plus historians later, would damn Metro for playing *Badge* on double features, not realizing this was standard policy for all but potential biggies the company handled. Wider release did find *Red Badge* occupying lower berths, but so did most other black-and-white Metros done at reduced budget, and Schary's mutilation was no diamond in the rough. There was little chance of *Red Badge* breaking out to attain sleeper status—not with audiences rejecting it wholesale as they continued to do.

Below: A lackluster poster campaign, including the one-sheet that promoted a "story of the Civil War," reflects internal studio conflict.

Variety spoke for a doubtful trade press as *Red Badge* went into general release, calling it "curiously moody." The paper added, "Big returns do not appear likely. Box office appeal in the general market is rather limited, and in this release [the] film will be best held to companion bookings." Critic Bosley Crowther of the New York *Times* concurred, saying the picture would be accepted only by "select audiences."

MGM's misgivings having been confirmed, the studio now sent out *The Red Badge of Courage* in support of features likely to perform better. In Boston it buttressed *Texas Carnival*, a program held over in mid-October thanks to interest in the Esther Williams starrer. The latter's eventual profit was $709,000. *Red Badge* played second fiddle to Mickey Rooney's noir *The Strip* in Denver, while Chicago and Detroit saw it beneath the Clark Gable western, *Across the Wide Missouri*.

The Red Badge of Courage had legs as weak as Metro's other punk release that month, *The Man with a Cloak*, which was yanked off a single berth in Cincinnati after four days and replaced with oldie combo *Luxury Liner* and *The Barkleys of Broadway*.

There were spasms of effort as 1951 wore down, with *The Red Badge of Courage*

Above: With an inaccessible and cowardly "hero," no love story, and grim depiction of a war that had been for the most part box-office poison, *Red Badge* steps to the plate with too many strikes against it. Below: An all-male cast, composed largely of character actors, and endless talk about who will stand and fight and who will run away from combat also hurt the picture.

booked into a pair of Los Angeles houses for December play with trade ads proclaiming, **MGM Is Proud of The Red Badge of Courage**, but the gesture came too late.

Admirable persistence put *Red Badge* back in Gotham—"three art spots," according to *Variety*—for a July 1952 encore that Metro marketers tied to publication of Lillian Ross's book, *Picture*, which compiled her five *New Yorker* articles about the misbegotten film. Toward hope of goosed receipts, ad copy read, "New York is still talking about the *New Yorker* magazine articles." Later-in-the-month trade headlines were direct: **Mag's Wide Publicity Fails to Hypo 'Badge.'** In fact, it performed below even modest art house expectation (the Trans-Lux 72nd Street house, for instance, took less than $2,000 for its week's run). Bitter experience had again taught MGM's sales force not to persist once hothouse plants were identified as such. Best to let them wilt, then disappear.

Final domestic rentals for *Red Badge* amounted to $789,000, with foreign as usual rejecting all themes Americana with $395,000. The $940,000 loss was no more disgraceful than for other Metro releases awash in red ink. The company's *Mr. Imperium* of high hopes and a Broadway opening went down in crushing defeat to $1.397 million lost, but who remembers that? Now well-separated from Metro, Louis Mayer seemed vindicated in his apprehension over *Red Badge* and belief that Civil War subjects invariably failed, save for the obvious exception of *Gone With the Wind*.

Ironic then was RKO's contemporaneous release of *Drums in the Deep South*, a more straightforward and action-packed Blue-Gray engagement, with square-jaws James Craig and Guy Madison far less tentative in the field than Huston's ragtag army had been. Trade support and a splashy Atlanta premiere—**TONITE ON STAGE: BARBARA PAYTON AND SOUTHERN BELLES**—greeted *Drums*, but a worldwide rentals total of $1.025 million actually fell slightly below *Red Badge of Courage*. Many public school showings lay in wait for John Huston's ruined masterpiece as state libraries kept it on hand and many a youngster sat for runs in history class.

MGM surprisingly withheld *The Red Badge of Courage* from its Perpetual Product reissue program in 1962–63, despite "World Heritage" groupings that would have seemed ideal. Television release came in a syndicated package for 1964, with *Red*

Stills are all that remain of deleted scenes like the one below that developed Henry Fleming's lonely odyssey on the fringes of the battlefield after he had turned and run from his first fight with the Rebs.

Badge among 40 titles that included *On the Town*, *The Stratton Story*, and *Love Me or Leave Me*. Revenue from *Red Badge* syndication totaled $118,000 as of April 1983, plus a non-primetime network run on the CBS Late Movie, which yielded an additional $34,000. By way of comparison, a pre-'48 from Metro, the Gable-Turner *Somewhere I'll Find You*, earned $149,000 from syndication through April 1983 and 1943's *Mrs. Miniver* $332,000.

Nontheatrical distributor Films, Inc. offered *The Red Badge of Courage* in its catalogue and said Huston's film had been "unjustly deemed a failure," neglecting to explain just what one *could* call it in light of rejection, deserved or not, by both its releasing company and a public that refused to embrace John Huston's bold, ultimately compromised, vision.

Above: Unpretentious kiddie take on the Civil War, *Drums in the Deep South*, competes on theatre battlefields with *The Red Badge of Courage*. Left: Atlanta welcomes *Drums* and star Barbara Payton with open arms—campaigning that *Red Badge* would never receive.

By the time he makes *On the Waterfront*, Marlon Brando is the hottest actor in Hollywood.

CHAPTER 18

COLUMBIA AND KAZAN'S WATERFRONT HAUL

Watching an adult picture and staying up late to do it was shared ritual for lots of us growing up, with *On the Waterfront* early among those I regarded seriously, as opposed to monsters and mayhem I forfeited sleep to look at. Now, it seems backlash has rooted among online thinkers. They're backing off *On the Waterfront* as settled paragon and asking themselves if this is an object more to be admired than enjoyed. I came away from a recent look, after 10 years' break, with similar mixed emotion. So how much do *we* change between viewings of a familiar show?

Darryl F. Zanuck counseled Elia Kazan and Budd Schulberg to avoid too much soap boxing over social themes during *Waterfront*'s early development at Fox: "I believe that the evil of the waterfront situation," said DFZ, "should be the background...and that the personal story must predominate." They'd halfway take his advice. Would *Waterfront* have been plainer film noir coming from 20th?

Now, it strikes me as even more political than the issue-oriented pics that Zanuck supervised to completion. What's more noirish is the bitter tea that so many drank for being eased off this *Waterfront*, cash and proper credit lost despite time and effort expended on a Best Picture (1954) winner's behalf. Elia Kazan argues his side compellingly in a '90s memoir, but others told a different story. The truth of success having many fathers got much confirmation on *Waterfront*'s road to revered status.

On the Waterfront excels for its on-location atmosphere and slice of gritty urban life. No wonder city folk flipped for it, as with 21 weeks at New York's Astor Theatre. You'd not top Kazan for knowing how to get the most out of locations. Neither was he far wrong calling Marlon Brando's the best performance that movies had tendered to that time, but was this actor's appeal so different from, say, Gary Cooper starting out? Both dealt quiet intensity and clicked best being diffident during love scenes. The difference was Cooper and golden-agers building on this toward stardom uninterrupted until death or retirement. Brando was ideally cast in *Waterfront*, then misstepped considerably from there. Could studio affiliation and careful grooming have yielded three *On the Waterfront*s for every *Desiree* instead of the other way around?

Here was Hollywood's most valued property in 1954, a name to guarantee any project going forward, and his psychiatrist is calling the shots. Studios wanted Brando so much that they'd put up with anything. There'd been a walkout on Fox's *The Egyptian* for which he'd ultimately be forgiven, and *Waterfront* producer Sam Spiegel spent weeks on bended knee getting Brando to sign for what won him a

Best Actor statuette. Certainly, it was this star people came to see in *On the Waterfront*. They'd wait for him to do another as good for years after, then give up by a '60s decline. Surprising it must have been by 1972 and *The Godfather* to realize that only 18 years had passed since *Waterfront*.

Darryl Zanuck was piqued when Budd Schulberg wrote in the New York *Times* of a studio executive, un-named but clearly DFZ, more dedicated to widescreen horse operas than films about real people. Kazan seized high roads as well, but then he could afford to after *Waterfront* broke big. Studio "ostriches" were an industry's bane, he said to *Variety* in December 1954: "They continue to stick their heads in the sand and make the same movies their fathers made before them." Here was a director fed up with "plain nonsense themes," speaking his mind freely now that industry doors opened widest to him.

Both Kazan and Schulberg would gloat over success of a gamble "that almost every major studio rejected at one time or another," but would Hollywood remember high-handed talk when later *A Face in the Crowd* came a cropper? I do admire Kazan's admitting how roguish producer Sam Spiegel manipulated him throughout *On the Waterfront*. "S.P. Eagle," as he was then known, gives the impression of one who'd duck out of hotels without paying the tab, as I'm sure he often did. What comfort it must have been for artists dealing with outright con men if not borderline criminals, but weren't the likes of Spiegel a reality that Kazan and Schulberg had known all their professional lives?

It's easy to forget the ruthless means by which most movies get made, that industry having always best served meat-eaters. *On the Waterfront* producer Sam Spiegel promised Frank Sinatra, fresh off a *From Here to Eternity* Best Supporting Actor win, that he would star. There were even costume fittings as everyone shook Frank's hand and told him how great he'd be. Then Marlon Brando got belatedly back in touch and said okay to *Waterfront*. Sinatra could get mad, but couldn't afford getting even. Frank being aboard would have meant a cheaper picture along the lines of *Suddenly*,

Top: Diffident Brando with sexy Eva Marie Saint. Above: *On the Waterfront* **opens in three big Los Angeles houses.**

Sinatra's next, but *Waterfront* with Brando became a fittingly bankrolled and *important* venture, one that Columbia tabbed to be 1954's *Eternity*.

There is conflicting info as to what *On the Waterfront* ultimately cost. *Variety* said in November 1954 it was $820,000; Kazan would claim years later a figure of $880,000. Either reflects a bargain rate in a period when "A"-pic tags were generally much higher. Chase National Bank staked half the production for Spiegel's Horizon company, with Columbia guaranteeing completion, this being Chase National's first dip into movie financing for years: "It's [Chase] policy now to accept only gilt-edged deals," said *Variety*, "with assurance that a major producer-distributor is backing the indie filmmaker." All concerned appreciated Marlon Brando's having supplied gilt to *Waterfront*'s edge for this borrowing occasion.

It was bold of Columbia to send a black-and-white flattie into box-office combat against color-wide opponents. B/W and standard-ratio *From Here* had come out a year's eternity ago and just before Cinemascope drew lines away from conventional screens. Fox had, in fact, dropped *Waterfront* in part because of a new season's switch to anamorphic, leaving Columbia to rely on character and content to put *On the Waterfront* over.

Sneak-previewing to generate word-of-mouth was a means of heating up the summer release, a hopeful twin for *The Caine Mutiny*, already in circulation and doing socko. Talk was of *Waterfront* hitting censor snags for rough language. Brando tells a priest to "Go to hell!" The PCA ordered that cut, despite similar epithets in Hal Wallis's recent *Cease Fire*. Buzz convinced Eastern metropoli that *Waterfront* was their kind of hard-hitter. Philadelphia's Stanley Theatre snuck *Waterfront* with Dean and Jerry in *Living It Up* and turned away crowds at said 2,900-seat palace.

By July and *On the Waterfront*'s siege of New York, **MUST SEE** was a label firmly attached. The Astor Theatre's old single-week record of $59,500 for MGM's stalwart *Battleground* fell to a *Waterfront* $68,000, that partly owing to increased ticket prices for Columbia's attraction. Patronage tendered from $1.25 to $1.85 for seats, with Saturday's a highest rate at $2.30. This was way bigger admission than any other Broadway house commanded, but crowds paid willingly. Elia Kazan would remember faces in line not unlike the rough customers populating *On the Waterfront* itself. It must have been like home movies for a beleaguered working class.

Toward everything old being new again, one can't help wondering if Marlon Brando was Jim Cagney reborn for this urban congregation. He was surely among the first since Cagney with whom

Columbia's July 24, 1954 trade ad for *On the Waterfront*.

FROM HORIZON PICTURES AND
Columbia

MARLON BRANDO
ON THE WATERFRONT
AN ELIA KAZAN PRODUCTION
co starring KARL MALDEN • LEE J. COBB
with ROD STEIGER • PAT HENNING and introducing EVA MARIE SAINT
Produced by SAM SPIEGEL
Screen Play by BUDD SCHULBERG • Music by LEONARD BERNSTEIN
Directed by ELIA KAZAN

Chicago's Woods Theatre links *Waterfront*
with earlier smash hit *Going My Way*.

they could identify. Ads called *Waterfront* "*Going My Way* with Brass Knuckles," a refer-back to that massive 1944 hit and not so inapt, what with both films' priestly presence and reform agenda.

Response to *Waterfront* was enough for Columbia to try shoehorning it in among entries to the Venice Film Festival, August a late date to apply, but who imagined that *Waterfront* would take off so big? Sam Spiegel pushed Venice placement hardest, as he'd been in Europe for funding to launch more projects. "I've never seen such a flood of money being offered," he told *Variety*.

Harry Cohn announced that Columbia would invest $10 million in forthcoming independent productions, this in addition to studio-made product. Much of that cash would be provided by Chase Bank, thanks to *Waterfront*'s showing; it earned $5,737,000 in domestic rentals. They'd even advance funds toward Sam Katzman's yearly "B" slate for Columbia.

Success, not unexpectedly, bred lawsuits. United Artists came after Sam Spiegel's *Waterfront* share for $459K they'd advanced him back in 1952 for a flop called *Melba*, while AFL dockworkers in Chicago sued Columbia for portraying its membership as thugs and hoodlums. Those who'd briefly been in on developing *On the Waterfront* also wanted a share now that it was paying off. Several filed claims and more could have. Darryl Zanuck waived recompense for time and $40,000 by which *Waterfront* was Fox-enriched—its dollars spent prepping the project before Zanuck let it go—satisfying himself instead with stern rebuke to ex-creative partners for the bad hand he felt they'd dealt him.

On the Waterfront stayed on the marquee a remarkable 21 weeks at the Astor. Columbia would ballyhoo this engagement to justify rich terms for subsequent play, with showmen fearing the same raw deal they'd gotten on *The Caine Mutiny*. "Why charge so much for product brought in for such a modest sum?" they asked, word being out that *Waterfront*'s negative cost to Columbia was less than half *Caine*'s total.

Waterfront held long enough at the Astor to push would-be opener *A Star Is Born* next door to the Victoria. *A Star Is Born* would also play the couple-blocks-away Paramount. Broadway houses were at a premium in days when a film's reputation lived or died on how it was received there. Unexpectedly long runs often meant reshuffling merchandise, or delaying bows. *On the Waterfront*'s Astor grossing might have continued into 1955 but for an ironclad December 19 start on Disney's *20,000 Leagues Under the Sea*.

An eight-Oscar *Waterfront* win kept the film in circulation and back at first-run venues where it was comboed with *The Caine Mutiny*. Columbia meanwhile pursued a buyout of profit participants Spiegel, Kazan, and Schulberg, rumor being their selling price totaled $3 million, although Columbia called that figure "too high." The company later followed up a successful *From Here to*

Eternity reissue in 1958 with another *Caine/Waterfront* parlay for 1959–60. "The pix...will be handled as if they were new films," said *Variety*, "with new advertising and promotion campaigns."

TV release came in 1963 among 210 post-'48 titles syndicated by Columbia. By April 1964, the package cleared the top-50 viewing markets and would play that year on 153 U.S. stations.

On the Waterfront survives notably as an actor's talisman. Brando inspired no telling how many to seek footlights after watching him here. Many performers born since 1954 call *Waterfront* a best-ever onscreen ensemble, drama timed perfectly to its first-run audience, amply rewarded by sturdy grosses, and living on as the foremost example of what teachers and students call "modern" acting technique.

Above: *Waterfront* pulls in crowds like this for its 21-week run at Broadway's Astor Theatre. Below: The *Waterfront/Caine* combo earns stellar box office from late 1954 into '55 and will again on reissue in 1960.

Merian C. Cooper and Fay Wray clown during a light-hearted still photo shoot for *King Kong*.

CHAPTER 19

THE MIGHTY MONARCH
OF MELODRAMAS

King Kong the success was born in 1933. *King Kong* the smash happened in 1952. "Sleeper of the Year" was among terms used by the *Motion Picture Herald*. Reissues were nothing new in the '50s. They'd been around since movies began. Major distributors stepped them up after the war, and some clicked beyond expectation. *The Wizard of Oz* finally got into the black based on earnings received from its 1949 encore, and Universal strengthened bottom lines with profits derived by leasing older titles to Realart Pictures.

RKO relied heavily upon reissues from that studio's inception. *Cimarron*, *The Lost Squadron*, *The Lost Patrol*, *Of Human Bondage*, and *Star of Midnight* were all brought back during the '30s, as was hands-down RKO library champ *King Kong*.

Kong was the surest revival thing outside *Snow White and the Seven Dwarfs*—a property distributed but not owned by the company. So many theatres were dedicated action houses, catering to patron appetite for westerns, thrillers, and adventures. They wanted shows to move and shunned those that dawdled. There was generally but one trip to the well for Constance Bennett mellers, but a *Gunga Din* could play forever—and seemingly did.

For RKO, *King Kong* defined evergreen. Exaggeration of its financial success became the stuff of many a press release. They said early on that *King Kong* saved RKO from bankruptcy, but didn't *Little Women* cost less and make more? Its domestic rentals of $1.337 million (and $663,000 foreign) against a negative cost of $424,000 resulted in $800,000 profit. *King Kong* took $745,000 in domestic rentals plus $1.1 million in foreign rentals to finish with a profit of $650,000. Upcoming *Top Hat* would surpass both *King Kong* and *Little Women* with a stunning $1.325 million in profit, the largest gain RKO would have on any release during the '30s, with the exception of Disney's *Snow White*. *King Kong* as studio savior became part of the character's mythology, and indeed he kept the wolves at bay for years beyond initial release in 1933.

Application for a Code Seal in 1938 necessitated infamous cuts whose retrieval some 40 years later enhanced Janus' commercial prospects when they took over *Kong*'s distribution. Audiences during the interim made do with a truncated version further compromised by lab-darkened prints designed to minimize gory visuals. The 1938 reissue coming but five years after initial release found many viewers recalling footage denied them now. There was $155,000 in domestic rentals for *Kong* that year, with

$151,000 foreign. The final profit was $200,000, excellent for a reissue. As of 1938, *King Kong*'s cumulative profits would now equal those of *Little Women*. Another *Kong* reissue in 1942 brought it neck and neck with *Top Hat*. On that occasion *King Kong* took $170,000 in domestic rentals and another $515,000 foreign. Note the disparity: *Kong* found its biggest audience by far in foreign territories. This time, there was $460,000 in profits.

With each reissue there were new prints, those from 1933 having been retired because of Code-banned footage. Fresh campaign material also was prepared. *King Kong*'s near-leading status would be overtaken in 1943 by *Mr. Lucky*, a Cary Grant vehicle that earned a remarkable $1.6 million in profits spurred by wartime attendance booms. It would be nine more years before *King Kong* would claim pride of place as greatest of all profit getters for its owner. Indeed, the Great Ape would leave his deepest imprint with the 1952 reissue. That would be the year in which *Kong* truly became the eighth wonder of the exhibition world.

The 1952 *King Kong* was a reissue whose time had come. Recent success of science fiction films had ripened the market for fantastic fare. RKO must have anticipated better-than-average grosses, as early trade ads reflect unusual confidence. In light of what *Variety* called "a degree of success with chiller combinations"—spurred by an earlier 1952 combo of *The Hunchback of Notre Dame* and *Cat People*—RKO had reason to believe *King Kong* would click.

In 1933 movie patrons stretch around the block for their date with the Eighth Wonder of the World. You'd almost expect Bonnie and Clyde to come careening around the corner, guns a-blazin'. But that's a different chapter.

Above, a seven-foot-long silk-screen banner promotes the greatest of apes in his 1952 re-release. It seems that bigger is always better when selling *King Kong*. Below: *Kong*, now nearly two decades old, takes his place with successful, brand-new RKO product.

RKO had tabbed few "A" features for summer 1952 release and experienced what trades called "a product dearth." As a result, the company pushed *King Kong* as if it were "first-time-around top product," said *Variety*, "with the coin outlay [for publicity] nearly equaling that of an initial launching." RKO's recent February '52 encore of *Snow White and the Seven Dwarfs* had proven reissues could sell when handled properly.

Midwest exhibitors weren't happy, though. They'd been "squeezed" by the distributor for a high percentage of ticket sales on *Snow White* and suspected RKO would follow through with similar terms for *King Kong*. The charge was leveled in early June by the Allied Theatre Owners of Indiana, their current bulletin warning members that "if you give RKO top terms [for *King Kong*], then reconcile yourself to paying outrageous terms for reissues from not only RKO but also from all other companies."

A midlands saturation launch found *Kong* in 400 theatres across five exchange areas—Detroit, Cleveland, Cincinnati, Indianapolis, and Pittsburgh—generally in tandem bookings with Val Lewton's *The Leopard Man*. Playdates were timed with schools-out attendance. RKO sent out four open-body trailer trucks to cities where *King Kong* was being saturated, these carrying replicas of the giant ape. The vehicles were 24 feet long and 8 feet wide. Truck sides and tail pieces were made up to depict a row of city skyscrapers, with the Empire State Building overlooking the center. The Kong figure towered 10 feet above the truck beds and had movable arms and head, while clutching a Fay Wray mannequin in his hairy paw. A portable light plant on each truck powered floods to illuminate the display at night. First-day shows saw grosses "the biggest in years," said *Variety*, in spite of outdoor temperatures reaching into the '90s in some situations.

Television spots, used but sparingly by distributors over the past two years, were more or less untried as a major selling device. There were, after all, only 109 stations on the air in 1952, and it

Small-town selling of the *King Kong* and *Leopard Man* combo puts locals to work on bally behalf.

188

THE GREATEST THRILLER OF ALL TIME...IN THE BIGGEST AREA PREMIERE IN SHOW HISTORY!

KING KONG

Booked into many top theatres in the Pittsburgh, Detroit, Cincinnati, Cleveland and Indianapolis Exchange territories beginning in Mid-June . . . A joining of more than 400 theatres . . . swept by a spectacular conflagration of explosive showmanship — including everything you've ever heard of and much you haven't — to launch anew the mightiest thriller of 'em all!

with
FAY WRAY
ROB'T ARMSTRONG
BRUCE CABOT

Here are some of the circuits participating:

Warners	Affiliated	Skirball
Schine	Y & W	Barnell
Publix	Alliance	Butterfield
RKO	Fourth Ave. Amus.	United Detroit
Chakeres	Denham	

—And just a few of the theatres:

Palm State, Detroit	Palace, Cincinnati	Indiana, Indianapolis
Rivoli, Toledo	Franklin, Saginaw	Clazell, Bowling Green
State, Ann Arbor	Palace, Canton	Emboyd, Ft. Wayne
Regent, Battle Creek	State, E. Liverpool	Rivoli, Muncie
Regent, Bay City	Robbins, Warren	Paramount, Anderson
Palace, Flint	State, Sandusky	Tivoli, Richmond
Michigan, Jackson	Palace, Lorain	State, Springfield, O.
State, Kalamazoo	Morrison, Alliance	Paramount, Hamilton
Strand, Pontiac	Rialto, Louisville, O.	Paramount, Middletown
Palace, Cleveland		Ben Ali, Lexington, Ky.

A June 1952 trade ad announces saturation bookings for *King Kong*.

was no good trying to sell color Hollywood spectaculars on snowy and dimly lit home screens. Many star contracts had clauses forbidding them to promote films on television. Obstacles were everywhere, yet the benefits of TV advertising could not be ignored.

The essential debate revolved around who would pay for it. Distributors felt exhibitors should at the least split television's promotional cost. Why should the former bear the sole expense of customizing trailers for bite-size video use? TV spots varied from 20 to 60 seconds. Film companies dropped between $2,000 and $5,000 on preparation of same. Rates for airplay in bigger markets were beyond the reach of most exhibitors, even if distributors supplied the promos for free. At New York's WNBT, a 20-second spot commanded $775 in "A" time and $500 during so-called "B" periods when fewer viewers were watching. There were volume discounts, but to be effective, a saturation campaign had to run at least 20 to 50 spots a week in support of a feature's local engagement. It required ten days to two weeks to hammer messages into home viewers for an upcoming theatre show, and such a blitz cost thousands even in smaller territories. RKO had previously spent in excess of $10,000 on TV time for the opening of *Sudden Fear* in Boston and 25 surrounding towns.

Above: Throngs greet *Kong*'s 1952 return at the Palace Theatre on New York's Times Square following 10 days of intensive radio and TV advertising. Below: Fay Wray, the original scream queen, proves alluring to a whole new generation, but note airbrushed cleavage in this art pose.

"KING KONG" IS KING OF THE YEAR'S BOXOFFICE!

The Gold Rush is on in the Middle West . . . in HUNDREDS of theatres in five Exchange Areas, including houses like the Palm State, Detroit; Palace, Cleveland; Palace, Cincinnati; Warner, Pittsburgh, and Indiana, Indianapolis . . . as grosses are hitting undreamed-of highs . . . sometimes *double* and *triple* the business for the top "A" pictures of the past three years! . . . And theatre owners are shouting "Hallelujah!". . . Backed by the RKO brand of "go out and blow the roof off" kind of showmanship, "King Kong" is not only the 8th wonder of the world, but the miracle of miracles of show business! . . . There hasn't been anything like this since "Hitler's Children" and "Behind The Rising Sun"! . . . Get ready for the big-money bonanza in your own territory RIGHT NOW!

Re-released by
R K O
RADIO
PICTURES

The Showmanship Company

By June 28, *Kong* is a roaring King of the Box Office. It wasn't unusual to get a week's worth of business in a single day during the mighty run of *Kong*.

Exhibitors agreed that television was being "horribly neglected" as a promotional device, but no one had the answer as to equitable sharing of cost between showmen and distributors. The situation is not unlike what we see today with installation of digital projection in theatres. Who gets the tab? Besides, there was still deep suspicion of television as dangerous and harmful competition. The thought of enriching video coffers was unimaginable to theatre men who'd assigned enemy status to the upstart medium.

RKO was prepared to shoot the works and invest $200,000 into *King Kong* TV spot buying. "In a lot of places where television didn't reach, our grosses on *King Kong* were off," said RKO's exploitation head Terry Turner. "In these situations, radio saturation held up the gross. But where we had neither radio nor television, such as places in Idaho, the picture had to be pulled."

There were problems as well in those cities in which a newspaper also owned a broadcast station. Buffalo and Milwaukee TV would not accept *King Kong* trailers at all. Publishers preferred that

The regular thrill partner for the Mighty Monarch in 1952 is Val Lewton's *The Leopard Man*. The duo scores big.

RKO spend greater money selling their movie with print ads, thus the freeze-out. Box office was down in these locations as a result.

Television had become *Kong*'s handmaiden in achieving what the *Motion Picture Herald* referred to as a "phenomenal gross" that summer. "Our use of television has increased the gross at the box office anywhere from 25 to 200 percent," said RKO, adding that "where *King Kong* was supported by TV trailers, the opening day was 40 percent above normal." *Variety* described this selling strategy for *Kong* as "the first all-out venture employing TV."

RKO's idea was to go region to region with *King Kong* and saturation-play it in each. Opening on multiple screens was the only way to justify the expense of television spotting, the cost of which was many times that of newspaper and radio ads. RKO had already dropped $50,000 supporting the first five cities that got *Kong*, more than even brand-new attractions warranted. The reward was considerable, however. House records were broken, for instance, at the RKO Grand in Columbus, Ohio, where an estimated 60 percent of tickets were bought by children and teens. To this was added "sock" business in popcorn, candy, and soft drinks, these a truest profit center for any theatre. *King Kong* quickly became known as the snack bar's benefactor.

July dates further snowballed receipts to the show-world's amazement. Long-percolating talk of RKO's film library being sold for ultimate play on the DuMont television network wilted before *King Kong*'s theatrical success, Howard Hughes nixing an offer worth $14 million from would-be Canadian buyers.

Even *Kong*'s producer, Merian C. Cooper, wanted back in the game. He had, said *Variety*, "activated a new exploitation project and will put it before cameras within the next 60 days." Cooper added that filming would take place on closed sets amidst strict secrecy, though his gimmick this time "will not be a giant gorilla."

By the time *King Kong* hit New York in August, the wheels of merchandising spun with utmost efficiency. RKO's fleet of four gorilla trucks took to Gotham streets, tossing in excess of a million tabloid heralds to passers-by. There would be a Broadway open at the venerable Palace Theatre, with wider netting to 150 neighborhood venues four days after. Palace management didn't appreciate the brief exclusivity they had. In the old days, clearance policy gave first-run houses dibs on cash to the exclusion of territorial others, but with vid promotion and the necessity of reaching as many patrons as possible in a short window, past times were truly passed.

The Palace had been a vaudeville house in glory days. Old habits dying hard, they still featured live acts with screen programming. Some of these performers dated back further than *King Kong*. Management was soon to realize that the kids storming their doors were there to see the big ape, not 65 minutes of, in this case, tap dancers, singing eight-year-old triplets, and a bicycle act for the curtain, 1952 vaudeville in descent sure as Kong's plunge off the Empire State Building.

Theatres everywhere were getting, in one day, audiences representing a week's average. Trade and even mainstream press were commenting on the *King Kong* summer phenomenon. "It was recently reissued," said exhib-aimed *Harrison's Reports*, "mainly for laughs, as we understand it—and lo and behold, it is again pulling 'em into the movie houses by the thousands and tens of thousands."

Harrison's viewed *Kong* as the ticket to greater dollars for revivals in general. "This is only one case out of many in which an old picture has been dusted off for another run and has proceeded to act like a fresh new smash hit."

The big guy hooks up with sleepwalkers and hits the road for RKO one last time in 1956. But now there's a new kid on the block who isn't intimidated by Kong's size and reputation.

With domestic rentals of $1.608 million generated, the 1952 *King Kong* did indeed trump first-run RKO releases of the same year. Compare *Kong*'s figure with domestic rentals received by the following in concurrent play: *Macao* ($1.1 million), *Tarzan's Savage Fury* ($750,000), *Rancho Notorious* ($900,000), *At Sword's Point* ($950,000), and *On Dangerous Ground* ($500,000).

Kong was walloping just-released product everywhere. *Time* magazine was moved to call it Picture of the Year, even as editors snickered at ancient biplanes on view and repeated the old canard of *Kong* having saved RKO from '30s' bankruptcy.

Showmen across the nation joined the hosannas. "A fine old picture, worth playing on your best time," said Charles R. Reynolds of the Marco Theatre in Waterford, California. "Did very well at box office. Good print and new sound, and priced right."

Prints were indeed fresh, as it was necessary for RKO to use the new safety stock for 1952 engagements, but were these prints actually good? Surviving 35mm from the reissue reflect all sorts of problems connected with long-ago loss of original elements and dictates imposed by the Code, still very much in effect as of 1952. In addition to cuts made in 1938, reels were now being printed out of frame and the picture remained too dark. The new generation discovering *King Kong* had no access to the picture as it looked in 1933, and so accepted and embraced this degraded *Kong* as cultural talisman for the baby boom, a status maintained and enhanced by RKO's sale of the feature, along with 741 others, to television in 1955, with runs to begin in 1956.

To squeeze final theatrical coin out of *Kong*, RKO reissued the venerable favorite one last time on June 13, 1956, as a combo with Val Lewton's *I Walked with a Zombie*. Why would RKO place a feature back in theatres so soon after selling it to television? Turns out the strategy not only generated more admission revenue for the monster classic, but also brought *Kong* head-to-head with imported-from-Japan *Godzilla, King of the Monsters!* (the exclamation mark being theirs, not mine). We know these giants battled seven summers later when Universal issued *King Kong vs. Godzilla* for 1963 school-outers, but here was a preliminary match all but forgotten.

"Based on its excellent showing on television during the past few weeks, *King Kong* will again be released for theatrical presentation by RKO," said company vice president Walter Branson in April 1956. "It has been withdrawn from future video airings and will be released in June."

Many assumed that *King Kong* remained on airwaves once New York's WOR-TV premiered it in March 1956. The week-long run, with broadcasts every day, had been a sensation. Kids tuned into every broadcast in great numbers. "This has been the biggest thing since *Davy Crockett*," said station management.

As it turns out, only two stations nationwide played the film during spring '56. Besides WOR, there was WHBQ in Memphis, Tennessee. Both were General Teleradio outlets and affiliated with new owners of TV rights in the RKO library. *King Kong*'s enormous success among limited home viewers did not go unnoticed. Theatrical distribution rights for the backlog remained with RKO, and they'd not forgotten *Kong*'s gangbusting 1952 box office, so why not try again?

Branson announced a 116-date saturation booking for June 1956 among carefully picked California venues. As before, summer vacation was adjudged most lucrative for a show with considerable youth appeal. A Val Lewton-produced oldie would go out with *Kong* same as *The Leopard Man* had for 1952 dates. This time it was *I Walked with a Zombie*.

The combo bowed at 12 Los Angeles locations on June 27. Here were two black-and-white full-framed ratio vaulties plopped down amongst widescreen blockbusters *Trapeze* at the Beverly Wilshire and *Cinerama Holiday* at the Hollywood Warner, with *Oklahoma!* and *The Man Who Knew Too Much* continuing long runs on neighboring blocks. *The King and I* in Cinemascope-55 would open at Grauman's Chinese the day after *Kong*.

More attuned to *Kong/Zombie*'s modest proportion was a horror/sci-fi coupling that started in 18 locations the same Wednesday as the RKO's. That was *The Black Sleep* and *The Creeping Unknown*, with "Glamour Ghoul" Vampira and consort Tor Johnson making lobby appearances in four of the hardtops. Even originals *Dracula* and *Frankenstein* played two neighborhood Los Angeles theatres the same night. For such an intersection of old with new, June 27, 1956, was stellar occasion for movie going in L.A., even as *King Kong*'s determined successor waited in the wings to knock the 23-year-old monster sovereign off his throne.

Makes King Kong Look Like a Midget! screamed ads for *Godzilla, King of the Monsters!*, its arrival (July 11) in 14 Los Angeles theatres and 7 drive-ins being but two weeks behind *Kong* and *I*

194

Walked with a Zombie. The latter combo had closed after a single week with prints headed for other territories to continue the summer run-off.

Godzilla's campaign made intentions clear. Here was the proposed new king of monsters, the title's exclamation mark giving emphasis to *Kong*'s displacement by a 400-foot-tall, fire-breathing gargantuan—instead of merely punching out a train, Godzilla *eats* it.

The *King Kong/I Walked with a Zombie* parlay continued successfully through summer 1956. Pittsburgh reported the combination doing surprisingly well, despite patron knowledge that both would likely be back on television before long; others of the RKO library had meanwhile fanned out on home screens nationwide.

The 1956 RKO reissue campaign of lobby posters for *King Kong* features fresh, full-color artwork for 116-date saturation booking in California. A pairing with fellow vintage full-frame vaultie *I Walked with a Zombie* produces successful box office, despite the fact that *Kong* has already transitioned to television.

A lobby card from the 1956 reissue of *King Kong* places the big ape back on top of the world—or at least the tallest building in New York City. Returns in the summer of '56 astonish exhibitors.

"Walked in with a home-run weekend. I'm still trying to figure out what or why," said incredulous showman Donald L. Rexroad of Falconer, New York's State Theatre, "To have given this to TV when it still has this much business in it is unbelievable." Rexroad's business with *King Kong* was reported at 30 percent above average, but of co-feature *I Walked with a Zombie*, he was more reserved. "This one did not hold up its end of the program—not enough thrills and chills to keep the audience interest at the peak *King Kong* had left it." Was RKO wise to have dualled these two? *Zombie* with its subdued effect couldn't help but pale beside *Kong*'s dynamic showmanship.

Exhibitors agreed that *King Kong* was still box office after all those years, unlike numerous oldies written off as decrepit even as they were TV bound. "Don't pay too much, and you can bank well on Monday," said manager Joe Meyer of Ione, California, after a profitable *Kong* weekend.

Ballyhoo updated for '50s consumption included a mechanized *King Kong* appearing "in person" on WFBM/Indianapolis during its daytime Open House Show, where the gorilla loomed over performing rock 'n' rollers. *Godzilla, King of the Monsters!* meanwhile played numerous situations in direct competition with *King Kong*.

CHAPTER 21

UNIVERSAL MAKES BOX-OFFICE MUSIC

We assume a lot about moviegoers in the 1950s and can speculate about reaction to *The Glenn Miller Story* and others of like success, but in the end, knowing that public's mind-set amounts to less fact than guesswork, especially as more of them pass on. There is what we know for truth, borne out by *Glenn Miller* revenues the likes of which Universal-International had not amassed before.

Some of the biggest hits of then are ones we seldom speak of now. *The Glenn Miller Story* was a right attraction at a perfect moment. It got people back into theatres who'd given up movies for barbecuing and evening softball. And said prodigals brought their kids, 1954 being a year when virtually every potential customer remembered Glenn Miller and wanted to see—and even more so, hear—his life story. Universal's biopic revived memories of what was pleasant about recently past war years. Youngsters who'd courted against the backdrop of Miller melodies now attended as married couples.

Fault lines that divided teens from the musical tastes of elders were opening, but the fissures remained narrow enough for showmen to manage a family audience and enjoy consensus among pleased patrons. Who foresaw surly youth busting up prized swing records just a year later in *Blackboard Jungle*? Decca pressed a soundtrack for *The Glenn Miller Story* in tandem with the pic's release, and selections from that zoomed up *Hit Parade* charts. The late bandleader sold again just as Al Jolson had when Columbia told his story in 1946, that one being the template for Universal's go at Miller's life, warts of which were scrubbed in deference to family and fans who viewed Glenn as Mister Congeniality among music makers. And who better to play him than James Stewart at his easiest-going?

Lots prefer Jim as neurotic in accordance with modern embrace of genres darkened, his westerns and Hitchcocks exploring avenues more to misanthropic likings. *The Glenn Miller Story* is a Stewart/Anthony Mann collaboration, along with *Strategic Air Command*, that cultists put in a sack and tossed to rivers. That happened decades after *Glenn Miller* socked bigger rentals ($7.5 million domestic) than any of their other teamings.

There's no use defending its sentiment, the by-numbers rise to fame having little to do with the facts of *any* bandman's history. It was, as with Jolson, all about the music, plus that aspect of Glenn Miller's life they wouldn't fudge, his tragic end in an air crash that everyone in 1954 recalled or had heard about. This for a finish guaranteed a solid femme turnout and wrung oceans of tears to wash down tunes folks loved hearing again. *Life* magazine stunted the openings to photograph women crying as they watched *The Glenn Miller Story* that February, along with couples adrift upon clouds of romance while Stewart and perfect movie wife June Allyson renewed their screen vows.

Who needed gloves-off biopics in 1954? Those were just around the corner in any case. MGM's *Love Me or Leave Me* of the next year was unrelentingly harsh, and *I'll Cry Tomorrow* from the same company added jiggers of alcohol to a getting-toxic mix. *The Glenn Miller Story* plays like pabulum beside these—and never mind ones further down the line. Nothing unpleasant happens short of Miller's plane going down, and that takes place offscreen. Stops are out, however, for Allyson's response. Here is grief clinically enacted by an actress for whom such display was the expected highlight of all her performances, a trio of which co-starred Stewart. People still attended movies in 1954 to weep as much as to laugh. Universal saw that reaffirmed in their other blockbuster from the same year, *Magnificent Obsession*.

Greater frustration lies in *The Glenn Miller Story*'s dawdling on the titular figure's slow climb to fame. A first half and part of the second is more about reverses and pawnshop detours, these forestalling songs we're there to hear. Best perhaps to tune in for its last 40 or so minutes, because that's where most all the Miller standards get loving recital. How potent a shot of adrenalin did his music get for being heard again here? An eBay search reveals multiple soundtrack releases through what remained of the '50s. There were albums, extended-play 45s, and Decca's stereo reissue of its platter in 1956. The film would become an object of movie-going nostalgia, as Universal happily discovered in 1959 when a Sindlinger & Co. poll revealed *The Glenn Miller Story* as the U-I backlog picture audiences most wanted back in theatres.

The survey was taken to measure the viability of reissues against the tempting alternative of television sale. Rival companies were gearing up for post-'48 surrender to the one-eyed monster and

This special one-sheet and corresponding trade ad tie into classic musicals and also call attention to the Glenn Miller Orchestra tunes that can be heard in the picture.

exhibs were apoplectic. Hadn't Universal been the small theatre's best friend? Now they looked for the company to stem a coming tide of recent features to home screens and promised favorable dates if only U-I would share vaulties with them rather than TV stations.

Sindlinger spent four weeks canvassing venues large and small to determine which Universal oldies, among 53 potential titles fielded, patrons would spring admissions to reacquaint with. Perhaps numbers got inflated for publicity's sake, but 23 million were said to want another round of *Glenn Miller*. Bosley Crowther doubted such a figure, and said so in a New York *Times* column, but millions of votes put U-I in full-blast selling mode, its energy on the pic's behalf being equal to that applied toward new releases.

A New York trade press luncheon saw Universal execs bandying estimates of $3.5 million in fresh rentals to come, plus claims they'd spend more pushing *Glenn Miller*'s revival than was expended for recent hit *Pillow Talk*. "If the picture were made today, it couldn't be improved upon," said marketers, so labs got out 100 new prints, and a rush was on for bookings starting March 1960.

By the time *The Glenn Miller Story* penetrated theatres, Warner Bros. was closing deals for many of its post-'48 biggest hits, and 20th Century Fox would follow suit with its own historic *NBC Saturday Night at the Movies* deal the following year. Television barn doors would thus open in 1960–61, and even *The Glenn Miller Story*, for all a public's willingness to come see it again in theatres, would be announced for airwave availability in December 1963.

Above: Music sells the picture and is tied into an in-house disc jockey talent show. Below: The soundtrack, also featuring Louis Armstrong, helps to put people in the mood.

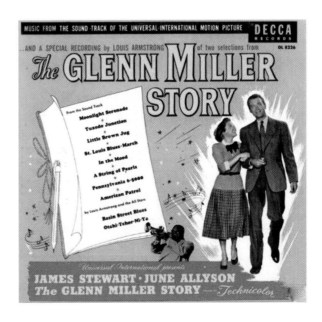

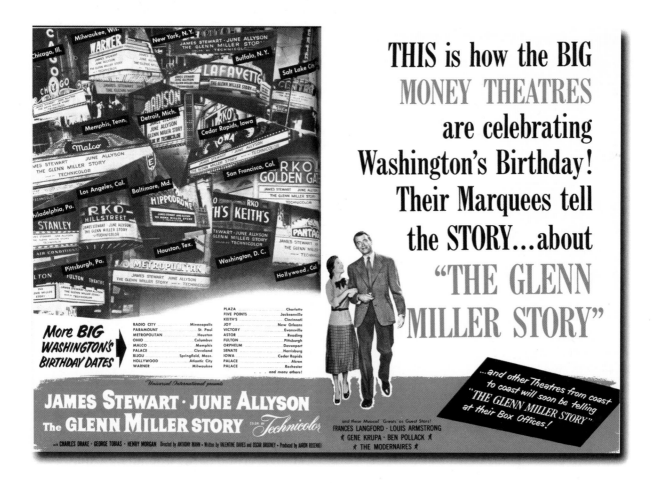

THIS is how the BIG MONEY THEATRES are celebrating Washington's Birthday! Their Marquees tell the STORY...about "THE GLENN MILLER STORY"

More BIG WASHINGTON'S BIRTHDAY DATES

RADIO CITY	Minneapolis	PLAZA	Charlotte
PARAMOUNT	St. Paul	FIVE POINTS	Jacksonville
METROPOLITAN	Houston	KEITH'S	Cincinnati
OHIO	Columbus	JOY	New Orleans
MALCO	Memphis	VICTORY	Evansville
PALACE	Cleveland	ASTOR	Reading
BIJOU	Springfield, Mass.	FULTON	Pittsburgh
HOLLYWOOD	Atlantic City	ORPHEUM	Davenport
WARNER	Milwaukee	SENATE	Harrisburg
		IOWA	Cedar Rapids
		PALACE	Akron
		PALACE	Rochester

. . . . and many others!

...and other Theatres from coast to coast will soon be telling "THE GLENN MILLER STORY" at their Box Offices!

Universal International presents
JAMES STEWART · JUNE ALLYSON
The GLENN MILLER STORY color by Technicolor

and these Musical "Greats" as Guest Stars!
FRANCES LANGFORD · LOUIS ARMSTRONG
★ GENE KRUPA · BEN POLLACK ★
★ THE MODERNAIRES ★

with CHARLES DRAKE · GEORGE TOBIAS · HENRY MORGAN Directed by ANTHONY MANN · Written by VALENTINE DAVIES and OSCAR BRODNEY · Produced by AARON ROSENBERG

Above: Showmen learn how to warm a winter's campaign in 1954.
Right: In 1960, *The Glenn Miller Story* still pushes the music, but this time in support of an animated feature starring the voices of Art Linkletter and Sandra Dee.

There was one more theatrical reissue for *The Glenn Miller Story*, a surprising 25 years after Universal's 1960 rollout. James Stewart had worked compatibly with the studio's sales force merchandising a package of Alfred Hitchcock features into theatres for 1983, and it was the actor who proposed *The Glenn Miller Story*'s encore as possible follow-up.

Stewart remembered stereo tracks having been recorded in 1954 and felt these might now be a lure for paying crowds to hear the venerable show as never before. A scouring of studio vaults bore little fruit, however, and it looked as though Stewart had been mistaken, and that Decca's song masters for the '50s soundtrack albums would be as close as they'd come to a stereo *Glenn Miller*. According to Universal publicity, a late-in-the-day pass through a Chicago storage depot yielded a hitherto unknown recording of the entire feature and the basis for an all-encompass-

GRAND STARTS TODAY! DOORS OPEN 12:30

YOUR HEART WILL SOAR THROUGH THE MIRACLE, MAGICAL, MUSICAL, MUSICAL LAND OF IMAGINATION!
THE BELOVED STORY-TELLER'S BEST-LOVED TALE... FOR ALL AGES OF THE HEART!

Hans Christian Andersen's THE SNOW QUEEN
ART LINKLETTER
SANDRA DEE
TOMMY KIRK
PATTY McCORMACK

A FULL-LENGTH FEATURE CARTOON IN RADIANT COLOR!

PLUS FOR YOUR RE-ENJOYMENT!
There's no music like the GLENN MILLER Music!

CHATTANOOGA CHOO CHOO
IN THE MOOD
MOONLIGHT SERENADE
STRING OF PEARLS
TUXEDO JUNCTION
and ALL THE GREAT GLENN MILLER MUSIC!

JAMES STEWART
JUNE ALLYSON Technicolor
The GLENN MILLER STORY

with CHARLES DRAKE·GEORGE TOBIAS·HENRY MORGAN and these Musical "Greats" as Guest Stars!
FRANCES LANGFORD·LOUIS ARMSTRONG·GENE KRUPA·BEN POLLACK·THE MODERNAIRES

Above left: Cue the tears. As seen in a card from the lobby set, Jimmy Stewart as a sanitized Glenn Miller is about to board the fateful plane. Above right: More than 30 years after production of the picture, Allyson and Stewart reunite in France. Below: The 1985 reissue campaign of *The Glenn Miller Story* places Dolby audio enhancement front and center, and features poster graphics like nothing that could have been produced in 1954, but audiences fail to respond.

ing Dolby mix. It seemed unlikely that a '50s feature could be tendered to TV-saturated customers. In this case, the discovery of this multichannel track became justification to go forward with theatrical dates.

Fresh poster art emphasized Dolby enhancement, and Universal got its refurbished *The Glenn Miller Story* a berth at the Cannes Film Festival held in May 1985. Stewart brought leading lady June Allyson along to thump for what both referred to as a "personal favorite," receiving 20 minutes' ovation at the fest unspooling.

The reception at Cannes encouraged the pair's continued touring with *The Glenn Miller Story*, Stewart presumably greased with a profit share per his original '50s deal with U-I, but black ink would not flow. A miserable $79,342 in domestic rentals was all this reissue could muster. Twenty years of televised access to *The Glenn Miller Story* had taken a toll in spite of stereophonic refreshment.

Sal Mineo and James Dean star in *Rebel
Without a Cause*. Within months Dean's
star will rise high, above his grave.

CHAPTER 22

WARNER BROS. AND THE JAMES DEAN CULT

Two-thirds of James Dean's starring work in films was yet to be released when he died on September 30, 1955. The only evidence of his fame was *East of Eden*, and that success led to one-sheets prepared for *Rebel Without a Cause* in which Dean was tagged "Overnight Sensation," with a future assured of playing leads. Never before had a star departed so prematurely. Rudolph Valentino rose, peaked, and began his decline before death intervened and conferred immortality. *Son of the Sheik* followed and became a rallying point for fans bereaved.

Youth snuffed out was, is, and always will be the stuff of morbid fascination for surviving youth. They'll not be denied a last glimpse. MGM would have shelved the unfinished *Saratoga* but for letters begging a screen farewell for Jean Harlow. Reviving her older films wouldn't do. Viewers wanted to ponder her closer to the end. The problem was collecting admission for such autopsies without appearing ghoulish.

That high wire is traversed yet when expensive projects lose a principal just before completion or release. Warner Bros. might well have dug out their Dean files when Heath Ledger died suddenly in January 2008, for what was this but corporate history repeating itself? Would *The Dark Knight* have proved such a smash had Ledger lived? There were ginger steps over how to sell it. Director Terry Gilliam called WB "white sharks" shamelessly capitalizing on the young actor's passing.

There's no easy out in merchandising when a thing like this happens. For all the acclaim given his performance in *The Dark Knight*, it seems unlikely that Heath Ledger will become a death cult figure on the order of James Dean. Times and circumstances are different. The mad rush for Dean echoed the frenzied reaction to Valentino's exit, even as that 1926 event flashed hotter—with near riots as he lay in state—and burned out quicker. Dean's built over months after September 30, was nourished with fresh product, and lasted longer; *Rebel Without a Cause* arrived in theatres soon after his death; *Giant* saw release a year afterward, followed by *The James Dean Story* in 1957.

Dean was his own best advance man for the romance of sudden death. "It's fast and clean and you go out in a blaze of glory," he said when reporters raised the possibility of early demise on a racetrack. And what of disquieting poses he'd struck when it seemed photographers recorded his every waking moment? Peering through a noose or nested in a casket, Dean looked intent on getting to the other side, as if a ticket to cult immortality had already been purchased and he was just waiting to cash it in.

Plenty of omens creeped out viewers in hindsight. Dean appeared with Gig Young on behalf of traffic safety in a spot intended for *Warner Brothers Presents*, the ABC series that played for a single season in 1955–56. It was part of a segment promoting *Rebel Without a Cause* and was filmed on September 17, 1955, but never televised. Two other promotions featuring *Rebel* players were broadcast on *Warner Brothers Presents* (Natalie Wood on October 11 and Jim Backus on November 1), but the Dean footage was shelved and not seen until it was included in *The James Dean Story*, released nearly two years later.

James Dean attended a preview of *Rebel Without a Cause* within hours of doing the safety spot. Warners' campaign was progressing and made references to Dean in present and future tenses. A new star was born, and there would be many triumphs to come. By October, however, those one-sheets were being sniped over with regards to Dean becoming the star of the year, little realizing that he'd become precisely that within a few short months, despite events of September 30, 1955.

The *Motion Picture Herald*'s Selling Approach column tried putting showmen at ease: "We believe that because James Dean was killed in an automobile accident a few weeks ago is no reason why his success as a star should not go on. Don't encourage your audience or any others to have any such qualms. It is one of the utterly mistaken notions of our industry—so let's keep his talent alive on our screens!"

This was November 5, and *Rebel* was filling houses everywhere it played.

Establishment critics, meanwhile, weren't giving Dean a pass just because he'd died. Bosley Crowther at the New York *Times* cited monotonous Brando-imitating among *Rebel* players, JD not excepted. Reported the *Motion Picture Herald*: "The perceived apathetic attitude of the American public toward motion pictures inspired

**Top: Natalie Wood and James Dean in *Rebel*.
Above: With tongue in cheek, the Dean of foreshadowing talks traffic safety with Gig Young.**

a group of Allied Theatre owners to launch their so-called Audience Awards," ballots for which would be filled out in lobbies and tallied by showmen.

The "Audies" were essentially grassroot Oscars, a democratic alternative to votes cast by Academy insiders. Elections held during fall box-office doldrums would culminate in a television spectacular (that never happened) comparable in its impact to the Academy Awards presentation, followed by bookings for winner films during notoriously slow pre-Christmas weeks. Among those selected for Audies were Tab Hunter as Most Promising Personality in *Battle Cry* and months-departed James Dean as Best Actor for *East of Eden*, the latter of which took WB unawares. "When I attempted to book *East of Eden* for a repeat run, I was advised that it had been withdrawn from distribution," complained one exhibitor.

A rush order went out to place more James Dean at nationwide theatres' disposal. On December 17, Warners announced a reissue double-bill for *East of Eden* with *Battle Cry*, its first recognition of a posthumous surge. Incoming letters rose to 8,000 a month, many asking for Dean bric-a-brac. Anxious teens sought the red zippered jacket Jim wore in *Rebel Without a Cause*. When studio replies suggested it could be had for $22.95 from Mattson's Hollywood clothier, which had

Dean, seen here in *East of Eden*, becomes shooting star of the year after his September 30 flame-out. One industry mag coaches showmen that a little thing like Dean's death "is no reason why his success as a star should not go on." Warner Bros. and theatres across the nation will embrace this concept for two years.

supplied the original, kids made a run on the place. Dean ranked #1 on *Photoplay*'s popularity poll by spring 1956, and high school students in 32 cities picked the late star as their fave.

The run-up to *Giant* was becoming feverish. Director George Stevens took his usual forever editing that long, long feature, trying cultists' patience. Warnings were issued that he'd best not cut a frame of Dean's performance.

"It's absolutely weird," said the veteran helmsman. *Rebel Without a Cause* meanwhile not only maintained but was doing splendid repeat business. Eventual profits of $3.374 million against a modest negative cost of $1.4 million put it right behind WB's biggest hits of 1955, *Mister Roberts* and *Battle Cry*. With *Giant* in the much-anticipated offing, was it any wonder so many Dean followers refused to believe he was really dead?

"A weird new phenomenon is loose in the land," said *Time* magazine on September 3, 1956 (the none-too-flattering article was called "Dean of the One-Shotters"). It seemed Dean-mania was getting out of hand. Mainstream bastions took note and were unanimous in their disapproval.

Showmen distribute heralds trumpeting *Rebel Without a Cause* not knowing that in short order, Dean will be a sensation for much more than *East of Eden*.

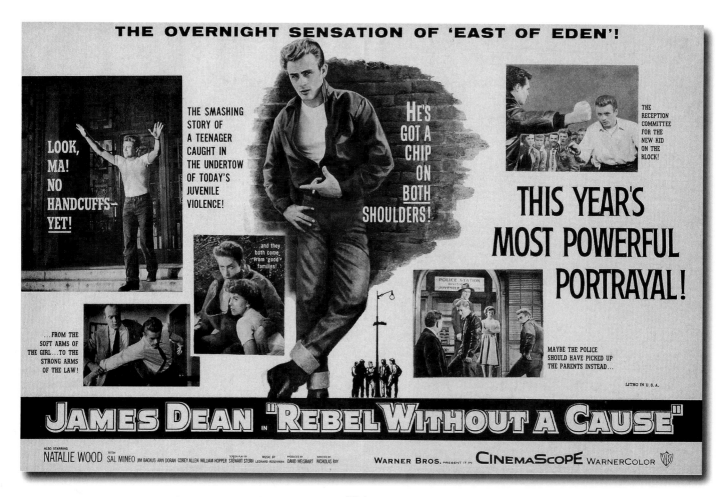

"The bandwagon that looks disconcertingly like a hearse" mirrored concern with an overlay of withering sarcasm. These were journalists, after all, who'd been in the game for years and weren't about to be taken in by such morbid folly. "This is really something new in Hollywood—Boy meets Ghoul." Were these publishers as miffed over rival magazines selling out aforementioned one-shot tributes to Dean?

Ezra Goodman reported for *Life*. "Delirium for Dead Star" headlined his condemnation of Dean-inspired excesses. By September 24, 1956, when the article was published, others joined the debate. Humphrey Bogart had spoken previously for an establishment Hollywood ready to apply the brakes. "If he had lived, he'd never have been able to live up to his publicity," said the actor.

Sick of it all, George Stevens minced fewer words as *Giant*'s premiere drew close, and he realized many were looking to his epic for a Jimmy fix and little else: "A few more films and the public wouldn't have been so bereft. He shortly would have dimmed his luster." All this as loosely hinged fans insisted their idol walked among us yet. Was Jimmy hiding out in Mexico to conceal disfiguring injuries sustained in the accident? Those sufficiently gullible could hope.

Grown-ups expressed concern now that *Time* and *Life* sounded their majority's alarm. Shouldn't Warner Bros. be engaged in healthier enterprise? A still breathing, if overworked, Tab Hunter suggested they might, as two 1956 releases proposed that ersatz heir to Dean's following and box office. Tab, however, lacked

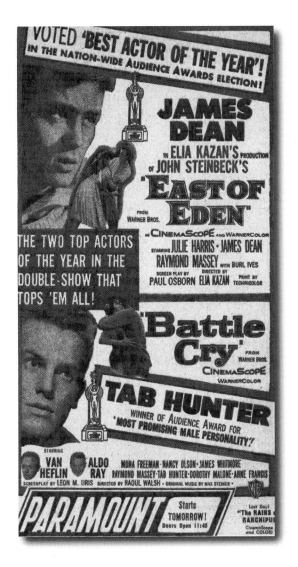

The rush teaming of Dean and Tab Hunter serves as first acknowledgment of "a weird phenomenon loose in the land."

JD's intensity and tragic grandeur. His dreamboat was no substitute for Dean's storm-tossed dramatics, despite the promising *Battle Cry*, and besides, Tab showed all intentions of staying alive to enjoy the underpaying benefits of Warner stardom. *The Burning Hills* and *The Girl He Left Behind* borrowed Dean's co-star and hopeful good-luck charm Natalie Wood to play opposite Hunter, her *Rebel Without a Cause* appearance in the foreground of publicity for both.

A sadder would-be successor to Dean was nakedly ambitious Nick Adams, his wholehearted immersion in the JD cult raising not a few eyebrows within industry circles. There were two fan magazine tributes under his byline, for which Nick relished his mail going up by 200 letters a week after the first magazine was published. They'd been close, you see. Jim left Nick poems he'd written, plus scarves, shirts, and belts, none of which the latter was disposed to share with fans. "I sleep with a loaded .32 automatic and a .45 automatic in my house," said Adams. "I keep all the stuff hid-

Above: Contracts with Rock Hudson and Elizabeth Taylor be damned; showmen drive Dean to the head of the bill. Below left: An already weird situation gets a lot more so when Nick Adams enters the mix and reveals how close he had been to Dean, even hauling all his JD mementos down from a "big strong steel box locked in the attic" to pose for photographers. Adams' popularity skyrockets. Below right: When the head of James Dean is removed from a display for *Giant* in Minneapolis, the local authorities post a detective and warnings. New patrons flock to the Radio City Theatre to find out what this Dean fuss is all about.

den in a big strong steel box locked in the attic." Adams hauled the bounty downstairs to pose Dean-like with his treasures: "I have police protection," he added. "The cops check my house eight to ten times a day."

Giant would open in October 1956, but theatres and drive-ins toward the back of the line made do with limited engagements Warners permitted of *Rebel Without a Cause* with *East of Eden*. James Dean photos came with admissions to many of these, and showmen noted grosses equivalent to first-run business. October also saw the release of soundtracks via MGM Records with Art Mooney and his Orchestra playing music from Dean films. "If we know the teenagers, they will go for it, by the millions," said the *Motion Picture Herald*. Warner Bros. meanwhile soft-pedaled JD in *Giant* publicity. The pressbook referred to him, as before, in the present tense. You'd never know the actor had died after reading press releases the studio had prepared.

Giant looked to audiences far beyond membership of the Dean cult, whatever that group's anxiety to see it. Contracted billing required Elizabeth Taylor and Rock Hudson in favored positions, but theatremen knew where their bread was buttered; thus, marquees brazenly sold Dean as main attraction. Newspaper ads were as culpable. Dean's image alone represented *Giant* in many of them, plus his name was often elevated above Taylor's and Hudson's. This sort of exhibitor free-styling was commonplace, as everyone sought to cash in on the Dean wave at its height.

Boxoffice magazine divined reality in its October 13 review and spelled things out for whoever booked *Giant*: "It is the presence and popularity of James Dean that will prove the most potent factor in attracting ticket buyers, particularly from the teenage groups." Discomfort over a phenomenon bordering on psychosis was offset by prospects of cash in the till. "It is his name that will bring the bobby-soxers in droves and will stimulate them into seeing the picture time and time again."

Sure enough, it *was* teens pulling four hours of *Giant* on repeated shifts. Bolder Dean devotees liberated poster materials out front, valuable publicity in itself for some situations. The Radio City Theatre in Minneapolis found its *Giant* display minus a James Dean head one morning, prompting rewards to be paid upon its return and placement of a sheriff's detective to guard a replacement bally. The warning sign they posted was enticement to both purloining fans and those who'd not yet paid admission to see what all the fuss was about.

Dean's relatives were dragged off Indiana farms to thump on *Giant*'s behalf. His

When showmen aren't able to book *Giant*, they settle for a limited engagement of *East of Eden* and *Rebel Without a Cause*. Some hand out a photo of the late star with every admission.

aunt, uncle, and a cousin showed up at an Indianapolis drive-in opening in late November and were duly recognized for service to the trade. It seemed a departed James Dean had no peer, let alone competition, for first placement among teen idols. That would change and soon, as many theatres coming off *Giant* play dates changed marquees to herald their next attraction—Elvis Presley and *Love Me Tender*.

It took Elvis to wash away tears we'd shed over the loss of James Dean. *Love Me Tender* began the healing with saturation bookings in November 1956. Unlike Warners' slow rollout of *Giant*, Elvis and company surged in with a record for 20th Century Fox—500 prints to make sure everyone wanting Presley got him then and there.

Love Me Tender came into many theatres right behind *Giant*, and lines announced youth's embrace of a fresh deity. Should 1956 Hollywood go forward with that proposed Dean biopic, why not let Elvis play Jimmy? It was considered, perhaps not seriously, but few concepts flew higher than a newly minted sensation enacting another just departed. Presley was a known Dean acolyte, but too fresh and untried a face to assume the burden of a posthumous image darkening with sad and sadder stories of how life and people had let Jimmy down.

"Kansas City filmmaker" Robert Altman—so identified by the trades—went in search of loner Dean with scriptwriter George W. George in a spec documentary project they'd begun in November 1956. *The James Dean Story* was, so far, 65 minutes of profile and interviews with Jim's relatives in Indiana. Months passed with bankrolls depleted by $20,000 as Altman and George shopped their project around for distribution. Would the Dean cult last as long as these two would take setting up a deal?

TV networks were better able to strike while Dean irons simmered. "He's hotter than

Above: A flip book available to showmen features the Chicken Run sequence from *Rebel*, with Dean behind the wheel defying death. Below: Proving that bad taste knows no millennium, the exhibitor at New York's Virginian Theatre takes a new approach to selling James Dean by serving up a smorgasbord of Abbott & Costello, the 3 Stooges, and Dracula live on stage "direct from Hollywood," plus the promise of Dean's ghost summoned from the grave. Predictably, the teenaged crowd grows rowdy before the end of the marathon.

218

anybody alive!" said one NBC exec. That web was repeating a *Robert Montgomery Presents* that Dean had done with Ed Begley and Dorothy Gish called *Harvest*, while CBS was giving third broadcast go-round to *The Unlighted Road*, a *Playhouse of the Stars* episode featuring Dean. CBS also reran *I'm a Fool* with Natalie Wood among Jim's support. All these were scheduled during a Dean-heavy month of November, 1956, when old anthology product with the actor regularly Trendex-trounced competing stations.

"All three shows exploited Dean's legend for frankly commercial purposes," said *Time*, but as any JD footage was so many ribbons of gold, how could you blame networks for mining them?

Warners, meanwhile, noted awards and nominations still coming Dean's way. Golden Globes went to him and Kim Novak in March 1957, while the Academy tabbed Jimmy among possible Best Actors for his work in *Giant*. It was time for WB to get serious about their backlog. No more limited engagements and catch-as-catch-can bookings for *East of Eden* and *Rebel Without a Cause*.

the hottest name* in show business today is yours for thanksgiving from 20th century-fox!

RICHARD EGAN
DEBRA PAGET
and introducing *ELVIS PRESLEY in
LOVE ME TENDER
CinemaScope
co-starring
ROBERT MIDDLETON · WILLIAM CAMPBELL · NEVILLE BRAND
Produced by DAVID WEISBART · Directed by ROBERT D. WEBB

Fox assures that its Thanksgiving release will be no turkey, and suddenly the James Dean phenomenon peaks.

"In response to the overwhelming demand," said ads, both would be reissued with a new campaign for nationwide combo runs in 1957. "Let kids pose with a Dean standee," said new pressbooks. "Tie in with local photog or use personal camera. Offer free pictures between 5 and 7 P.M."

Still taboo was mention of the actor's death in publicity. "A psychologist or member of the clergy could give talks at the theatre on the meaning of James Dean to teenagers" was the closest they'd come to dealing with the cult and its cultural ramifications—but what right-minded showman would furnish a lectern for such?

Flip-books of the Chicken Run sequence from *Rebel Without a Cause* were made available to whet darker patron appetites, while taglines trumpeted the Academy nomination for *Giant*. *Eden/Rebel* played percentage and fattened many an exhibitor's purse, in addition to enabling recent Dean converts to catch up with his limited output.

As time passed, Dean cultism faded toward the margins. Kids were ready to ease up and have a little fun with it. Enter the spook showman. If fans were so eager to bring Jimmy back, well, that could be arranged. New York's Virginian Theatre offered "The Materialization of James Dean" as part of a stage show wherein JD shared residency with Count Dracula in a so-called house of the living dead. So much for respectful tribute. The press reported a teen girl found slumped and writhing in her seat in the wake of shock and convulsions sustained during the show's climax. Two male rowdies had been fighting in an adjacent aisle and one of them kicked her in the head while the lights were out. All this followed said materialization, which consisted wholly of the showing of an illuminated photograph of Dean's face during one of innumerable blackouts.

Hooliganism became an increasing problem as youth patrons emulated antisocial behavior they observed on screens playing *Blackboard Jungle*, American-International delinquency pics, and yes, *Rebel Without a Cause*. Increasingly raucous spook rallies did little to restore calm. A dozen uniformed NYC police were on hand to quell the effects of electric shocks, face-slapping from invisible hands, and a roving gorilla named Gargantua at one spook rally. Ushers with luminous-painted features chased up, down, and between rows as horrific screen attractions unspooled.

Others prepared meanwhile to exploit gothic possibilities of ongoing Dean fascination. Faded-from-airwaves Maila Nurmi (a.k.a. Vampira) saw profit potential in her one-time association with JD. They'd been friends, maybe more, she implied. Anyhow, the Dean factor fleshed out an act gone stale on fading memories of Vampira's single year hosting horrors on Los Angeles television, and she'd make the most of it. Maila claimed to be in communication with Dean beyond the veil, and was not averse to on-stage discussions regarding the black magic curse she'd placed on the departed actor for having spurned her.

Said Maila, "Jimmy's fans called out to me: 'Did you kill him?' I didn't answer them."

The Vampira act was useful adjunct to shilling she'd done up and down the California coast during April 1957 for United Artists' double-chiller bill of *Voodoo Island* and *Pharoah's Curse*. The restless spirit of James Dean was now inexorably linked with carny-inspired freak fairs and low-budget horror-thons. All this as someone else won the Academy Award for which he'd been nominated.

Sensing perhaps a need to dignify, if not honor, Dean's memory, Warner Bros. lent support to a worthy (at last) gesture in his name. California's blackest year from the standpoint of traffic deaths was recorded in 1956. An exhibitor who was also Public Information Director for

Vampira is a well-known horror hostess and alleged intimate of James Dean. Had it been her black-magic curse that killed him? She might tell you, upon paid admission.

the California Traffic Safety Foundation submitted a script to WB for a short subject highlighting the problem. Would they consider making a public service film with *Cheyenne*'s Clint Walker as onscreen host? Television division exec William T. Orr volunteered studio resources for a subject that would ultimately go to National Screen for distribution. One hundred fifty California first-runs got it free for a week beginning June 26, 1957, with drive-ins and other venues to follow after the July 4 holiday.

Within that week, another Presley feature opened. *Loving You* would further chip away at Dean's youth idol preeminence. An Elvis craze was sweeping the country, and it was bigger than Jim's ever was. *Jailhouse Rock* would be along in October with the promise of many more to come.

Warners had, meanwhile, dragged its feet committing to distribution for Robert Altman and George W. George's documentary. *The James Dean Story* was finally announced for WB release in June 1957, but they'd first need to polish it up with studio sheen missing from the barely more than an hour's content sub-

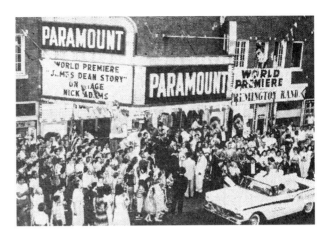

Above: The world premiere of *The James Dean Story* coincides with the end of the Dean cult cycle. Below: Soon, *Dean Story* is supporting *A Face in the Crowd*.

mitted by the Kansas City filmmakers. A musical score was added and rocker of the moment Tommy Sands sang a theme tune, *Let Me Be Loved*, penned by veterans Jay Livingston and Ray Evans. A heavy score by Leith Stevens and doom-laden narration by actor Martin Gabel emphasized the downer aspects of Dean's life, as though early death was, for him, just another sad chapter laid atop those many preceding it. Warners fleshed out the running time to 83 minutes with screen tests Dean had made for *East of Eden* and at last permitted public scrutiny of that road-safety spot with Gig Young intended for *Warner Brothers Presents*.

There would be an August 13, 1957 near-hometown premiere for *The James Dean Story* at the Paramount Theatre in Marion, Indiana. The state governor and Indiana's U.S. senator were in attendance. Ever-ready Nick Adams flew in from Hollywood, and opening festivities were coordinated with the annual county fair in full swing. A huge night parade featured school bands, saddle clubs, girl and boy scouts, plus the Strategic Air Command in flight. Nick Adams, then-reigning Miss Fairmount, and other dignitaries visited Dean's old high school and his grave, with a barbecue for

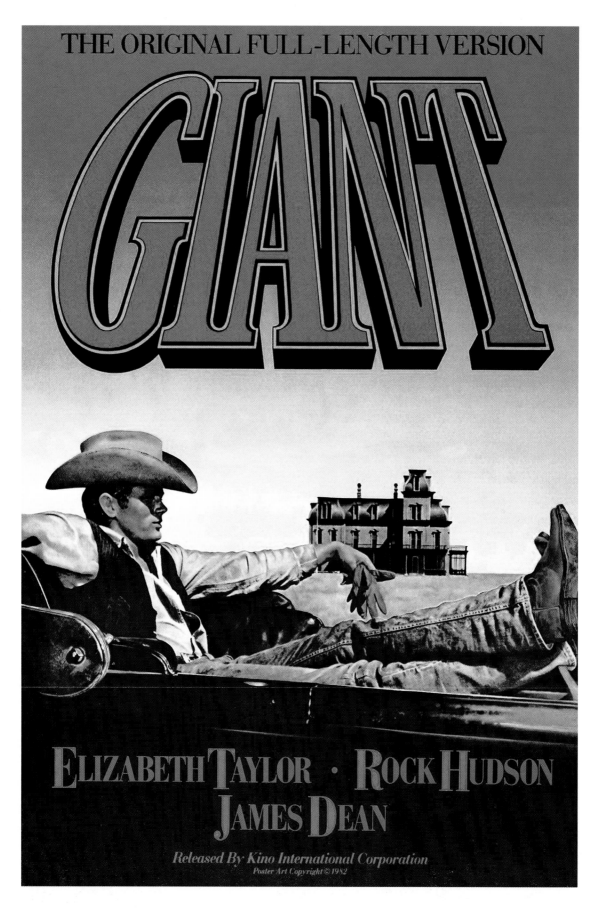

all capping festivities at the Winslow Farm where Jimmy had lived with his aunt and uncle. A 12-foot monument unveiled for the premiere may or may not still be standing, though WB presumably stood good on its pledge to donate opening proceeds to a Fairmount school for aspiring actors.

Seventy-three Indiana theatres played *The James Dean Story* after its regional premiere. Then business fell off. Hindsight suggests Warners waited too long to get the documentary out. New York's double feature playdate at the Paramount Theatre found *The James Dean Story* supporting *The Black Scorpion*, while other situations put it in second position behind *A Face in the Crowd*.

Time's review was expectedly dismissive: "It exploits a ghoulish clamor for Dean's voice to echo once more from the grave, but it does so with a mortician's lugubrious solicitude for the living."

Soft domestic rentals of $335,000 for *The James Dean Story* suggested a cult having run its course. Warners' modest pickup cost of $50,000 assured they'd get a profit, and that in the end amounted to $200,000. This would be the third and last James Dean release since his death. There was nothing left to sell.

By mid-1958, WB had Jimmy's dramatic successor launched in a western slated originally for Dean. *The Left-Handed Gun* is one of those films where you can shut your eyes or ears and summon up JD doing the lead. Paul Newman, as Billy the Kid, had an early career enacting parts Dean might have enjoyed if not for 9/30/55. The two even screen-tested together for *East of Eden*. Would Warners have given Newman such late '50s opportunity with Dean still living?

The sad dispersal of *East of Eden* and *Rebel Without a Cause* to televised oblivion happened in summer 1960. Both were dumped into late shows and 90-minute berths nationwide. For these two features carefully composed for Cinemascope projection, the loss was especially ruinous. It would be years before either would be seen properly by audiences discovering Dean.

Giant was television-withheld for ongoing theatrical reissues. The first of these in 1963 played Dean's participation way down. The trailer spotted him fleetingly and near unrecognizably in a scene where he's covered with oil. That seven-years-later campaign was all about "Liz and Rock," with their names towering high in previews. Why promote Dean and give emphasis to the fact you're peddling an old movie?

The cult of yore was surely a spent thing by 1963. It would echo, if faintly, when Warners' 1970 reissue trailer appeared. By then, a nation of disaffected youth had thrown its net over most filmland product, as witness narration: "The star who became a legend, who spoke for all the restless young as no one has before or since."

Domestic rental take for *Giant* that year was $539,000. Marketing of *Giant* since has been given over altogether to Dean's image. Kino's 1982 reissue featured him alone on its one-sheet, while Warners DVD distribution finds *Giant* absorbed into a boxed-set tribute to the actor.

Opposite page: The iconic James Dean will emerge by the 1982 Kino reissue, and *Giant* will be remembered as *his* picture and not that of higher-billed stars Rock Hudson and Elizabeth Taylor.

This unretouched photo shows just how fair-skinned and sun-sensitive Doris Day has always been. Rex Harrison, meanwhile, displays a roadmap of hard living on his 52-year-old face.

CHAPTER 23

I CALL IT "FASHION NOIR"

I don't know if success ever spoiled Ross Hunter, but it certainly blew his critical reputation. He's the producer that Douglas Sirk was said to have risen above to give us *All That Heaven Allows* and *Imitation of Life*, while his *Portrait in Black* and *Midnight Lace* rank high among Bad Movies We Love.

Will latter-day cultists ever come to embrace Hunter's signature Fashion Noir? He had a determinedly superficial concept of what movies should be. "I gave audiences what they wanted—a chance to dream, to live vicariously, to see beautiful women, jewels, gorgeous clothes, melodrama."

So how are legacies preserved upon such craven appeal to lower appetites? Hunter never cared. His was the sensibility of a movie fan turned loose to make the sort of movies *other* fans dreamed of seeing. I'm not ashamed to watch his shows and thoroughly enjoy them. You can have the camp readings and ironic overlays too, for I'll take my Ross Hunter straight up and leave deeper insight to academics and postmodernists.

I showed *Midnight Lace* to girlfriend Ann in secure knowledge she'd like those very things Hunter listed above, and it having been 1968 since I last saw it, we both waited in suspense for the would-be killer to be unmasked. This clearly isn't Hitchcock, but such things as *Midnight Lace* and *Portrait in Black* offer much by way of simple pleasure others might dismiss as trash wallowing. How much expectation should you bring to any picture whose credits read "Gowns by…" and "Jewels by…"?

A Ross Hunter story was always secondary to lifestyles he celebrated. Having taught English in high schools, he applied just enough polish to flatter that level of his targeted audience—women, teens, and so-called young adults. Hunter had a teacher's good sense to know these were about the only groups still buying tickets to movies by 1960. The sun was setting upon an industry's outreach to a fan-driven, glamour-for-its-own-sake public. Soon enough, they'd be gone to the counterculture, and sensibilities like Ross Hunter's would perish with the transition.

By 1970 and his last big hit, *Airport*, the producer himself would represent old Hollywood in graceful retreat, his exit, like that of Doris Day, Lana Turner, Sandra Dee, and all the rest who'd made his output so much fun, being seen as the necessary giving way of a discredited old to make way for a knowing and more sophisticated new.

It's no good watching *Portrait in Black* right after *Vertigo*—both being suspense thrillers set, and at least partially shot, in San Francisco. You'll be let down, but then again, maybe not. As with all Ross

HOLD YOUR SUMMER PLAYING TIME FOR THIS HOT ONE FROM UNIVERSAL!

LANA TURNER · ANTHONY QUINN · SANDRA DEE · JOHN SAXON

CO-STARRING
LLOYD NOLAN · RAY WALSTON · VIRGINIA GREY · RICHARD BASEHART
as "Matthew Cabot" ANNA MAY WONG
AND ALSO STARRING

Directed by MICHAEL GORDON
Screenplay by IVAN GOFF and BEN ROBERTS
Produced by ROSS HUNTER

A ROSS HUNTER PRODUCTION

Portrait in Black
IN EASTMAN COLOR!

THE STARS OF
"IMITATION OF

THE PRODU
DIRECTOR
OF "PILLOW T

Above: A trade ad captures the Ross Hunter formula in a nutshell: stylish coiffures, perfect makeup, simulated sex, and breathless shock. Below: Ross Hunter ogles Lana Turner.

Hunter, you must surrender before you can enjoy. *Vertigo*, indeed much of Hitchcock, takes endurance and commitment.

Portrait in Black has all the comfort of an electric blanket with sugared donuts besides. You consume, and maybe come away a little sullied, but it was pure pleasure being there, and what's more engaging than a movie one can feel so superior to? Balls-out melodrama is a necessary corrective to excesses of civility we get from pictures that critics like. Give me confrontation, faces slapped, and pistols in handbags. Let it be actors slumming but never condescending to the material as they would, and do, nowadays in woebegone efforts like *Down with Love* and *Far from Heaven*, two that tried spirit-rapping with a departed Ross Hunter.

Lana Turner spent a lifetime and attendant marriages, gone-sour loves, and even a real-

life bedroom killing to qualify herself for *Portrait in Black*. That is credibility you don't come by with thesping lessons, and reason withal why modern actresses can never heft the weight she did at what she did. Turner performed best in courtrooms and nightclubs. That was all the preparation needed for frankly silly movies featuring her in middle age. Clothes made this woman (and her previous incarnation as Sweater Girl), and even if Lana never knew her Ibsen, she sure had tinseled reality down pat. She exhibited infallible instincts and was wired to those who paid quarters for magazines she'd posed in for 20-plus years.

Portrait in Black director Michael Gordon accused Turner of "impoverished taste," but I'm betting he was the clueless one; certainly it was she and not he walking away with whopping gross percentages on these Universal mellers.

"Lana was not a dummy," said the director, "and she would give me wonderful rationalizations why she should wear pendant earrings. They had nothing to do with the role, but they had everything to do with her particular self-image."

On the contrary, Mr. Gordon, I'd submit that Lana Turner, like her producer Ross Hunter, knew well that earrings—and gowns and furs—*were* the role. Nothing beyond these was really consequential in films like *Portrait in Black*.

In fact, Lana's hair drove ticket sales in many situations. Universal tied in with Seligman and Latz beauty salons to highlight a Lana Turner-inspired, frosted platinum-blonde hairdo in department stores wherein S&L had parlors. National advertising tied to saturation bookings was becoming the norm with high-profile releases, but Universal still leaned on exhibitors to get the word out locally. Toward that end, special kits were supplied in advance of regular pressbooks. "This is not a do-it-yourself kit, but one which tells you what you can do with the picture if you want to become a showman," said introductory paragraphs.

Against so loud a countrywide drumbeat, had grassroots management gotten lazy and as willing to let Universal tote the heavier load? May be, but they were also loudest to complain when increased-percentage demands reflected distributor effort to get back some of what had been spent on

In selling *Portrait in Black* to showmen, Hunter zeroes in on the only demographics not glued to televisions: women, teens, and young adults, and even families, although ads pitch "an evil spark," forbidden romance, and murder that tie into Lana's recent involvement in the Stompanato case.

large-circulation magazines and network television ads. Selling *Portrait in Black* in 21 publications, including virtually all those geared toward feminine readers, was said to have reached 140 million, but how many of these actually paid admissions to see the feature? Theatre attendance was seriously declining after all. It was enough for most women to check out photos of Lana Turner sporting her new "champagne blonde" style in the pages of *Redbook*. Why buy tickets and bother with her emoting too? Sobering indeed was the measure of those 140 million readers against $3.2 million in domestic rentals Universal realized on *Portrait in Black*.

The fraction of folks going to movies grew ever smaller as the '60s dawned, and for a company like Universal, seldom vaulting far over a single million in rentals, $3.2 was a more-than-respectable number. Others were surely getting by (or not) on far less. You really had to work to drag people away from their televisions. Star touring was essential. Lana Turner, Sandra Dee, Virginia Grey, Anna May Wong, and even *Portrait in Black* script girl Dolores Rubin canvassed 40 cities and towns, a heavier plow to pull than merely working on the film itself.

Universal applied wake-up calls in many spots by comping news scribes with wining and dining that their paychecks could otherwise ill afford. Suspiciously kind reviews followed. "Exhibitors will find their local newspaper and radio people well-conditioned on *Portrait in Black*," said a confident Universal. Well fed and lubricated might have been a franker choice of words.

Spinning off the previous year's *Imitation of Life*, a monster hit also with Lana Turner, and memories of l'affaire Stompanato assured that mother/daughter conflicts would segue to *Portrait in Black*'s scenario and be emphasized accordingly in ad art. Wasn't this, after all, what Turner's image was all about?

MULTI-MEDIA LUSTRE-CREME PROMOTION

COMPLETE COPPERTONE CAMPAIGN

Opposite page: Hunter sees satisfaction when *Portrait* sells big. Above: Cover girl Sandra Dee proves to be a multimedia sensation who makes cash registers jingle. Cross-promotion for *Portrait in Black* will include Lustre-Creme and Coppertone. Below: "Every mother's dream" makes a hometown personal appearance at the height of her popularity.

It's said that Sandra Dee became "every mother's dream." She was perhaps the last of the white-glove ingénues. Butter wouldn't melt in her mouth, but that arose as much from having subsisted since childhood on a diet of lettuce heads and Epsom salts. Childhood was an elastic term in any case, as Dee seems never to have had one. She played beyond her years from the age of eight, called ten by her ultra-aggressive stage mother looking to jump-start employment in teen roles.

Sandra Dee was cresting just when *Portrait in Black* made its summer 1960 landfall. She'd been featured on two dozen fan mag covers so far that year. Veteran Universal still photographer Ray Jones called hers "the most kissable lips in Hollywood, comparable only to those of Clara Bow." Two years prior to *Portrait in Black*, Dee had nuzzled John Saxon on camera in *The Restless Years* and pretended all the while to be 18, abetted by a studio anxious to move her up to adult parts. She inspired girls to buy Coppertone and Lustre-Creme, while being kept clear of peers on the lot lest one damage the valued merchandise Dee was.

It was still possible for movie stars to revisit hometowns in triumph. Sandra Dee's was Bayonne, New Jersey, where she'd be received in that delirious way that young celebrities just off assembly lines were. A local showman would welcome both a visiting star and the unaccustomed sight of his house filled to capacity. A customized Sandra Dee, like other studio models catering to fad and fashion, could thrive but for a moment when a public embraced the idealized teen she personified. That having ended, "Whatever became of…" was a question few even bothered to ask. Dee was a soft object for ridicule once her era came under a succeeding decade's microscope, but what in the end was more pathetic—being cruelly spoofed in *Grease* (1978) by a song called *Look at Me, I'm Sandra Dee*, or having it sung by a cringingly over-aged Stockard Channing who was three months *older* than Dee at the time she played a teenager in that geriatric musical with its leading lady Olivia Newton-John a ripe high schooler of 30?

The frightful revelations set forth in *People* magazine and her son's book, *Dream Lovers: The Magnificent Shattered Lives of Bobby Darin and Sandra Dee*, at long last revealed Dee's true age and crushed any illusions fans might have clung to, leaving one with little but satisfaction for not having been a movie star like she so unfortunately was.

Another Ross Hunter Fashion Noir, the thriller *Midnight Lace*, didn't make history in

Another unretouched portrait shows the faith that Doris Day, #1 Box-Office Attraction in America, put in the airbrusher on duty. Rex Harrison shows wear and tear courtesy of the recent loss of his bride, Kay Kendall, who died of leukemia at just 33.

1960 as did its genre companion, *Psycho. Midnight Lace* was merely functional in its day and is little remembered now. Who cares that it played, and very successfully, but months in the wake of Hitchcock's smash? Both were offered up as exercises in polished suspense. The not unfamiliar device of encouraging audiences to arrive not later than the picture's beginning was gently pursued by theatres showing Ross Hunter's confection, while Hitchcock's similar but hard-and-fast edict on *Psycho*'s behalf, was actually written into exhibition contracts and enforced at ticket windows.

Having opened in October, *Midnight Lace* provided balm for audiences undone by Hitchcock's relentless assault upon genre conventions. The mystery of *Lace* was as reassuringly elemental as its outcome was predictably resolved. To challenge viewers would be to distract them from matters of greater concern, namely clothes and décor that would center merchandising strategy and deliver a success on the order of previous Hunter hits.

Midnight Lace represents the triumph of the superficial thriller, one that might emerge if an artist like Hitchcock were to shoot and release the barest skeletal outline of a coming project. By 1960, the guessing game as to villainous identity was one practiced nonstop on televisions everywhere, what with schedules awash in whodunits and series like *Perry Mason* making armchair sleuths of us all. The point of a *Midnight Lace* had to be something other than which character was seeking to terrorize Doris Day. The imperative must be what Day was wearing while the unknown he/she was about it.

Howard Hawks had been canny enough to observe the impact of relentless video recycling of westerns, and so put greater emphasis on character and bantering comedy in 1959's *Rio Bravo*, cowboy formulae now being all but

Above: Fashion Noir titles knew how to pre-sell, setting *Midnight Lace* up for box-office triumph. Below: Hitchcock's see-it-from-the-beginning policy for *Psycho* goes arm in arm with padlocks, while *Midnight Lace* asks politely for cooperation.

impossible to deliver fresh. The ubiquity of old movies at home was indeed forcing Hollywood to remix paints, especially with regards familiar genres.

Ross Hunter was something of an industry's Ashley Wilkes. He so wanted Hollywood to remain that place of glamour others knew was dying. Almost poignant was his conviction that all of what once made movies great could somehow be recaptured in the likes of *Midnight Lace*. Toward such ends, he invited monuments of an already vanished studio era to sprinkle stardust upon pictures designed to remind patrons of theatre going at its romantic summit. Myrna Loy was among red herrings in *Midnight Lace*, but her larger purpose was to evoke larger-than-lives she'd essayed back when Hunter, and most of his audience, were thrilling to oldies since consigned to the late, late show.

"They don't make them like they used to" was a chorus sung by middle-agers who'd stopped going to theatres in any case, and the producer's idea was to lure them back along with his now-loyal core of women both teenaged and young adult. To these he presented Doris Day at the very moment of her coronation as Number-One Box-Office Attraction in America, with *Midnight Lace* arriving in the wake of Universal's phenomenal *Pillow Talk*.

To read Day's straight-faced account of traumas she suffered enacting her victimized heroine in *Midnight Lace*, we're all the more impressed at how earnestly stars of her generation applied themselves to what viewers would now charitably call high camp. Part of my respect for *Midnight Lace* and others like it derives from cast refusal to betray their condescension to what most of them knew was pulpy material. Doris Day recalled projecting onto her character to a point of on-set breakdown and three days needed to recover. Within a few years, players briefed on irony and the knowing wink would convey their indifference all too well, and sensibilities like Ross Hunter's would run out of avenues for expression.

Despite the fact that they're working on the fabled *Phantom of the Opera* stage, Herbert Marshall, Myrna Loy, and Doris Day appear to be thoroughly bored during production of *Midnight Lace*.

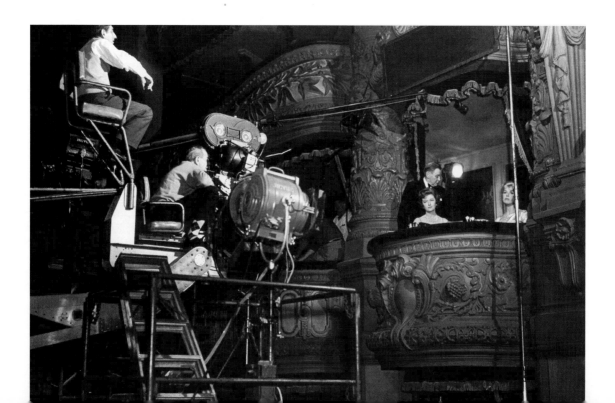

A FASHION FIRST

NEVER BEFORE SUCH A *Powerful* PACKAGE
TO PRE-SELL YOUR PICTURE
TO *The Women of* THE WORLD!

FREE PROMOTIONAL FILM
"High Style Elegance"

Starring

DORIS DAY

IRENE
The Famous Designer

and her

Fascinating Fashions
in
"MIDNIGHT LACE"

No. 1900-P37
Doris Day and noted designer Irene discuss
"MIDNIGHT LACE" wardrobe.

No. 1900-Ex5

A 6-MINUTE FASHION FEATURETTE
IN GORGEOUS COLOR

See it at your Universal Exchange — Then show it as a part of your Regular Screen Show as a Fashion Extra. It will prove a sensation . . . and it's FREE!

No. 1900-P36

IMPORTANT NOTE

After you have played this Fashion Featurette in your theatre program, contact the Department Store (see list on next page) carrying the Irene, Inc. line of Women's Fashions and arrange for them to show a 16mm print of the same featurette in their auditorium during fashion shows and special events.

No. 1900-Ex6

No. 1900-Ex7

No. 1900-Ex1

No. 1900-Ex2

No. 1900-Ex3

No. 1900-Ex4

No. 1900-Ex8

I assume there's still a fashion industry, but does it thrive as in 1960 when Universal marshaled its forces on behalf of *Midnight Lace?*

"Hollywood must regain its place as Glamour Capital of the world, and clothes is what made Hollywood just that," said Ross Hunter as the studio's aggressive tie-up with retailers nationwide left the feature almost an afterthought in the wake of Doris Day-inspired outfits designed by Hollywood's renowned Irene. She'd been in movies since Keystone days, first as would-be actress, and later more successfully as dressmaker to the stars. Ross Hunter built much of his *Midnight Lace* campaign around Irene's wardrobe for Doris Day. There was a six-minute short, free to exhibitors, made up of costume tests for the film, and this was fanned out by Universal field men to department stores in every key location playing *Midnight Lace.* Prints in 16mm were shown to clerks in advance of shopper arrival and display windows were festooned with outfits seen in the film.

In Kansas City, for instance, the sales staff of Harzfeld Clothier, a mainstay in that city since 1891, confabbed with studio reps at a closed screening of *Midnight Lace* with accompanying fashion short. The idea was to acquaint management and 36 sales staffers on how best to merchandise both the movie and clothing displayed during it. An original Irene suit as seen in the film would be a grand prize in contests held at the store. Initiative on the part of Universal exploiters created *Midnight Lace* consciousness running weeks in advance of the show's opening. As with *Portrait in Black* and its beauty salon tie-ins, this was surest to target femme patrons and inspire commerce both at Harzfeld's and the National Theatre circuit, which had booked the feature into houses it controlled throughout the territory.

Why I Would Like to Be Doris Day for a Night was the subject of contemplation for over a hundred women who responded to the Center Theatre's contest appeal in Corpus Christi, Texas. It seemed not a foolish inquiry in light of the popularity of this performer. There were scores nationwide who wanted to be Doris Day all the time, or at least spend whatever they could spare of it watching her films. Much of that appeal had to do with luxuries Day was thought to enjoy. *Pillow Talk* was as much about lavish lifestyle as laughs, and *Midnight Lace* would be more of the same, only this time gracious living would be salted with comparatively mild thrills. Doris on screen (and fans assumed off) consumed much of what money could buy, so to *be* Doris Day was to wear the latest and buy the mostest. No more would roles find her in humble circumstance. She was tied inexorably to products sold on her image and/or endorsement. Representing an ideal to patrons now

Mrs. Fran Lowley is crowned Doris Day for a Night and accepts a floral tribute and a $50 bill before being whisked off in a Chevrolet Impala for her elegant Hollywood-style dinner, not at Trocadero on the Sunset Strip, but at Luby's Cafeteria in Corpus Christi, Texas.

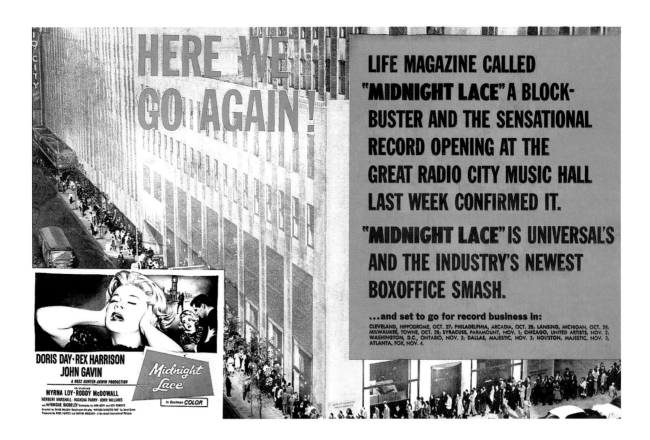

During a very hot streak in the career of Doris Day, *Midnight Lace* enjoys a big opening week at Radio City Music Hall in New York City.

meant shopping for them as well, so why not be Doris Day for a night when that amounts to having your wish list filled?

The contest winner in this instance would enjoy a night on the town consistent with those DD might routinely experience, provided one bought into Hollywood as High Life Incarnate, an illusion still tenable, but for not much longer, in December of 1960 when Mrs. Fran Lowley of Ronstown, Texas, had her big night out. She and extended family, including kids not unlike ones Doris had in that year's *Please Don't Eat the Daisies*, were driven 17 miles in a 1961 Chevrolet Impala sedan on loan from a local dealer, with color commentary by a radio announcer brought along to broadcast the event. There was supper in the spacious dining room of the luxurious Luby's Cafeteria in Corpus Christi, followed by a star entrance into the Center's lobby and an interview on stage that was transmitted live to listeners. Mrs. Lowley then took receipt of gifts presumed worthy of a Doris Day and by courtesy of town merchants—transistor radio, vinyl jacket, cigarette lighter, and crisp new $50 bill in addition to 12 months of free admission to the Center. It wasn't a wardrobe by Irene, but this being 1,500 miles east of Hollywood, it would do.

Whatever glamour dust was needed to supplement this temporal Doris Day would be supplied by *Midnight Lace*, for which Universal collected $3.5 million in domestic rentals, its biggest profit taker for 1960 next to *Operation Petticoat.*

Even a still with Vera Miles and John Gavin posing by an empty chair can raise hackles.

CHAPTER 24

PSYCHO SALESMANSHIP

What a shame the startling effect of a groundbreaking new film can be felt only by those who come to it first. My initial exposure to *Psycho* was via television, so I can't relate to seismic shocks off initial release during that summer of 1960. A biggest problem with a life spent in adoration of classic movies is the rocker punch of first-runs being something the younger, or still living, can only imagine. We can read about opening nights of *Gone With the Wind*, *A Star Is Born*, or *House of Wax*, but never mind feeling what they felt, no matter the restorations set before us. Chasing a sensation like that experienced long ago in crowded and excited auditoriums is tempered by realization we'll never come within hailing distance, armed with nothing other than a DVD and good intentions.

Reliable accounts say many screamed and fled from *Psycho*, with police called to calm disturbances. I've read of such incidents during early engagements of *Frankenstein* in 1931, but weren't we past this by 1960? Maybe, but was this only because there'd been no one like Hitchcock to take up the challenge of upending us anew? *Psycho* demonstrated it was still possible to shatter senses on a mass scale.

Taking critics off the loop for advance screenings was nothing so radical in 1960, but barring exhibitors from same was a near declaration of war. "Who can help launch a film better than an exhibitor who has seen it?," asked Pete Harrison in his June 6, 1960 *Reports*. "Paramount's excuse can only make theatre-men suspicious of the hidden feature's merit."

Harrison despaired of *Psycho*'s critical fate as well: "Furthermore, it is understood that Paramount will not screen the film for trade reviewers before it opens at a theatre. Under such conditions, even the fairest of critics will have trouble viewing the film objectively."

Indeed, Hitchcock had gambled his dollars, reputation, and showman goodwill in a go-for-broke campaign that might easily have backfired and cost the director everything he'd built up over a 20-year career in the United States. Had grosses not been so extraordinary, would the excesses here have finished Hitchcock, as many predicted after seeing *Psycho*? It took nerve to put one's name on the line for product rough as this, and no precedent gave assurance that audiences would sit still for it. A similar gamble with *Peeping Tom*, also from 1960, damaged the career of British director Michael Powell.

If ever a filmmaker read the pulse of his constituency, Hitchcock did that summer, for *Psycho* lured business vast beyond the wildest expectation of ordinary shockers—so much so as to suggest he'd invented a new genre. One could opt for a simplistic explanation and dismiss the new Hitchcock as upscale William Castle, and indeed, he envisioned *Psycho* as a riposte to Hammer, AIP, and, yes, Bill Castle pics nipping at the master's heels.

Summer of 1960's release schedule is fun for the glimpse it affords of *Psycho*'s thriller competition. Bowing before and after Hitchcock was American-International's *House of Usher* (June), Universal/Hammer's *Brides of Dracula* (July), and Columbia's *13 Ghosts* (August).

Castle was a particular thorn in Hitchcock's side, as their marketing techniques often overlapped, and the latter didn't enjoy his work confused with the likes of *The Tingler* and *House on Haunted Hill*; writer applicants to AH faced veto for having worked on previous Castle shows.

Was Bill the Hitchcock doppelganger—a cut-rate Bruno Anthony to the master's Guy Haines? Comparisons would end at the ticket window, for neither Castle nor fellow shockmeisters ever realized anything near *Psycho* grosses. Of those three competing with *Psycho* that summer, only *House of Usher* cracked a million in domestic rentals, while *Psycho* took $8.9 million. This might have proven a mixed blessing for Hitchcock, as adult expectations of star-laden, and more or less civilized, suspense were now supplanted by newly won youthful acolytes awaiting a topper to horrific thrills he'd furnish with *Psycho*, and later, *The Birds*.

I distinctly recall the letdown attendant upon my family's beach vacation outing to see *Torn Curtain* in August 1966. Owing to the reputation of his last two, this 12 year old craved stronger meat than Paul Newman and Julie Andrews playing at tepid espionage behind the who-cares iron curtain. Hitchcock was by then trapped in his own house on a haunted *(Psycho)* hill, and immature fans such as myself weren't disposed to let him out.

There was a pair of teaser trailers in addition to the six-minute deluxe preview wherein Hitchcock hosted a tour of the Bates Motel and environs. The latter attained legendary status and was bootlegged/sold by collectors for years to come. Universal included it among DVD extras, but the teasers have remained obscure. One was a plea urging top secrecy regarding the content of *Psycho*, while the other set forth policy for all bookings of the feature.

See It from the Beginning was a dodge they'd used since movies began, but never was it actually enforced with

Employing a highly unusual and highly personal ad campaign, Alfred Hitchcock's *Psycho* opens at two theatres in New York City to strong returns.

Surely you do not have your meat course after your dessert at dinner. You will therefore understand why we are so insistent that you enjoy PSYCHO from start to finish, exactly as we intended that it be served.

We won't allow you to cheat yourself. Every theatre manager, everywhere, has been instructed to admit no one after the start of each performance of PSYCHO. We said no one — not even the manager's brother, the President of the United States or the Queen of England (God bless her).

To help you cooperate with this extraordinary policy, we are listing the starting times below. Treasure them with your life—or better yet, read them and act accordingly.

Hitchcock's ad campaign reveals his personal stake in the production. The master asks potential moviegoers—using his usual deadpan style and intellectual wit—to view his "extraordinary entertainment" by "beginning at the beginning." He begs people who have consumed his picture not to reveal the ending, and assures that neither President nor Queen could enter the theatre late.

Having lived with PSYCHO since it was a gleam in my camera's eye, I now exercise my parental rights in revealing a number of significant facts about this extraordinary entertainment.

First of all, I must warn you that PSYCHO was designed to be as terrifying as possible. Do not, however, heed the false rumor that it will frighten the moviegoer speechless. Some of my men were doomed to disappointment when they hopefully sent their wives to a preview. The women emerged badly shaken but still vigorously vocal.

To learn how false the rumor really is, you have only to come to the theatre and listen to the screaming. A few may mumble incoherently, but they will definitely not be speechless. Be sure to bring your wife. A miracle may occur.

I would also like to point out that PSYCHO is most enjoyable when viewed beginning at the beginning and proceeding to the end. I realize that this is a revolutionary concept, but we have discovered that PSYCHO is unlike most motion pictures. It does not improve when run backwards. This applies even to that portion of the film in which I make a brief but significant appearance.

I have therefore asked that no one be admitted to the theatre after the start of each performance. This, of course, is to help you enjoy PSYCHO more.

More important — I insist that you do not tell your friends the amazing secrets of PSYCHO after you see it.

I know that you feel grateful for all this valuable information, but I must in all fairness point out that in bringing it to you I am not entirely without selfish motives. Thank you very much.

starring
ANTHONY PERKINS · VERA MILES
JOHN GAVIN co-starring MARTIN BALSAM · JOHN McINTIRE

and **JANET LEIGH** as MARION CRANE
Directed by ALFRED HITCHCOCK · Screenplay by JOSEPH STEFANO
Based on the Novel by Robert Bloch · A PARAMOUNT RELEASE

regards arriving patrons. Embattled showmen happy to get their quarters any way they could were alarmed to find such uncompromising terms written into *Psycho* contracts.

"Our opening playdates have proved, beyond the shadow of a showman's doubt, the success of this required policy," said Hitchcock in an appeal to exhibitors that ran in the trades. "If the word 'required' startles you, please try to think of a box office besieged by patrons anxious to purchase tickets. Feel better?"

Hitchcock forecast that theatre owners would be "happily startled all the way to the bank" if only they'd comply with his absolute bar against late arrivals to *Psycho*. For first-run houses with definite start schedules, this was well and good, and promotional budgets at metro venues allowed for stunt emphasis on Hitchcock's edict, with Pinkerton guards, off-duty officers, and the like, but what of grind situations down the line where double and triple billing prevailed and start times were uncertain at best? My guess is the policy, or at least enforcement of same, was abandoned after the first month or so of general release, though scrambling for prints of *Psycho* aroused the ire of circuit heads denied early run privileges.

Said Allied Theatre's North Central president: "Here is a black-and-white picture for which Paramount could make up at least 100 more prints for 'peanuts' and take advantage of the publicity the picture is now receiving. It could then be booked into the smaller towns and earn thousands of more dollars and help keep the small-town exhibitor alive."

The age-old problem of popular titles going stale before less-populated areas could get them was an ongoing grievance among rural showmen, as addressed by the same Allied Theatre exec: "Can the revenue derived from the comparatively few who are lured from their communities to the big cities possibly compensate the film company for the losses resulting from the local theatres' lessened prestige and the positive manner in which such sales policies date a picture and render it passe in the minds of local theatergoers?" This

Top left: Hitch's nemesis, William Castle, goes on the stump for *13 Ghosts* with his moppet "fan club" in Detroit. **Center:** Hitchcock finds a way to spell *Psycho* success, Gotham style, but how will he reach that far? **Bottom:** Six letters on the marquee of a California theatre say it all.

was a question not unreasonably put by more than one manager standing at the back of playdate lines.

The backlash stung as *Psycho* limped its way into the sticks. "Not as good as William Castle's *Macabre*," was manager Chuck Gerard's dismissal in the wake of patrons' migration to catch *Psycho* in Iowa City or St. Louis rather than wait months for Warsaw, Illinois' modest house to book it.

Among questions still taboo in celebrity interviews, one has endured and, I suspect, always will: "How much were you paid?" There's an impertinence factor there, the code unwritten. You just don't ask people what kind of money they earn. Otherwise probing journalists back off in the face of such personal inquiry. Of all the Hitchcock interviews I've seen or read, no one broached the topic, yet for me, it's the most arresting of all the master's mysteries. We're told of his gifts in negotiation and of arts he practiced, that of the deal being perhaps supreme among them. Hitchcock did cash checks in the millions for his end of the *Psycho* payout. Given access to the director, this would have been my first avenue of interrogation, though I've no doubt a frosty reception, if not a security escort off the Universal lot, would have ensued. Still, transcripts of closed-door conferences between Hitchcock and superagent Lew Wasserman would at the least offer perspectives undreamt of by scribes who never looked and interviewers that didn't ask.

Hitchcock died fantastically rich, more so than any Golden Era director I can think of, except possibly art collector Billy Wilder, and not knowing details of Hitch's business acumen represents a large gap in our understanding of the man and his career.

Above: A would-be patron cows before Hitchcock's stern edict—and the uniformed guard intent on backing it up. At far left of frame, a spectral figure with crossed arms keeps watch. Below: Ozoners in the New York metro area yield electrifying results.

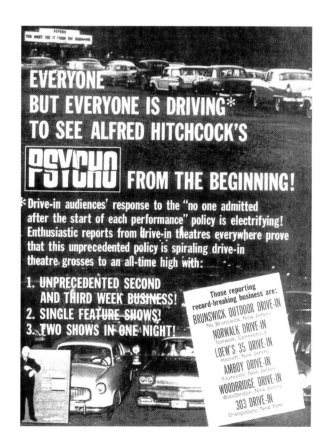

241

Commonly accepted is the notion that Hitchcock owned 60 percent of *Psycho* after agreeing to largely finance the show himself in the wake of Paramount's expressed reluctance to do so. Hitchcock historians tell of how he filmed the shower scene, but information about his deal with Paramount has always been sketchy. In fact, I'm guessing they're guessing about a lot of what went on with regards ownership and compensation. Has anyone examined the contract? It's bound to exist and must be fascinating.

Paramount had an eight-year distribution deal with Hitchcock, after which all rights to the *Psycho* negative would revert to him. This meant Paramount had the right to handle a 1965 theatrical reissue of *Psycho*, plus initial sales to television. For both of these, they received a distribution fee plus an agreed-upon percentage.

The 1965 run of *Psycho* brought back $1.2 million in domestic rentals. This was the biggest grossing reissue Paramount had in the '60s, with the exception of *The Ten Commandments* in 1966 ($8.8 million). Hitchcock participated in new ads emphasizing the now-legendary status of his five-year-old thriller. Said he, "The first time we wouldn't let you in except at the beginning. Now you can come in and be shocked anytime."

With *Psycho* a smash, Hitch thanks patrons for respecting his "see it from the beginning" edict.

Publicity emphasized "the shower-bath sequence and other grisly goodies," while Hitchcock's signature appeared below warnings that *Psycho* "is again on the loose in your fair city." For the first time, Anthony Perkins was shown in advertising holding a knife, an acknowledgment of patrons long since in the know as to the picture's denouement.

The next major *Psycho* sighting was an aborted one; on September 23, 1966, the *CBS Friday Night Movie* had scheduled *Psycho* to make its network television premiere after NBC had passed (that network thought *Psycho* "too rough" to broadcast, according to *Variety*). Controversy was rife among affiliates. Conservative markets were aghast that CBS would broadcast such a thing. A sum of $800,000 was tendered to Paramount for two runs.

Four days before liftoff, *Psycho* was postponed. CBS released a statement on Monday, September 19. Out of deference to the family of Senator Charles Percy of Illinois, they would not be showing the film. An intruder entering Percy's house during the previous weekend had murdered his daughter in her bed. The horrific crime remains to this day unsolved. I was 12 then and hadn't read the news, so imagine my chagrin when the *CBS Friday Night Movie* instead showed Frank Sinatra and Natalie Wood in *Kings Go Forth*!

Network execs lamented the loss they'd sustain in the event *Psycho* was cancelled altogether, while press hounds inquired as to an eventual broadcast date. It was summer 1960 all over again, with *Psycho* at the eye of a public relations hurricane. CBS maintained it would be shown later. Toward that end, they previewed a sanitized version in December for New York *Times* reporter Peggy Hudson. She timed both versions of the shower scene and found the TV version shortened by 45 seconds. "The murder is still shown, but the repeated stabbings have been cut," being Hudson's summation. As if to reassure readers that some vestige remained of *Psycho*'s impact, she closed with a faint endorsement: "Viewers are left with a sense of shock, but perhaps not with the sense of stark horror felt by movie audiences."

CBS president William H. Tankersley was chided for his defensive attitude on the topic of rescheduling. "Possibly in the spring," he said, while bristling at suggestions that nine minutes excised for network broadcast weren't enough. "To rule out the way we've edited it would be to rule out any good murder mystery." Huh?

By December 18, CBS had surrendered to public and affiliate pressure: A firm decision was made *never* to broadcast *Psycho*. Syndicators were now free to package the feature among titles for an upcoming broadcast season. *Psycho* would be crown jewel and assured ratings-getter for local stations with nerve enough to telecast it.

Our own Channel 9 out of Charlotte took the plunge in fall of 1968. Station buyers were furnished with complete prints. The 16mm negatives weren't cut, so local standards could dictate how much footage to trim.

Again I took my place in front of the Zenith, this time at home with both parents (unfortunately) watching. WSOC began with a s-l-o-w text crawl warning of extreme adult content in the film we were about to see. "It may be well to send the children to bed," came the damning words. My now-alerted parents let that pass, though I found myself disparaging Hitchcock for that first scene with Janet Leigh and John Gavin lolling about half-naked in a hotel room. Sure enough, off went the television, and off I was sent to bed.

Local censors would now have their turn at *Psycho*. TV stations in

So visceral was the *Psycho* experience that five years later, on first reissue, those who couldn't make it inside the theatre in 1960 are enticed to try again by a bra-clad Leigh, a beefcake Gavin, a shower-bath, and BLOOD!

those days edited with seeming hacksaws. Movies were cut by thirds, even halves, to accommodate time slots a fraction of intended length. Dollar-an-hour staff hovered over dimly lit benches and mutilated Hitchcock's design until little was left but the title.

I finally caught *Psycho* when Channel 9 ran a late show repeat in 1970. Was it complete? Perhaps, but how could one know, not having seen *Psycho* theatrically? A subsequent primetime airing on Greenboro's WFMY was interrupted by a sudden splice occurring just as the darkened figure approached Janet Leigh's shower, eliminating altogether what should have come next. No stabs, no knife, not a scream, but at least Channel 2 was spared complaints, and so what if viewers were suckered into watching under false pretenses?

I wonder how aware Hitchcock was of such wholesale abuse. It wasn't confined to North Carolina broadcasts. Stations everywhere were taking safe ways out and gelding *Psycho* for dubious benefit of standards and practices. The director was powerless to intervene, as these weren't theatre exhibitors he could dictate to. **See It from the Beginning** was a grim joke in the face of prints shorn by entire reels so they could fit into a 90-minute slot. Ever resourceful, Hitchcock found a way of turning such carnage to his advantage for Universal's first theatrical reissue (1969) of *Psycho*.

See It the Way It Was Originally Made! screamed new ads. **Every Scene Intact!** The master's unsmiling countenance promised **The Version TV Didn't Dare Show!** and a newly introduced ratings system assigned the since-discarded "M" classification, limiting access to mature audiences. The reassertion of 1960's **No One Will Be Admitted to See Psycho Except from the Very Beginning** policy was likely ignored by showmen catering to patrons at the least familiar with every bump in this show, having seen it several times at home, if not previously in theatres.

To reissue a feature fresh out of heavy television rotation was near unprecedented in the late '60s, but a complete *Psycho* still had the allure of forbidden fruit, with fans yet willing to pay an admission to get a bite—Universal realized $262,000 in domestic rentals for this 1969 reissue. Meanwhile, 16mm rental houses proudly displayed *Psycho* in their show windows. Paramount exercised some residual rights here, for early nontheatrical prints bore the studio logo and were in fact much superior to muddy 16mm editions Universal would later generate for similar markets.

A '60s deal with Hitchcock gave Universal all rights to *Psycho*, which they exercised for the 1969 reissue below. By now Hitchcock's edict is back in place: You must see it from the beginning—"it" being the original picture that TV didn't dare to unspool.

244

Left: Another great film on the *CBS Friday Night Movie*? Almost. Above: 16mm rental terms are $125 for a one-day *Psycho* booking—much more around Halloween.

This collector made many an inquiry to dealer contacts before springing for a *Psycho* liberated from some warehouse or depot. Does it have a Paramount logo? If not, forget it. Those pursuing legitimate rental engagements were confronted with terms in excess of what other Hitchcocks commanded. Swank Motion Pictures, Inc., wanted $125 for a day's 16mm *Psycho* booking in 1979; $200 if you played it between October 5 and November 5. *The Birds*, on the other hand, could be had for $95, up to $125 around the time of All Hallows' Eve.

Universal was meanwhile tying anchors to designated "special" *Psycho* by placing it among barking dogs in a syndicated group known as Universal 53, where Hitchcock's classic warded off the stench of bunkmates *Angel in My Pocket*, *The Ballad of Josie*, and *The Far Out West* (adapted from episodes of the Ann Sheridan series *Pistols 'n' Petticoats*). You'd think these would be specimens TV **Wouldn't Dare Show**, but most were at least in color, a main criterion for station buyers during those multihue-besotted days.

And so *Psycho* thrives yet in a second century. Pictorial quality of Blu-ray discs may surpass that of 1960 release prints. Certainly there is more detail here than most of us can recall seeing elsewhere, leaving little doubt of *Psycho* being the most valuable black-and-white property Universal owns. That's likely to remain the case, given the seeming impossibility of monochrome films ever making a comeback.

Starring Yvonne Monlaur and David Peel, *Brides of Dracula* seeks differentiation from competitors in the marketplace.

CHAPTER 25

A MEMPHIS SCREAMIERE

The Malco Theatre in Memphis, Tennessee, might have seemed an unlikely place to jumpstart a nationwide campaign for *Brides of Dracula*, yet this is where the Hammer horror classic had its world premiere, on Friday, June 3, 1960. Three-thousand patrons, most of them teenagers, lined the block around Main and Beale Street, jamming the house to capacity.

Combined efforts of Malco staff and Universal field agents brought them here. Evidence at hand suggests movie going reached a state of grace that night. Film history books don't have a lot to say about that fraternity of men at the vanguard of picture selling. Their bows were taken at ticket booths and deposit windows, where success counted most.

"It's fun," said Malco vice president Richard Lightman, as he coordinated the arrival of Count Dracula in a mule-driven antique hearse found in a Kentucky junkyard. "You can't just take a horror thriller and put it on the screen. This type of picture must be ballyhooed."

Lightman understood the need for novelty to merchandise monsters, especially when so many of them competed for a kid's allowance dollar. The very week he played *Brides of Dracula*, a neighboring palace was head-to-head with *Circus of Horrors*.

Universal faced the challenge of differentiating its shocks from those served up by rivals. Already there had been complaints about the plethora of Dracula themes. *Harrison's Reports* rebelled two years earlier when confronted with *Blood of Dracula*, *Return of Dracula*, and *Horror of Dracula*, all in simultaneous circulation and causing no end to confusion among patrons and promoters.

Said Pete Harrison: "The average moviegoer, unlike those of us who are in the motion picture business, does not remember the exact title of a picture he or she has seen unless it happened to be a truly exceptional film. There is no telling how many moviegoers who will see one of them will unwittingly pass up either one or both of the other pictures in the mistaken belief that they are one and the same."

Now, schools were letting out for a 1960 summer that much *more* saturated with horror subjects, and here was Universal entering yet another contestant in the Dracula sweepstakes. An expert would be needed to sell this one, so they called A-Mike Vogel.

A-Mike (just Mike to friends) was an exhibition genius from way back (1919), having conducted, among other things, the Manager's Round Table section for the *Motion Picture Herald* from 1933 to 1942. A-Mike could pound ad copy in his sleep, a dangling cigarette and crumpled hat his trademarks, a seeming merger of Walter Winchell, Billy Wilder, whom he actually resembled, and *A Star Is Born*'s Matt Libby into one flamboyant package.

By 1960 Vogel had his own advertising and exploitation agency in San Francisco. "Let's get in and pitch," said he to exhibitors as Universal turned this merchandising whirlwind loose on *Brides of Dracula*. "Find a newly married couple willing to spend their wedding night in the graveyard!" fairly captured the spirit of A-Mike's strategy. His Dracula Bat-Flying Derby took the shape of kid-built kites looming over marquees. Science and shop classes from school would be certain to tie in, promised Vogel.

Book merchants received assurance that Monarch's paperback novelization would feature a cover impregnated with special-type perfume. Having acquired my own copy several years ago, I reexamined same, only to find it sans odors, other than musty ones owing to the encroachment of age.

Potential hit singles on the Coral label included *Brides of Dracula Cha-Cha-Cha* and *Transylvania Polka,* complete with David Peel and Yvonne Monlaur on the sleeve—talk about latter-day collectibles! *I'm a Mummy* had been Universal's pop single accompanying a previous Hammer horror they'd distributed, and who better than airwave disc spinners for getting the word out to kids?

Saturation openings were planned for June, and Memphis would lead off. Lightman and the Malco had been angling for this premiere since a proposed bow for *The Mummy* fell through a year before. Malco's reputation was built selling chillers. Now they'd establish a template for showmen nationwide to follow.

Getting capacity audiences was tougher by 1960. A barn like the Malco gathered lots of dust among 3,000 often-empty seats. "Only a monster movie will fill the house," said management. One local reporter noted "teenagers who flock to these goosebump spectacles with glowing eyes, as if it were something wonderful."

Above right: A newspaper ad for the Malco premiere. Below right: Shown hovered over a typewriter, exhibition genius A-Mike Vogel merges Walter Winchell, Billy Wilder, and *A Star Is Born*'s Matt Libby into one flamboyant package.

Clockwise from top left: Richard Lightman stands beside his antique hearse; patrons queue up; a bride goes for a walk; serenaded by a German band and shrouded in fog, Dracula appears in person to take a new bride; the Vampire Gift Shoppe, run by theatre manager Elton Holland (left) and Watson Davis (right), sells out an hour before showtime; and the Malco racks up a strong three-day gross.

News coverage of the *Brides of Dracula* premiere revealed a condescending tone typical of mainstream attitudes toward horror films and their audience. "The picture was about what one would expect," sniffed Memphis' *Commercial Appeal*. "One of those creations which are completely ridiculous but which will quiver your spine anyway if you aren't careful."

Richard Lightman understood the reality of pushing thrillers: "It has been our experience that with a show of this type, the business just won't hold up over a week."

Long runs were unknown where films like these were concerned. Many "A" venues avoided them altogether. Horror favorites we now revere opened as drive-in second features in many major cities. Hardtops usually played them off within two or three days. Lightman's prophecy would be fulfilled yet again with *Brides of Dracula*, as it too would exit after seven days, ceding place to a reissue of *The Greatest Show on Earth*.

Films like *Brides of Dracula* were indeed all about heavy exploitation and a brief run. Silly stunts such as those recommended by A-Mike Vogel worked best. Sidewalk ballyhoo was commonplace. Pedestrians barely flinched at the sight of vampires and festooned femmes on various city corners. Such things were almost taken for granted in those days of busy downtown shopping.

Below left: The Malco run becomes proof of the viability of Hammer's new entry. Below right: Universal tempts showmen with the promise of saturation area bookings around the nation, which will result in a strong summer run for the picture.

A man walking the streets in a barrel, his sign proclaiming **I Just Saw Brides of Dracula and It Scared the Pants Off Me!** heralded Malco's premiere night. "Werewolf whistles" and a Do-It-Yourself Vampire Kit were available in advance of the opening. Accessories included two sharpened stakes, a small wooden mallet, a silver bullet, garlic cloves, and wolfbane, all for a quarter.

The stage show was pushed hardest. Advertising director Watson Davis' efforts were abetted by Universal "technical expert" Heidi Erich, a self-proclaimed descendent of Elizabeth Bathory, history's only legally convicted vampire—I Googled her, and yes, Bathory was a notorious vampiress during the 1500s.

Members of the Memphis Little Theatre would perform a ritual of unholy matrimony wherein assorted girls were accompanied down the aisle by a German band, while the Malco's mighty Wurlitzer rose up from below floor level to herald the arrival of Dracula himself. Brides inclined to resist were tied to mock-ups of various medieval torture instruments to await the ceremony, while a "heckler" plant in the audience was dragged from his seat and beheaded on a guillotine to college glee-club accompaniment.

Ushers working in the guise of Frankenstein, Quasimodo, and the Wolf Man doubled as stage performers—a complete script of the pageant was made available to exhibitors wishing to stage their own effort. A Vampire Gift Shoppe in the lobby sold out its inventory an hour before the premiere.

Bally maestro Watson Davis specialized in horror film promotion; he had constructed a 20-foot high Tyrannosaurus Rex to promote the Malco's subsequent booking of *Dinosaurus,* and would later assume hosting duties for WHBQ's *Fantastic Features,* wherein he was billed as Sivad. That series of Memphis TV horrors lasted from 1962 into the '70s, and made Davis a legendary local figure. The Malco thrives to this day, albeit restored to its original name, The Orpheum, which had been given birth in 1928 as a vaudeville and variety site. Now a performing arts center, the venerable house hosts concerts and special events.

Brides of Dracula goes national after the Malco premiere. Above: In A-Mike Vogel's hometown of San Francisco, sex sells the picture. Below: In Milwaukee, it's a student in Dracula garb.

251

It's a long way from '30s glamour for these two, but *Baby Jane* will pay off big for Bette Davis and Joan Crawford.

CHAPTER 26

EXHIBITION'S BABY JANE BLASTOFF

It was a sure enough dismal fourth quarter looming when members of the Theater Owners of America met in July 1962. Distributors had long been hoarding better product for holidays and summer release, leaving crumbs (and crummy pictures) for showmen to get by on during slower months. "The leanest in industry history" was how TOA's investigating committee characterized a bleak autumn to come.

So how to induce the majors to release something good to alleviate said drought? The group made its presentation to Warner Bros., a company they felt was best equipped to supply them with a high-quality feature justifying the effort and expense their promotional project would entail. Would Warner Bros. agree to move up the release date for *What Ever Happened to Baby Jane?* from February 1963 to November 3, 1962 in return for guaranteed extended playdates and assurance of intensive selling efforts by TOA members and cooperating showmen?

The announcement came on August 20, 1962. *Baby Jane* would lead the charge of so-called Hollywood Preview Engagements, a plan calling for nationwide saturation, patron contests, and month-in-advance drumbeat to create anticipation and excitement. This was the bolt of lightning that would galvanize Robert Aldrich's gothic shocker and place it on a fast track to a whopping $3.5 million in domestic rentals.

Few modestly budgeted, black-and-white independent projects had it so rich. The fact Aldrich delivered more than goods expected was so much icing. Jack Warner likened sneak audience reaction to "a match lit in a paint factory." Watch *Baby Jane* on DVD and imagine how those shudders reverberated over 100 rows of seats.

Aldrich had started out with a good story, plus Bette Davis and Joan Crawford, neither of whom stimulated interest or dollars among prospective studio backers. Elliott Hyman, he of the legendary purchase of Warner Bros.' pre-'48 library, put up cash and an edict that *Baby Jane* be shot in six weeks. Warners was brought aboard to release, but was not otherwise invested. Press at the time took Aldrich on his word that the shoot was completed for $825,000, though his career files indicate the negative cost ran to $1.025 million, still an amazing bargain for an "A" picture in 1962.

The Theatre Owners of America announcement came in the midst of filming *Baby Jane*. Time would now be of far greater essence. A release moved up from February to November required post-pro-

duction be done at a dead run. Aldrich told it to the New York *Times*. "We finished shooting on schedule on September 12. Exactly one month later, we held our first sneak preview at the State Theatre, in Long Beach, California. That we were able to get the picture in shape in this incredibly short time is due to a group of dedicated craftsmen who performed above and beyond the call of duty—and almost beyond physical endurance—who worked virtually around the clock to meet our schedule."

As Aldrich sweated completion of *Baby Jane*, exhibitors coast to coast were vying for $1,750 in prize money being awarded for the most creative campaign, to be judged by Bette Davis and Joan Crawford, among others. The TOA's locomotive had left the platform. Exhibitors aboard were expected to get their ducks in a row early. That meant special trailers promoting the Hollywood Preview Engagement, plus an additional cross-plug preview to be shown in rival theatres. And why would competing houses agree to push *Baby Jane*? "Remind them that they may be playing the next Hollywood Preview Engagement and will be anxious for your cooperation," said the distributor, And indeed, there would be a follow-up HPE venture, *The Courtship of Eddie's Father*, in spring of 1963.

TOA and Warners also sponsored a contest for patrons. There were 1,200 prizes, including round trips for two to Hollywood or New York via American Airlines Astrojet. Participants were to compose essays in 50 words or less as to which scenes in *What Ever Happened to Baby Jane?* were most exciting, and why.

Warners had 400 prints ready for the November dates, a fairly high number in 1962, even for saturation openings. The whole idea of Hollywood Preview Engagements was to make audiences feel they were getting something ahead of everyone else. Bookings totaling 116 covered neighborhood theatres throughout the New York-New Jersey metropolitan area, certainly wider-than-usual coverage for that territory. Bette Davis rode a Greyhound bus for weekend openers as far as White Plains and wide as Astoria, stopping in 17 houses for raucous on-stage appearances wherein she handed out Baby Jane dolls and yelled herself hoarse thumping on behalf of the picture. A

Top: Davis, Warner, Crawford, and Aldrich in J.L.'s office. Center: Showmen and execs dream up the TOA concept. Bottom: The Hollywood Preview Engagement would help to return $3.5M for *Baby Jane*.

A happy and congenial Bette and Joan embark upon production of *What Ever Happened to Baby Jane*.

visit to Jack Paar's program found Bette Davis regaling the host over Hollywood's initial reluctance to back her and Crawford as co-stars.

"We wouldn't give you a dime for those two old broads" was self-deprecating humor to roll viewers in the aisles, but Crawford was less amused. Her letter the following day asked that Davis not refer to her as an "old broad." This may have been where enmity between the two had beginnings, for Davis was nothing if not outrageous during interviews and cared less about maintaining the dignity Crawford cherished. The latter would surely not have submitted to a sketch on the *Steve Allen Show* called "What Ever Happened To Baby Fink?" but Davis did, and was game besides to record a twist variation of *Baby Jane*'s theme song. Her performance of that was seen on *The Andy Williams Show*, and it's happily part of Warner's special edition of the film on DVD and Blu-ray.

Two years before Susan Sontag analyzed and immortalized the term, *Baby Jane* was camp on the verge of camp's recognition, though in 1962 this picture was sold and consumed as straight gothic terror. The prospect of gorgons like Blanche and Jane living just off Hollywood Boulevard was no leap of faith for viewers who indeed wondered whatever happened to familiar faces from late-night television. They'd fed on '30s movies since TV began, but never so many as had been broadcast in the six years prior to *Baby Jane*'s release.

Bette Davis seemed to have divined those camp sensibilities *Baby Jane* would eventually appeal to. She embraced full-out performing needed to put this one over, both onscreen and as uninhibited promoter for the film. It was OK by Davis to see her early emoting submitted to ridicule during opening flashback sequences detailing why *Baby Jane* never made it as an ingénue player.

Parachute Jumper and *Ex-Lady* were the Warner programmers excerpted, long before historians discovered joyous potential in studio pre-Code vaults. Davis spent years declaring them wretched movies. TV runs by 1962 were sporadic, and revival theatres took little interest in titles so obscure. Davis had scant opportunity to see such pics again and realize how much fun they were, especially in comparison with overwrought WB melodramas she'd make during the '40s. Mining by William K. Everson in the mid-'70s and his New School showings began the slow rehabilitation for these and other worthy pre-Codes.

Above: Plain-speaking Bette pitches *Baby Jane* on *The Andy Williams Show*. **Below:** Joan goes old school to promote her book and decries the death of establishment Hollywood and the decorum of its stars.

While Davis twisted on behalf of *Baby Jane*, Crawford burned. She'd mourn the romance and glamour her beloved industry had forfeited. Hollywood could thrive again if only they'd make stars the way they used to, and by extension, if ones like Davis would behave with decorum befitting their legendary status.

Crawford made many adjustments to stay hep with the times for going on four decades. Now, she was wagging fingers at newcomers like Liz Taylor and Marilyn Monroe with a sort of don't-do-as-I-once-did-do-as-I-say-now attitude. There's an illuminating Crawford interview with British historian Philip Jenkinson wherein she longs for times as vanished as those Blanche and Jane Hudson clung to and refers to herself as having been a *teenager* during silent days at MGM!

Davis picked up on ironies lost to insular Crawford. The former's cheeky *Variety* want ad for acting jobs after the triumph of *Baby Jane* would never have occurred to uptight Crawford. Indeed, it may have been the latter's awareness of that plus resentment of such antics that led to Crawford's campaign against Davis' bid for an Academy Award.

Both actresses had books out when *Baby Jane* hit theatres. Still, their public knew far less of their lives than we'd learn from biographies later on. Press inquiry revolved around ego clashes surely to come of co-starring these two. As early as July and before shooting began, columnists said there'd be fireworks. Would Davis and Crawford act in accordance with characters they'd played in all their movies? If so, expect a donnybrook.

Did Davis kick Crawford in the head and leave an injury requiring stitches? Hopefully, yes. Did Crawford weigh herself down so Davis would wrench her back hauling the actress across floors? Surely she would, if for no reason than to avenge having her head kicked in. "People who loved the violence of it thought it was inherent, but it wasn't," said Aldrich. Tales of on-set combat were/are distorted, but they're hard to resist in view of physical and emotional carnage in *What Ever Happened to Baby Jane?*

As star exposé and icon dismantling got grubbier in the '70s, Davis loosened restraints for writers telling her side of the Crawford story. *Mother Goddam* was a 1974 bio with Davis commentary tempered by Joan still being alive, but later *This 'n That* in 1987 saw gloves coming off. Crawford's alcoholism and unbridled vanity were on the table now, and *I'd Love to Kiss You: Conversations with Bette Davis*, published shortly after BD's death in 1989, found her referring to JC's past venereal diseases as possible reason for the actress's hygienic obsession.

The cracked doll head was my introduction to *Baby Jane* in 1962 newspaper ads. I didn't even ask permission to go see the picture. That image ran a close

Bette Davis pursues a killer schedule to stump for her picture in New York City.

257

second to *Devil Doll* for me as the 1960's most disquieting. *Baby Jane* was and still is a decathlon among horror films. People bragged then for having got through it. I was packed off to bed the Sunday night of *Baby Jane*'s network broadcast premiere shortly after Blanche was served her rat dinner. That moment was treasured among members of my age group at the time. Ten years later, a college sorority played it in our student commons lobby because, outside of *Psycho*, *Baby Jane* was considered about the scariest picture around.

I never heard anyone laughing at *Baby Jane* until well into the '80s. Camp following must have hardened sensibilities, for I watched the film again recently and was as traumatized as ever. This is one epoch maker for cruel and nasty. My fast-forward spared me much of BD's shrieking and JC's agony but did slow down whenever Victor Buono undulated onto the scene. Whether slurping cereal or heaping invective upon his suffocating mother, Buono is humor's godsend in a picture otherwise relentless in its assault upon nerves.

I've read that director Aldrich couldn't afford process screens and so had Davis driving down Hollywood streets as his camera rolled alongside, economy thus tipping us to what a drab and bleached-out location L.A. had become by 1962. The Hudson house is a convincing fall from grace, probably not unlike places a lot of old stars live in yet. Blanche's movie relics on television are shot through with obnoxious announcers and dog food commercials, a time-honored object of industry scorn since the early '50s, then more recently when Billy Wilder had Jack Lemmon trying to watch *Grand Hotel* on his TV in *The Apartment*.

Baby Jane's overlength comes of bodies dragged or dragging s-l-o-w-l-y: Davis with a housekeeper she's hammered to death and Crawford's agonizing crawl down a flight of stairs. Maybe people mock *Baby Jane* to relieve intensity otherwise unbearable. I know I was glad to see it finally end.

Above: Some *Baby Jane* ads are raw in their depiction of the evening's entertainment ahead. Opposite page: The all-out selling blitz includes a contest to describe in 50 words the most exciting scene in the picture, for which the trip of a lifetime is grand prize.

HOLLYWOOD PREVIEW ENGAGEMENT MAKES IT ALL POSSIBLE!

WIN A TRIP FOR 2 TO FABULOUS HOLLYWOOD OR GLAMOROUS N.Y.*

OR ANY ONE OF MANY EXCITING PRIZES FOR EVERYONE IN THE FAMILY!!!

Arrangements by AMERICAN AIRLINES!

IN NEW YORK YOU'LL STAY AT THE WORLD'S TALLEST HOTEL, THE AMERICANA. IN L.A. YOU'LL STAY AT THE LUXURIOUS AMBASSADOR, A SCHINE HOTEL AND ENJOY A NIGHT AT ITS WORLD FAMOUS COCOANUT GROVE.

*3 GRAND PRIZES!!!
1200 PRIZES IN ALL!!!

HERE'S HOW YOU WIN: see Bette Davis and Joan Crawford in their long-anticipated first screen appearance together and in fifty (50) words or less describe what you felt was the most exciting scene in the shock-packed, screen-shattering suspense drama, "WHAT EVER HAPPENED TO BABY JANE?". Bring or mail your entry to this theatre. Be sure to include your name and address. Contest closes January 31, 1963. Judges decision final. Prizes are non-transferable and cannot be redeemed for their cash value.

SEE! BETTE DAVIS and JOAN CRAWFORD WHAT EVER HAPPENED TO BABY JANE?

Heroes for the counterculture Bonnie and Clyde give audiences the same thrill that 20th Century Fox's Jesse and Frank James had 28 years earlier.

CHAPTER 27

WARNER BROS.' BULL'S-EYE SELLING OF BONNIE AND CLYDE

There's less celebration of *Bonnie and Clyde* as decades pass. Recognition of its fortieth anniversary in 2007 seemed lukewarm. Generational struggles the picture once represented aren't relevant anymore, as the disapproving establishment circa 1967 is mostly gone now, and victors who claimed cultural dominance are themselves under siege by revisionist-minded youngsters in diapers or not yet born when *Bonnie and Clyde* was released. A few even dared to acknowledge merit in the scabrous Bosley Crowther review that set off a firestorm when the film was new and led to the critic's forced retirement after years with the New York *Times*.

A 1960s-bred generation still flatters itself for having pulled down a decaying critical hierarchy too moss-bound and obtuse to "get" *Bonnie and Clyde*. Grayed rebels clinging tenaciously to their myths won't acknowledge that they were but lemmings enticed to ticket windows by what I'd call a plain inspired sales plan by Warner Bros. Wait—weren't they supposed to have bungled distribution and fought against Warren Beatty's vision all the way to those cast-off drive-ins where *Bonnie and Clyde* was allegedly dumped?

One latter-day columnist addressed the fortieth anniversary thus: "Warner Bros. thought so little of the film that they released it as a "B" movie, primarily to drive-ins and second-tier theatres." That's a damning reference to territorial openings common at the time. What more insulting for New York critics and their acolytes than having the season's pet movie open in Texas and across the South prior to saturation in urban markets far better able to appreciate such a groundbreaker? The fact that *Bonnie and Clyde* went wide first in the South was something elites would never get over. To this day, they call it a black mark against Warner Bros.

Once again, it helps to have been there. We got *Bonnie and Clyde* at the Liberty on September 13, 1967. That was a month before Pauline Kael's review in the *New Yorker*, which is supposed to have further stoked the tempest. Down where I lived, *Bonnie and Clyde* was an unknown quantity. The limited openings in New York had taken place August 13 after a Montreal film festival showing on the fourth of that month. Saturation bookings in the South and Southwest would be the public's first wide exposure to the film.

Warner Bros. based much of its campaign on the positive reviews *Bonnie and Clyde* had received after the Canada and New York bows. Naysayers like Crowther were more than offset by raves else-

'Bonnie and Clyde' Opens Film Festival

Mr. Exhibitor:

Your next attraction, 'BONNIE AND CLYDE', had its world premiere at a time and place, and in circumstances that brought it world attention.

- The picture was the official United States entry in the International Film Festival held in Montreal in August, 1967, as part of exciting Expo 67;

- It was accorded the honor of being the film that opened the entire festival;

- Producer and star Warren Beatty, co-star Faye Dunaway and director Arthur Penn attended and received top attention from the international press and the knowledgeable first-night audience;

- Reactions were overwhelming.

The New York Times, reporting from Montreal on this major cultural event, noted that the film was "wildly received with gales of laughter and given a terminal burst of applause."

Expo 67 was knocked dead by 'BONNIE AND CLYDE.' Now it's your turn to knock 'em dead with 'BONNIE AND CLYDE.' You can start by planting with your local outlets the news story, (right) which describes the prestigious and successful premiere of 'BONNIE AND CLYDE' in Montreal.

'Bonnie and Clyde' Cheered In Canada

The exciting new film, of "Bonnie and Clyde," which opens ...... at the .... Theater, provided a smash opening for Montreal's Eighth International Film Festival. Doubly honored by being chosen as the official United States motion picture entry in the festival and as the opening-night feature presentation, "Bonnie and Clyde" captivated the critical first-night audience and the international press covering the event.

Jacob Siskind, film critic for The Montreal Gazette called "Bonnie and Clyde" a "blockbuster" and "one of the most engrossing American motion pictures I have ever seen." His colleague on The Montreal Globe and Mail, Joan Fox, wrote: "I've seldom experienced such a public reception for a film and can only go along with the enthusiasm and report 'Bonnie and Clyde' is Arthur Penn's chef d'oeuvre. This film should establish him as a director of the first rank."

The festivities which marked the start of such an important film festival were heightened by appearances of the film's stars, Warren Beatty and Faye Dunaway. The director, Arthur Penn, was also present for a round of press conferences and for the gala opening night parties.

The Warner Bros.-Seven Arts release, "Bonnie and Clyde," kicked off the 15-day film Montreal festival which included entries from all the major motion picture - producing countries. An important cultural feature of Expo 67, the festival was held in the new 2,000-seat Expo Theater.

The Technicolor action-packed film which created international interest at Montreal comes here after a major opening in New York following the world premiere in Canada. In the title roles are Warren Beatty as Clyde Barrow, and Faye Dunaway as Bonnie Parker. The other members of the notorious Barrow gang, which ripped through the Southwest in the 1930's robbing banks, include Michael J. Pollard, Gene Hackman and Estelle Parsons. The fascinating film about a group of thrill-seekers on a crime spree was directed by Arthur Penn and was the first venture produced by Warren Beatty.

"VERY MUCH WORTH SEEING! A BEAUTIFULLY MADE FILM AND AN EXCELLENT ONE TO BOOT! ONE OF THE FINEST AMERICAN FILMS OF THIS YEAR!"
—*Judith Crist, Today Show*

"A JUMPING UP AND DOWN RAVE! A WORK OF CINEMATIC ART! The screen is strewn with violence, but the violence is meaningful, vital to an understanding of these real people. UNFORGETTABLE! HOMAGE TO ALL!"
—*Ladies' Home Journal*

"STUNNING DIRECTION, SENSITIVE PERFORMANCES AND BEAUTIFUL CAMERA WORK!"
—*Seventeen*

"AN AMERICAN WORK OF ART—POSSIBLY THE BEST FILM OF THIS YEAR! 'Bonnie and Clyde' has been brought perfectly to the screen! The action stuff is simply overwhelming. Warren Beatty gives the greatest performance of his life. JUST GO SEE THIS PICTURE. YOU WILL NEVER FORGET IT!"
—*Cosmopolitan*

"EXPLOSIVE! JAZZY! POWERFUL! WARREN BEATTY AND ARTHUR PENN MAY WELL BE APPLAUDED!"
—*Coronet Magazine*

"VIVID, VIOLENT TALE! UNUSUAL! FASCINATING! Captures a sense of the period and attempts to understand the twisted motives of the young man and his girl who went on a prolonged bank-robbing and killing spree. Exceedingly well made – astonishingly good performance by Warren Beatty."
—*Saturday Review*

"I SUGGEST VERY STRONGLY THAT YOU SEE IT! One of the finest films I have ever seen coming out of Hollywood!"
—*Women's Wear Daily*

"★★★★! BOLD AND BRASSY, BRUTAL AND BRILLIANT! The pace – furious. The cast is perfect. No one can help but marvel at the film's technical virtuosity!"
—*N.Y. Daily News*

WARREN **BEATTY**
FAYE **DUNAWAY**

BONNIE AND CLYDE

ALSO STARRING
MICHAEL J. POLLARD · GENE HACKMAN · ESTELLE PARSONS
WRITTEN BY DAVID NEWMAN and ROBERT BENTON · MUSIC BY Charles Strouse · PRODUCED BY WARREN BEATTY · DIRECTED BY ARTHUR PENN
TECHNICOLOR® FROM WARNER BROS. - SEVEN ARTS

Elements of *Bonnie and Clyde*'s marketing campaign include an ad speaking to exhibitors (above left) a review one-sheet (above right), and a two-page trade ad with verbiage speaking to the counterculture (below). Opposite page: Bullet-riddled windshields bring to mind the ballyhoo of days gone by.

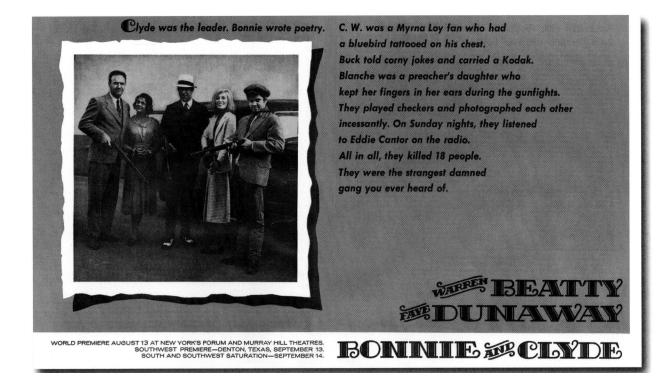

Clyde was the leader. Bonnie wrote poetry.

C. W. was a Myrna Loy fan who had a bluebird tattooed on his chest. Buck told corny jokes and carried a Kodak. Blanche was a preacher's daughter who kept her fingers in her ears during the gunfights. They played checkers and photographed each other incessantly. On Sunday nights, they listened to Eddie Cantor on the radio. All in all, they killed 18 people. They were the strangest damned gang you ever heard of.

WARREN **BEATTY**
FAYE **DUNAWAY**

BONNIE AND CLYDE

WORLD PREMIERE AUGUST 13 AT NEW YORK'S FORUM AND MURRAY HILL THEATRES.
SOUTHWEST PREMIERE—DENTON, TEXAS, SEPTEMBER 13.
SOUTH AND SOUTHWEST SATURATION—SEPTEMBER 14.

where. The pressbook was salted with laudatory quotes. Better still for exhibitors was a free package of accessories that normally would have run upwards of $10 for rental.

I noticed the set of door panels right away when the Liberty started *Bonnie and Clyde*, and a bullet-hole decal on the back windshield of a parked car out front was reminiscent of ballyhoo they'd done back in 3-D and Cinemascope days. It was only when Colonel Forehand gave me the pressbook that I realized these extras were gratis, courtesy of Warners' sales force. This wasn't the first time they'd done a little something extra for showmen. Bookings for *Chamber of Horrors* in 1966 included a free Fear Flasher/Horror Horn standee with powered lights and sound effects.

There was something distinctly ahead of the curve about Warner campaigns. They'd been trend setting and showing up the competition for more than a year prior to *Bonnie and Clyde*. I'd submit that modern movie advertising began with Warner Bros. Note sassy appeals to seen-it-all patrons encouraged to share a wink with Paul Newman's *Harper* in February 1966, among the first camped-up and deliberately sarcastic ad appeals for a straightforward detective thriller. That same month saw *Inside Daisy Clover* and an almost confrontational tagline—**and a special word of thanks to all the slobs, creeps and finks of the world**—ideally suited to product demands of fashionably disaffected youth. *Who's Afraid of Virginia Woolf?* (June 1966) was marketed with precise awareness of its eventual impact. Cunning Warner salesmen had painted targets on the backs of sophisticated moviegoers nationwide by the time *Bonnie and Clyde*'s campaign hit the drawing board.

A plan this good would *still* work. **They're young...they're in love...and they kill people.** Is that brilliant or is that brilliant? Anyone claiming Warners botched this sale must have rocks in their head. Warners' several alternate ads suggest what I'd consider a major reason for *Bonnie and Clyde*'s fantastic success. Each are knowingly hip and cutting edge. The pressbook refers to the film's "dry wit" and violent punch. Advertising delivery on both is what put this show over. Stark contrast is furnished by way of Fox's conventional effort on behalf of *The St. Valentine's Day Massacre*, a not dissimilar product released within months of *Bonnie and Clyde*. There was nothing wrong with Roger Corman's movie, other than its ultimate loss of $264,000, with an arthritic sales force pushing *St. Valentine's* as though it were *Little Caesar*—and what misguided staffer proposed a tie-in for George Segal's *Yama-Yama Man* banjo album?

Few pictures have had the ingenious kind of tell-at-a-glance exploitation assist offered by Warner Bros.-Seven Arts to exhibitors due to play 'BONNIE AND CLYDE.' A reproduction is shown on these pages. The item is made of clear, heavy-duty acetate over-printed in three colors. The tagline, "Bonnie and Clyde was here" is done in red to simulate the scrawl of a lipstick. The item is manufactured in a size of 11 by 15 inches and carries clear adhesive top and bottom so that it may easily be affixed to side or rear car windows (NEVER TO WINDSHIELDS) or to any glass surface such as storefronts, mirrors, doors. You'll want to have your allotment out working as soon as possible. THE SUPPLY IS LIMITED — FIRST COME, FIRST SERVED. Quantity is LIMITED — 25 copies to a theatre. If you want this item — DON'T WASTE TIME. Request it right away.

Here is how to use the sensational 'BONNIE AND CLYDE' exploitation item!

• Make it hard to get, a prestige gimmick, something that not everyone can have, something that everyone will want to be the first on his block to own;
• Do that by tieing-up with a deejay, for instance, and have him offer it as a special prize for a 'BONNIE AND CLYDE' contest;
• Or, let an auto supply store or a car dealer be the only one to give it away in return for purchase of a given amount of merchandise, or a new car; naturally, you get cross-plug advertising or promotion in return;
• Tie-up with a big supermarket, have them give out one to a store to customers who meet given qualifications.

Philips Records has planned a smashing campaign to promote the album by George Segal "The Yama Yama Man." Segal plays the notorious Pete Gusenberg, head gunman for gang leader Bugs Moran in "The St. Valentine's Day Massacre." Shown here is a 4-foot standee of Segal holding the album which captures the sounds of the 20's, with Segal accompanying himself on the banjo. It is Segal's first album -- the young, popular dramatic star branching out to conquer new worlds in entertainment.

Exhibitors should not miss this excellent opportunity to make tie-ins with record stores and to make displays in windows, on store counters and in theatre lobbies. Contact 20th Century-Fox fieldmen for assistance in this valuable promotion. They have the list of Philips managers and promotion representatives throughout the country.

Who is "the Yama Yama Man?" It's George -- George Segal, that is! The exciting young star, who turned millions on with his Academy-Award nominated performance in "Who's Afraid of Virginia Woolf," is ready to let loose as he goes on record with his singin' and strummin' new side that will excite millions!

So be sure to let that boyish charm reach out and grab 'em -- Use this special 4-foot die-cut display wherever "The Yama Yama Man" is on sale!

All this and a top 40 single too!

THE YAMA YAMA MAN

and

YES SIR, THAT'S MY BABY

Old school versus new in the mid-1960s shows the campaign for Fox's *The St. Valentine's Day Massacre* (top left and right) versus three innovative campaigns from Warner Bros. in support of *Virginia Woolf*, *Harper*, and *Daisy Clover*.

Thick with irony is the fact that *Bonnie and Clyde* filmmakers so cleverly utilized the same instrument to augment their soundtrack, as I well remember rushing out to buy that 45 rpm single of *Foggy Mountain Breakdown*. I'm betting the *Bonnie and Clyde* craze was no accident, despite what others have written. Warners knew it would take off in the South, and that's why we got it early. For us, it was *Thunder Road* all over again.

Dixie territorial openings have a noble history. After all, weren't we first to get *Brides of Dracula*, *The Ghost and Mr. Chicken*, and *The Wild Bunch*? Snobs up north accused, and maintain, that Warners abandoned *Bonnie and Clyde* thusly. The Liberty's problem was *retrieving* this show once audience demand tied up available prints. By late fall these were exhibitor equivalents of Faberge eggs. Everybody wanted *Bonnie and Clyde*, and in those days 400 prints in circulation was the norm, as opposed to 3,000 to 4,000 we'd later see on opening weekends. It took Colonel Forehand until May 25 the following year to score a return booking.

My fervent embrace of *Bonnie and Clyde* resulted in two trips to the Liberty during that one-week en-

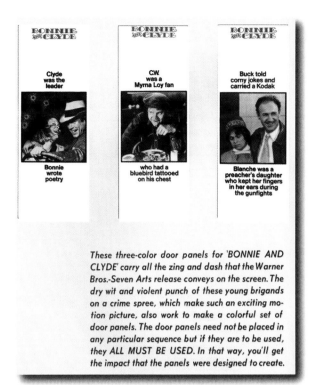

These three-color door panels for 'BONNIE AND CLYDE' carry all the zing and dash that the Warner Bros.-Seven Arts release conveys on the screen. The dry wit and violent punch of these young brigands on a crime spree, which make such an exciting motion picture, also work to make a colorful set of door panels. The door panels need not be placed in any particular sequence but if they are to be used, they ALL MUST BE USED. In that way, you'll get the impact that the panels were designed to create.

A set of door panels caught my eye at the Liberty and served as part of an effective sales campaign in support of *Bonnie and Clyde.*

gagement. I realized early on the price I'd pay in the final third for fun I'd had in the first. That may be why I didn't revisit the DVD for an anniversary look. More than 40 years have passed, but Estelle Parsons' screeching in the back seat of that blood-soaked car is still a daunting prospect.

Bonnie and Clyde may take credit for stoking the revolution, but that's been over a long time now, and even though their side won, that still doesn't make it easier to sit through an at times very unpleasant show. Could this explain so few throwing birthday parties when *Bonnie and Clyde* hit 40? A handful of web sites rose to the challenge of explaining *Bonnie and Clyde* and why it matters, or doesn't. The younger ones come across a little doubtful. They missed going straight from university-town showings to marches on the chancellor's house back in 1967. All that's left to them is the movie, and how likely is that to pack a wallop equal to what it did four decades back?

Much of *Bonnie and Clyde*'s initial reception was weighted down with politics and social issues largely forgotten now. I wasn't aware of all that when I was 13 and seeing it new. That's just as well, for it compels me less to defend the film now against justified revisionist criticism. We've all had occasion to accept a film's greatness on someone else's authority, and that someone is usually the person who saw it brand new and can summon up memories of impact and emotion we'll never feel. *Bonnie and Clyde* will not again deliver the goods as once it did, though I'm glad I was there to flinch with other first-run-shocked observers. But what of all those great shows I missed by accident of (too late) birth? Have my perceptions of these been largely shaped by impressions my viewing elders passed down?

CHARLOTTE CHRYSLER-PLYMOUTH and

Big WAYS—Radio 61
Charlotte's Santa Claus
WILL BABY SIT FOR YOU AT
The Big CAPRI Theatre
WHILE YOU DO YOUR CHRISTMAS SHOPPING!

YOUR CHILDREN WILL ENJOY A
BIG 3 HOUR PROGRAM OF FUN & LAUGHS!

- ★ **The Beatles**
- ★ **Dave Clark 5**
- ★ **3 Stooges**
  WALT DISNEY'S
- **3 Bears**
  IN YELLOWSTONE
- ★ **16 Color Cartoons**
- ★ **Tom & Jerry**
- ★ **Road Runner**

You Can See It FREE!

GET YOUR FREE TICKETS FROM
BIG WAYS
400 Radio Road
CAPRI THEATRE
For Further Details
Listen To
Radio 61
B-I-G WAYS!

PRESENTED AS A COMMUNITY SERVICE . . .
In A Special Effort To Give Parents A Place To Leave Children
While You Do Your Shopping!
Leave the Kiddies at the CAPRI!

Tickets Also At CHARLOTTE CHRYSLER-PLYMOUTH, 1615 S. Tryon St.

5 BIG DAYS! # MON. thru FRI., DEC. 20-24

OPEN 9:30 A. M. DAILY — 3 Hour Show 10:00 A. M. — 1:00 P. M.

BIG CAPRI THEATRE
3500 E. INDEPENDENCE BLVD.

ADMISSION WITHOUT FREE TICKET
All Seats **50c**
First Come . . . First Served
Seating Limited To Capacity

Come Early For A Seat! — Only 1,000 Persons Admitted Daily!

EPILOGUE

LIGHTS OUT

So when and why did showmanship fade? I place decline's start around the mid-'60s. Others might argue it was sooner, that exhibition's party was over well before then. It helped that we in small towns kept main-street theatres open beyond wider trends of boarding up and giving up. The Liberty clung to grassroots promoting as long as it could. There's happy memory of a pony cart that Colonel Forehand dressed out and sent to our elementary school in 1962 to carry kids the less than half a mile to see *Papa's Delicate Condition*, and delighted we were to find an authentic racing car parked in front of the Liberty on *Redline 7000*'s opening day in November 1965. These were but last gasps of a bally tradition fading fast, and stark contrast to photos Col. Forehand had of past campaigns, including a street parade to herald *The Greatest Show on Earth* in 1952, with crowds lining Main Street in front of the Liberty and blocks surrounding it. I could only dream of being there—*born too late again!*—but locals would speak of it and some remember still.

Newsprint ads shrunk and posters got uglier as Hollywood depended more on TV promotion and saturation bookings. We were, of course, a couple months behind the larger towns these covered. I'd see *Goldfinger* advertised on all three networks in winter 1965, knowing it would be well into spring before the Liberty would have it.

Colonel Forehand gave me pressbooks for every show he played. They told of stunts other theatres used to sell tickets, but the Liberty by then could barely maintain ad presence in our twice-weekly, and that was mere recital of titles and start time, with no art or graphics to dress the limited space bought.

For reasons best known to the maturity level of a 14 year old, I decided to volunteer myself as ongoing movie critic for a rival gazette in which the Liberty did not advertise—was that why I got the job? My audition was a snarky review of *King Kong Escapes*, that akin to shooting fish in a barrel, but the publisher was amused. I came to better understanding in that 1968–69 season just how far movies

Opposite page: A mid-'60s peak of Main Street showmanship on the eve of changed times and decline for grass-roots promoting. Charlotte's Capri Theatre teams with a leading radio station and plays Santa Claus to parents in need of babysitting while holiday shopping gets done (Presented as a Community Service). Neighbor merchants are happy to hand out free tickets for the show, linking with the Capri in a best tradition of co-op between exhibition and surrounding business. Alas, there wouldn't be many more Christmases like this for hometown moviegoers.

had sunk and why people were staying home with their televisions. Much as I sought to apply an even hand, it was tough singing praise for *Skidoo*, *Lady in Cement*, and *The Horse in the Gray Flannel Suit*. Sometimes my editor would juice a headline over reviews to emphasize my displeasure, as in **The Green Slime Is Repudiating Movie**. The only unqualified rave I submitted was for *The Wild Bunch*.

My reviews ended when the upstart newspaper itself folded. From there, the Liberty kept lights on, but drew lines to but few attractions: a *Patton* here, a *Billy Jack* there (*BJ* was huge in my town). Colonel Forehand wanted to stop weekday matinees, but the owner, Ivan Anderson, who'd been exhibiting since talkies arrived, wouldn't hear of it. The doors finally closed in 1974, but not for long. A local businessman who'd ushered at the Liberty as a teenager reopened the venerable site the following year and bisected an auditorium that had once seated 700, turning its balcony into a projection booth for two screens. What I remembered most fondly of the Liberty thus fell before market realities and knowledge that the good old days at the movies, at least for me, were spent for keeps.

I'd be foolish to argue that showmanship is dead but would maintain we've lost it at a grassroots level. Promotion today is high-tech and expansive beyond the dreams of exhibition as it thrived/struggled in a classic era this book commemorates. What has evolved in its place is undeniably progress, even as much of hometown hoopla and individual initiative were sacrificed to get there. As the American experience becomes more homogenized, so too does the selling of movies. What's still here to enjoy, at least, are souvenirs of showmanship that heralded the coming of features now regarded as classic, such artifacts richly evocative of days when treasured shows were new.

CHAPTER NOTES

Chapter 1: About Those So-Called Good Old Days...

Much of the information regarding showmanship and exhibition came from the recollections of those who operated and/or worked in theatres and, in some instances, spent lifetimes in the trade. They include Roy Forehand, Dale Baldwin, Garland Morrison, Eddie Knight, Homer Hanes, Mike Cline, Don Jarvis, Tom Osteen, Moon Mullins, Bill Wooten, Wesley Clark, William Sears, Dan Austell, and Geoffrey Rayle. Veteran booker Bill Cline offered details regarding Popeye Clubs during the 1930s. Roy Forehand, Dale Baldwin, and Mike Cline gave me specifics on movie cowboys who appeared in person at small-town theatres in North Carolina. Dan Austell told me of his experiences with kiddie and teen stage shows at his Carolina Theatre in Winston-Salem, North Carolina, back in the '60s. Homer Hanes spoke of late shows and vintage movies that continued playing his Hickory, North Carolina, venue well past presumed sell dates. Phil Morris shared anecdotes of performing on theatre stages as "Dr. Evil" and gave me ad art done for his traveling spook shows. Trade magazines of the classic era were rich with showman accounts of hard and happy times in the theatre business: *Boxoffice*, *Exhibitor*, the *Motion Picture Herald*, *Showmen's Trade Review*, *Harrison's Reports*, the *Independent Film Journal*, *Moving Picture World*, and others spoke vividly to realities of operating a theatre when movies were a dominant mode of entertainment.

Chapter 2: All Aboard the Mutilation Express

This was based in large part on a fascinating *Moving Picture World* account (12/17/21) of the cross-country train trip during which *Foolish Wives* was edited to its New York premiere length. I also found useful info in the *Universal Weekly*, a publication the studio maintained in order to get word out on movies in production or going into release. There was information in vintage *Blackhawk Bulletins* about Arthur Lennig's restoration of *Foolish Wives* and availability of the film in 8mm and 16mm from Blackhawk. Helpful too were outstanding books on von Stroheim by Thomas Quinn Curtiss, Richard Koszarski, Joel Finler, Herman G. Weinberg, and most definitively, Arthur Lennig's biography of EvS, *Stroheim* (University Press of Kentucky), published in 2000.

Chapter 3: Titillated to Distraction

Much insight was supplied here by trade publications of the pre-Code era. Nothing sums up lean times like letters to editors informing them of a theatre gone broke or shows unable to meet their rental costs. Dr. Karl Thiede was the usual font of information with regard to profit and loss on pre-Code features. Product annuals, specifically RKO's from 1932–33, were very illuminating. Theatre ads and trade accounts of promotions for shows like *The Blonde Captive* and *Freaks* were vivid in detailing how such films were sold. Original photos and theatre ads were from my collection.

Chapter 4: When RKO Flew Down to Rio

Veteran showman Garland Morrison supplied much insight as to small-town promotion of *Flying Down to Rio* when it was new in 1933. Information on producer Merian C. Cooper came from *Living Dangerously: The Adventures of Merian C. Cooper, The Creator of King Kong*, by Mark Vaz (Villard, 2005). RKO's 1933–34 product annual was source of info as to initial casting for *Flying Down to Rio*, and original theatre ads from the film's Radio City Music Hall opening showed how the film was sold on Broadway. *Variety* was a source for further insight as to this and other first-runs, and RKO's pressbook had much in the way of colorful ad art. Dr. Karl Thiede furnished box-office data for *Rio* and other RKO features referenced.

Chapter 5: Metro and the Marxes

Dr. Karl Thiede filled me in on costs and rentals on comedies the Marx Brothers did at Paramount and MGM as well as supplying context as to other Paramount features from around the same period. Trade ads and imagery from the *Motion Picture Herald* were helpful in showing what went on with regard to promotion of *A Night at the Opera*, and Mark Vieira's fine biography, *Irving Thalberg: Boy Wonder to Producer Prince* (Fletcher Jones Foundation Book in the Humanities) (University of California Press, 2009), gave me insight into that producer's methods. Original theatre ads helped to illustrate Chico Marx's live act during the '40s and a Chicago first-run for *A Night in Casablanca*. Finally, it was our local community college English instructor Bill Moffitt who made it possible for me to see *A Night at the Opera* for the first time in 1974 when he loaned me a 16mm Films, Inc. rental print.

Chapter 6: Metro's Jean Harlow Closeout Sale

David Stenn's definitive Jean Harlow biography, *Bombshell: The Life and Death of Jean Harlow* (Doubleday, 1993), was a source of context for the actress' career as she approached *Saratoga* and her 1937 death. Dr. Karl Thiede provided rental figures. *Variety*, the *Motion Picture Herald*, and *Harrison's Reports* had much to chronicle the process of salvaging *Saratoga*. The original pressbook for *Saratoga* made suggestions and proposed ideas to soften morbid aspects of a post-passing Harlow vehicle. MGM trade ads reflected tact toward the selling of *Saratoga*, but at the same time sold it hard.

Chapter 7: The Pair That Curled Your Hair

The *Motion Picture Herald* and exhibitor comments published therein helped illustrate reaction to the *Dracula/Frankenstein* combo, and there was additional data in *Boxoffice*, the New York *Times*, *Harrison's Reports*, and *Variety*. Jean Cannon at the University of Texas Austin's Harry S. Ransom Center supplied trade articles. Pressbooks and theatre ads from 1938, 1947, and 1952 were helpful in showing how the double feature was promoted. Background on Arthur Mayer and his legendary Rialto Theatre came from his own memoir, *Merely Colossal: The Story of the Movies from the Long Chase to the Chaise Longue* (Simon and Schuster, 1953). Dr. Karl Thiede had the negative cost figure for *Son of Frankenstein*. William Brandt's letter to Realart came from the 1952 *Dracula/Frankenstein* pressbook. I found info on New York's Victory Theatre at the indispensable Cinema Treasures web site. John Story sent Realart theatre ads from his own Indiana territory, and lastly, Richard Watson was the generous soul who drove me to the Starlight Drive-In in August 1968 so I could see *The Curse of Frankenstein*.

Chapter 8: The Great Jesse James Box-Office Raid

Background on the location shoot of *Jesse James* came from Larry C. Bradley's colorful *Jesse James: The Making of a Legend* (Larren), published in 1980. Jerry Williamson was host to those of us who saw the very rare *Stark Love* at Appalachian State University. Data from the *Motion Picture Herald* showed how exhibitors responded to both *Jesse James* and its sequel, *The Return of Frank James*. Dr. Karl Thiede gave insight as to how well the pair continued doing in reissues. Longtime booker Bill Cline had info on the later days of *Jesse James* in North Carolina theatres. Ace showman and former venue manager for the ABC Southeastern chain Mike Cline gave me all the dope, plus ad art, on *Jesse James* as a 1972 "project picture" for his company.

Chapter 9: John Ford's Evergreen Stagecoach

John Newman found microfilm to aid my search for *Stagecoach* bookings in North Carolina during the '60s. Russ McCown filled me in on *Stagecoach* lore and put me by way of a nice 16mm print. Matthew Bernstein's excellent book, *Walter Wanger: Hollywood Independent* (University of California Press, 1994), had fascinating info on John Wayne's *Stagecoach* casting. Scott Eyman's *Print the Legend: The Life and Times of John Ford* (Simon & Schuster, 1999), has an illuminating chapter on the making of *Stagecoach*, as does Tag Gallagher's book, *John Ford: The Man and His Films* (University of California Press, 1986). The *Motion Picture Herald* and *Stagecoach*'s original pressbook, plus one for the 1948 reissue with *The Long Voyage Home*, had much that was useful, and account ledgers from the Liberty Theatre told how much *Stagecoach* cost to rent and how it performed. Dr. Karl Thiede had rental data on *Stagecoach* and other westerns from 1939. Gerald Haber was the collector whose 1948 print of *Stagecoach* enabled me to see just how good the picture could look.

Chapter 10: The Three Million Dollar Splurge

The MGM strategy for release of *The Wizard of Oz* was covered by *Variety* through a latter half of 1939 and into 1940, along with comparisons of *Oz*'s reception with that of Paramount's *Gulliver's Travels* and the earlier *Snow White and the Seven Dwarfs*. MGM trade ads and pressbooks for the 1949, 1955, and 1972 reissues gave insight to devices used to update *Oz* for new generations of patronage. The Independent *Film Journal*, *Boxoffice* and the *Motion Picture Herald* had much to say about *The Wizard of Oz* coming to television in November 1956, as did *Broadcasting* magazine. Dr. Karl Thiede supplied rental figures for *Oz*'s initial release and subsequent revivals.

Chapter 11: Campaigning for Kane

Dr. Karl Thiede had financial data for not only *Citizen Kane*, but other RKO releases from the same period of 1941–42. RKO's product annual illustrated an upcoming *John Citizen, USA*, later to be *Citizen Kane*. Orson Welles' objections to the delay of release for *Kane* was reported in *Variety*, the *Motion Picture Herald*, and the New York *Times*. J.A. Aberdeen's book, *Hollywood Renegades: The Society of Independent Motion Picture Producers* (Cobblestone Enterprises, 1999), told of Samuel Goldwyn's Reno tent showing for *Up in Arms*. The *Motion Picture Herald* detailed Palace Theatre preparations to open *Citizen Kane* in New York. There were two separate pressbooks issued by RKO to support *Citizen Kane*, each offering a distinct approach for selling the film. Collector/Showman Mike Cline made rare stills available, including the one with Alan Ladd. Dr. Karl Thiede had information on C&C's withholding of certain RKO titles, including *Citizen Kane*, from television until the 1956 reissue played out. *Variety* reported on Bryant Haliday and Cyrus Harvey, Jr.'s art-house revival of *Kane* in February 1956 that led to a nationwide reissue later that year. The *Motion Picture Herald* reported showman successes with the 1956 reissue of *Citizen Kane*, including one in Dallas, Texas. United Artists Associated's *Movietime USA* catalogue offering television rights to the RKO library was furnished to me by Fred Santon. Films, Inc.'s 1971 16mm catalogue, *Rediscovering the American Cinema*, described the terms of nontheatrical rental of *Citizen Kane*. Dr. John Schultheiss at USC was the instructor who first showed me *Citizen Kane* in 1975.

Chapter 12: The Thinking Man's Exploitation Shockers

Val Lewton background came from two fine books, Joel E. Siegel's *Val Lewton: The Reality of Terror* (Viking, 1973), and *Fearing the Dark: The Career of Val Lewton* (McFarland, 1995), by Edmund G. Bansak. *Films in Review* had articles by DeWitt Bodeen about writing for Val Lewton. The *Motion Picture Herald* featured ballyhoo on Arthur Mayer's part at his Rialto Theatre on Broadway. The New York *Times* profiled Mayer and his status as a "Merchant of Menace." The Cinema Treasures web site had much useful information on the Rialto Theatre. RKO product annuals were a rich resource for colorful ads announcing Lewton films to come, including a few promised but not actually made. Exhibitor comments on Lewton films were published in the *Motion Picture Herald*. Costs and rentals for the series were supplied by Dr. Karl Thiede. *The TV Feature Film Sourcebook* from the Broadcast Information Bureau, Inc., was a source for Lewton series' placement in various syndicated packages. William K. Everson told me about 16mm prints of *The Ghost Ship* that originated from Harris Films in England. The St. Louis premiere of *The Body Snatcher* was detailed in RKO's pressbook for that film as well as in pages of *Boxoffice* and the *Motion Picture Herald*. John Newman made it possible for me to acquire the original ad for the Missouri Theatre's premiere of *The Body Snatcher*.

Chapter 13: Stateside Theatres of War

Insights into wartime conditions in theatres were supplied by trade journals of the period, including the *Motion Picture Herald*, *Boxoffice*, and *Exhibitor*, plus first-hand recollections from showman Dale Baldwin and concession operator Wesley Clark. Original ads from our own Liberty Theatre indicated some of the propaganda shorts that accompanied features during WWII. Trade ads vividly captured merchandising of *Flying Tigers*, *Across the Pacific*, and *Somewhere I'll Find You*. Pressbooks yielded promotional accessories not only on behalf on these films, but for the war effort in general. Dr. Karl Thiede provided shooting dates for *Somewhere I'll Find You* as well as cost and rental figures for *Flying Tigers*, *Across the Pacific*, and *Somewhere I'll Find You*.

Chapter 14: Paramount's Road to Sunset Boulevard

The *Motion Picture Herald* covered the March 1949 Paramount reception that reunited old-time stars as well as revivals of silent comedies and Robert Youngson's *Fifty Years Before Your Eyes*. Paramount trade ads publicized Gloria Swanson's goodwill tour and their pressbook for *Sunset Boulevard* offered TV spots referenced. Movie star endorsement ads for *Sunset Boulevard* were also sampled in the pressbook. Dr. Karl Thiede provided cost and rental figures for *Sunset Boulevard*.

Chapter 15: Wilder's Ace Goes in the Hole

Separate pressbooks for *Ace in the Hole* and *The Big Carnival* were illuminating as to changes in how the film was merchandised. The *Independent Film Journal*, *Showmen's Trade Review*, and the *Motion Picture Herald* each covered *Ace in the Hole* and later *The Big Carnival*. Paramount trade ads conveyed the studio's position with regard to the film's title change. *Variety* kept tabs on how *Ace in the Hole* performed and was a source regarding audience and exhibitor response. The *TV Feature Film Sourcebook* from the Broadcast Information Bureau, Inc., had information as to *The Big Carnival*'s circulation on television, and Films, Inc.'s 16mm catalog for 1974 included nontheatrical rental terms for *The Big Carnival*. Dr. Karl Thiede provided cost and rental figures for *Ace in the Hole/The Big Carnival*.

Chapter 16: Forgotten But Not Gone: My Son John

Laura Boyes at the North Carolina Museum of Art in Raleigh made it possible for me to finally see *My Son John* (in 35mm!) in November 2007. *Boxoffice*, *Harrison's Reports*, *Showmen's Trade Review*, the *Independent Film Journal*, the *Motion Picture Herald*, and *Exhibitor* all covered *My Son John*, with emphasis on its controversial theme. *Harrison's Reports* in particular dealt with the American Legion's interest in promoting the film. Paramount's pressbook also was informative with regard to groups eager to spread word about the film. The New York *Times* had several articles about Leo McCarey and ongoing production of *My Son John*. McCarey also spoke to the *Times* about the influence Alfred Hitchcock had on his film. Dr. Karl Thiede provided cost and rental figures for *My Son John*.

Chapter 17: Metro and the Red Badge Blow Off

The *Motion Picture Herald*, *Boxoffice*, and *Variety* followed *The Red Badge of Courage* and publicity surrounding publication of Lillian Ross's essays in the *New Yorker*, these collected in a later book entitled *Picture* (Rhinehart & Company, 1952). There also was helpful info in John Huston's memoir, *An Open Book* (Knopf, 1980), as well as Dore Schary's *Heyday* (Little, Brown, 1979). Margaret Booth, who edited *The Red Badge of Courage*, gave a rare interview to *Focus on Film* for their Summer/Autumn 1976 issue. Dr. Karl Thiede provided cost and rental figures for *The Red Badge of Courage*.

Chapter 18: Columbia and Kazan's Waterfront Haul

Rudy Behlmer's book, *Memo from Darryl F. Zanuck: The Golden Years at Twentieth-Century Fox* (Grove Press, 1993), had useful data on early development of *On the Waterfront* at Fox. Elia Kazan and Budd Schulberg were quoted in the New York *Times* and *Variety* regarding *On the Waterfront*. Kazan's autobiography, *Elia Kazan: A Life* (Knopf, 1988), had an informative chapter about the film. *Variety* reported on censorship concerns as well as the Astor Theatre opening and success of *On the Waterfront*. Original theatre ads from Chicago first-runs illustrated how earlier hit *Going My Way* was evoked to help sell *On the Waterfront*. The *Motion Picture Herald*, *Boxoffice*, *Exhibitor*, and the *Independent Film Journal* dealt with release and audience reception for *On the Waterfront*.

Chapter 19: The Mighty Monarch of Melodramas

Dr. Karl Thiede supplied financial data for *King Kong*'s 1933 release and subsequent reissues as well as *King Kong vs. Godzilla* and *King Kong Escapes*. *Variety* and the *Motion Picture Herald* in particular focused on the success of *King Kong* in its 1952 revival. The New York *Times* and *Time* reported on *Kong*'s continuing popularity and its warm reception on television in 1956. *Harrison's Reports* addressed the surprise hit of *King Kong* as a summer 1952 attraction.

Chapter 20: "100 Percent Pure Gravy"

Variety had articles about the successful New York test engagement for *Little Caesar* and *The Public Enemy* that led to a nationwide reissue for the pair. *Boxoffice* reported tentative efforts to suppress the two gangster films, and the *Motion Picture Herald* featured multiple trade ads during that 1954 winter when *Little Caesar* and *Public Enemy* made a hit with a new generation of patrons. Warner's pressbook for the combo featured updated ad art with Robinson and Cagney in recent imagery to play down dated aspects of *Little Caesar* and *Public Enemy*.

Chapter 21: Universal Makes Box-Office Music

I found coverage on *The Glenn Miller Story*'s 1954 release and 1960 revival in *Boxoffice*, the *Motion Picture Herald*, and *Exhibitor*. There were details of later showings in *Billboard*. The New York *Times* covered Universal's reissue program for 1960, which included *The Glenn Miller Story*. Original trade and newspaper ads illustrated how the film was sold in various releases.

Chapter 22: Warner Bros. and the James Dean Cult

There was much information and a number of editorials about the James Dean fad in the New York *Times* and in *Time* and *Life*. Trade magazines like *Boxoffice* and the *Motion Picture Herald* followed exhibition's dawning realization that James Dean was a bigger star in death than he had been in life. George Feltenstein kindly supplied information concerning broadcast dates of *Warner Brothers Presents* episodes that highlighted James Dean and *Rebel Without a Cause*. The pressbook for *East of Eden* and *Rebel Without a Cause* as a combo reissue was a source for devices used to promote the pair, including the "chicken run" flip-book. Dr. Karl Thiede provided cost and rental figures for each of James Dean's films, along with *The James Dean Story*.

Chapter 23: I Call It "Fashion Noir"

In A.E. Hotchner's *Doris Day: Her Own Story* (William Morrow, 1975), the star told of her experience making *Midnight Lace*. Michael Gordon spoke of directing Lana Turner in a book of interviews compiled by Ronald L. Davis, *Just Making Movies: Company Directors on the Studio System* (University Press of Mississippi, 2005). Pressbooks for *Midnight Lace* and *Portrait in Black* were helpful in showing how each film was promoted. The *Motion Picture Herald*, *Boxoffice*, and *Exhibitor* covered the release and ad support extended by Universal-International, along with tie-ins and contests staged by individual showmen.

Chapter 24: Psycho Salesmanship

Harrison's Reports was a source of info on the release of *Psycho* and the controversy among small exhibitors over slow availability of prints. A special sales manual issued by Paramount to support *Psycho* was useful for showing how Alfred Hitchcock customized a nationwide campaign for his thriller. Trade journals *Boxoffice*, *Exhibitor*, the *Independent Film Journal*, and the *Motion Picture Herald* addressed reaction to *Psycho* by audiences and exhibitors who were obliged to close admittance doors after each performance of the film began. The cancellation of *Psycho*'s network TV showing by CBS was covered in the New York *Times* and various trades. *TV Guide* ran ads and promotion for a Friday night network premiere cancelled at the eleventh hour. The *TV Feature Film Sourcebook* from the Broadcast Information Bureau, Inc., had information regarding placement of *Psycho* in TV syndication packages afterward. Pressbooks for the 1965 and 1969 reissues illustrated modifications Hitchcock made to latter-day merchandising of *Psycho*. Swank's 16mm film rental catalogue gave figures as to the cost of *Psycho* as a nontheatrical attraction. Dr. Karl Thiede provided rental figures for various releases of *Psycho*.

Chapter 25: A Memphis Screamiere

The *Motion Picture Herald*, *Boxoffice*, and *Harrison's Reports* covered the *Dracula* deluge from 1958 into 1960, as well as *Brides of Dracula*. Its premiere was an event for showmen countrywide to emulate, so trades followed Memphis events closely. The film's pressbook and a 1960 Monarch paperback novelization for *Brides Of Dracula* gave insight as to how Universal's release was sold to summer 1960 patronage. Historian and Memphis film critic for the *Commercial Appeal* John Beiffus supplied valuable information as to past and present circumstances of the Malco Theatre, host to the 1960 premiere of *Brides of Dracula*.

Chapter 26: Exhibition's Baby Jane Blastoff

The New York *Times* printed articles about *What Ever Happened to Baby Jane?* in 1962, which included remarks by director Robert Aldrich. The latter's career was well documented in a 1986 book, *The Films and Career of Robert Aldrich* (University of Tennessee Press, 1986), by Edwin T. Arnold and Eugene L. Miller. Trade journals *Boxoffice*, *Exhibitor*, and the *Motion Picture Herald* covered *Baby Jane* and the Hollywood Preview Engagements concept devised by the Theatre Owners of America. Bette Davis spoke of Joan Crawford and *What Ever Happened to Baby Jane?* in two books, *Mother Goddam* (Hawthorn, 1974) and *This 'n That* (Putnam, 1987), the latter with Michael Herskowitz, along with *I'd Love to Kiss You: Conversations with Bette Davis* (Pocket Books), published in 1990. *Mother Goddam* and *I'd Love to Kiss You: Conversations with Bette Davis* were both written by Whitney Stine. The Warner Bros. pressbook for *What Ever Happened to Baby Jane?* was a useful guide to contests and promotions utilized to sell the 1962 film. Dr. Karl Thiede provided rental figures for *What Ever Happened to Baby Jane?*

Chapter 27: Warner Bros.' Bull's-Eye Selling of Bonnie and Clyde

The New York *Times* and the *New Yorker* published reviews in 1967 by Bosley Crowther and Pauline Kael, respectively, that set the whole *Bonnie and Clyde* phenomenon in motion. Warners did the rest with a pressbook and special campaign materials that I used for illustrations in this chapter. Pressbooks and advertising materials for *Harper*, *Inside Daisy Clover*, *Who's Afraid of Virginia Woolf?*, and *Chamber of Horrors* supplied further evidence that WB was at the top of its promoting game when *Bonnie and Clyde* went into release. For contrast, there was 20th Century Fox's wan merchandising of *The St. Valentine's Day Massacre*, as indicated by its own pressbook.

INDEX